I0462699

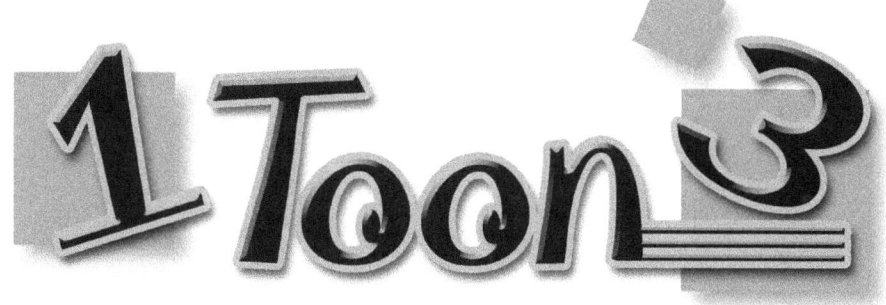

A step by step drawing guide
for creating innovative
cartoon characters

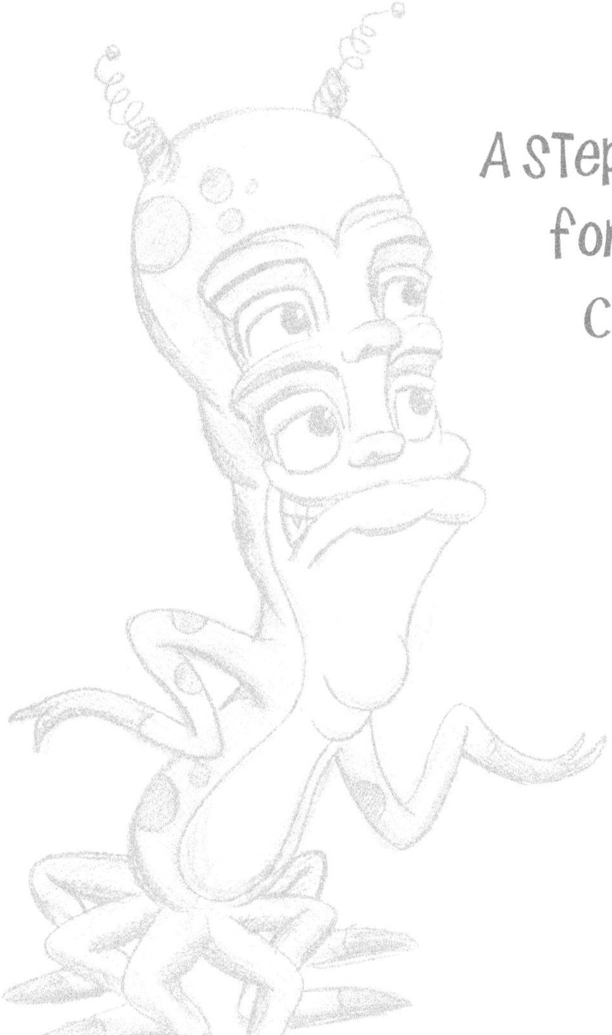

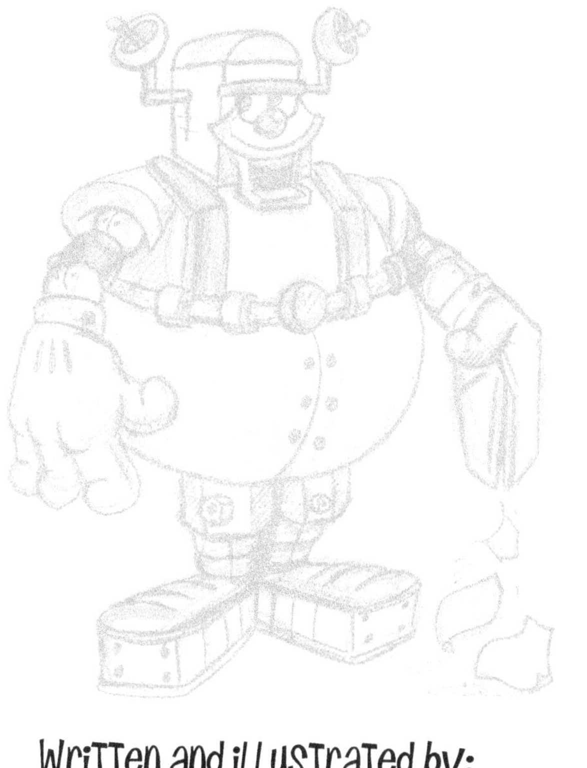

Written and illustrated by:
Rene D. Erazo

# Table of Contents

# Chapter 1 Basic Shape Lessons

## Basic Shape Lessons
## Adding Limbs for
## Legs and Arms To Shapes

STep 1.  Draw a basic foundation shape or a distorted shape.

STep 2. Find a Limb point on The shape and make a floor
Line as your reference for feet or gravity pLanes. AppLy other
designated points or reference shapes in order
To extend out Limbs.

STep 3.  Begin To add Leg and arm Lines by connecting The Limb points
To The fLoor Line or To designated points. ATTach Them To The
main shape. Finish construction of Legs and arms by
connecting aLL parts and cLosing shapes as seen in
The foLLowing shapes featured in This chapter.

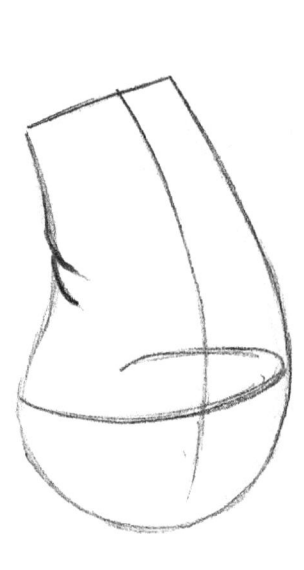

STep - #1

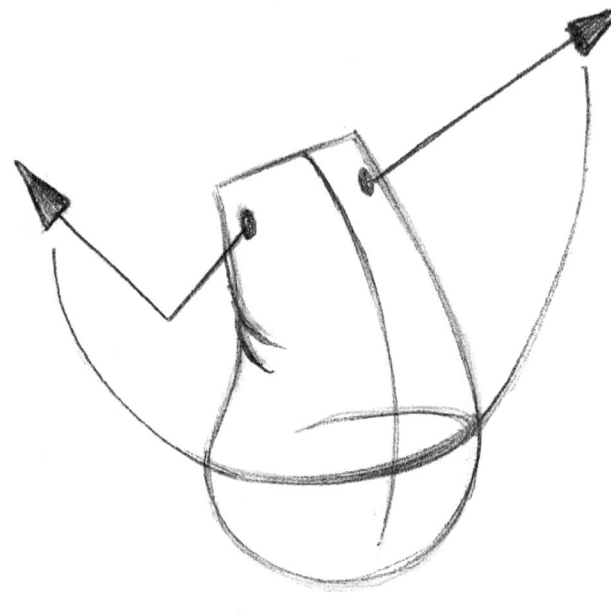

STep - #2

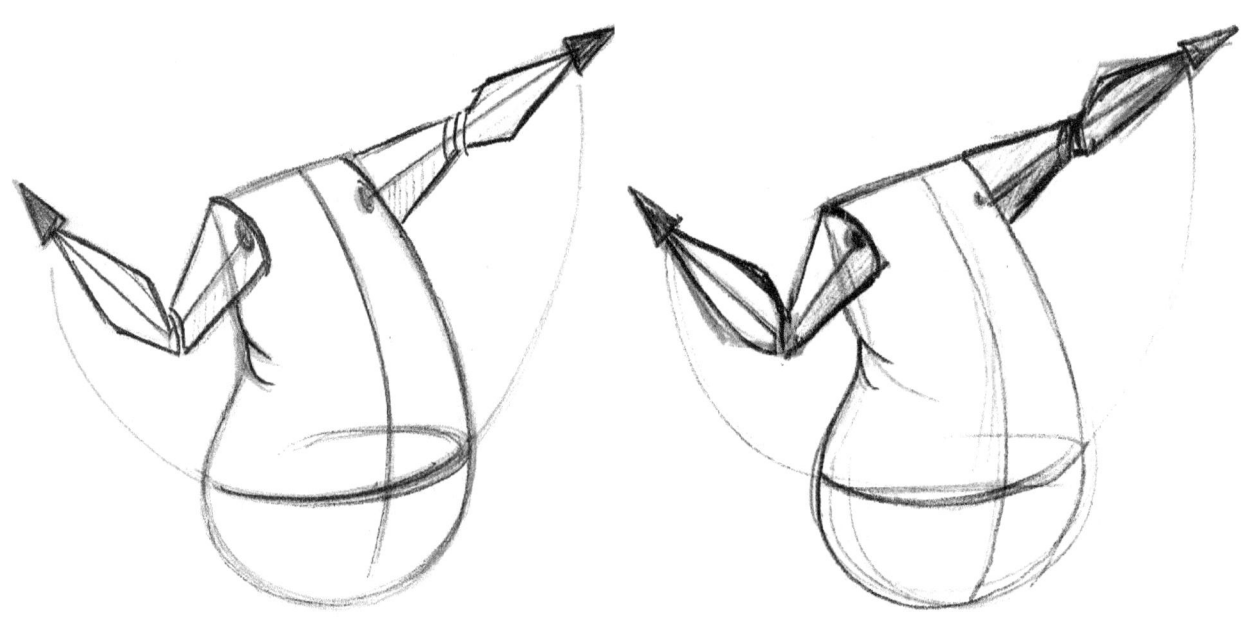

STep - #3

Toon SkeTch

2.

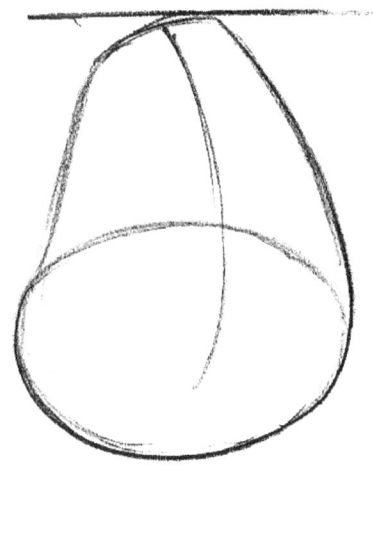

STep - #1

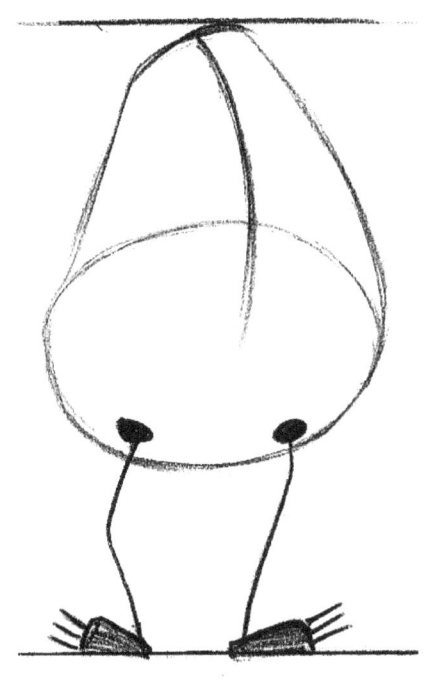

STep - #2

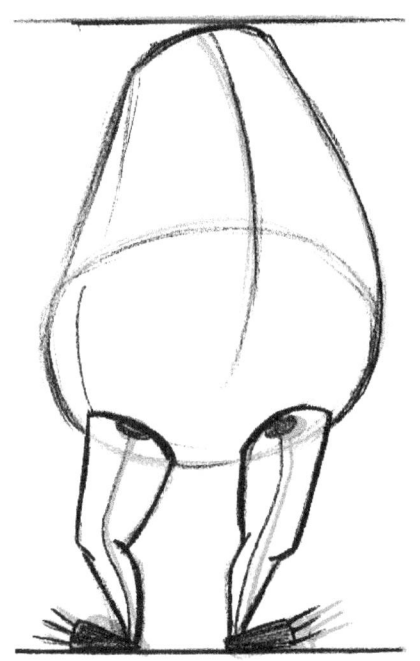

STep - #3

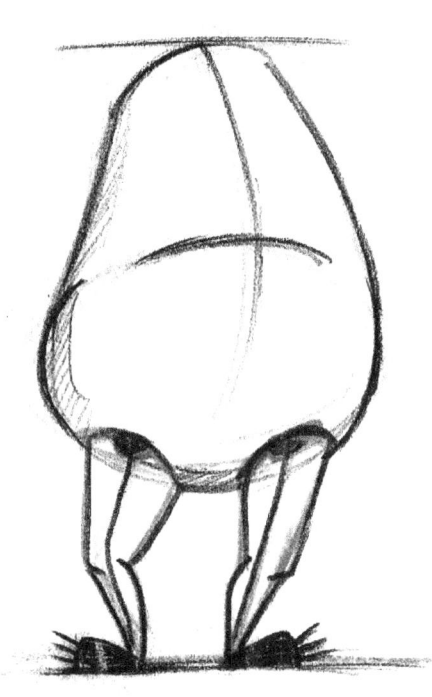

Toon sketch

3.

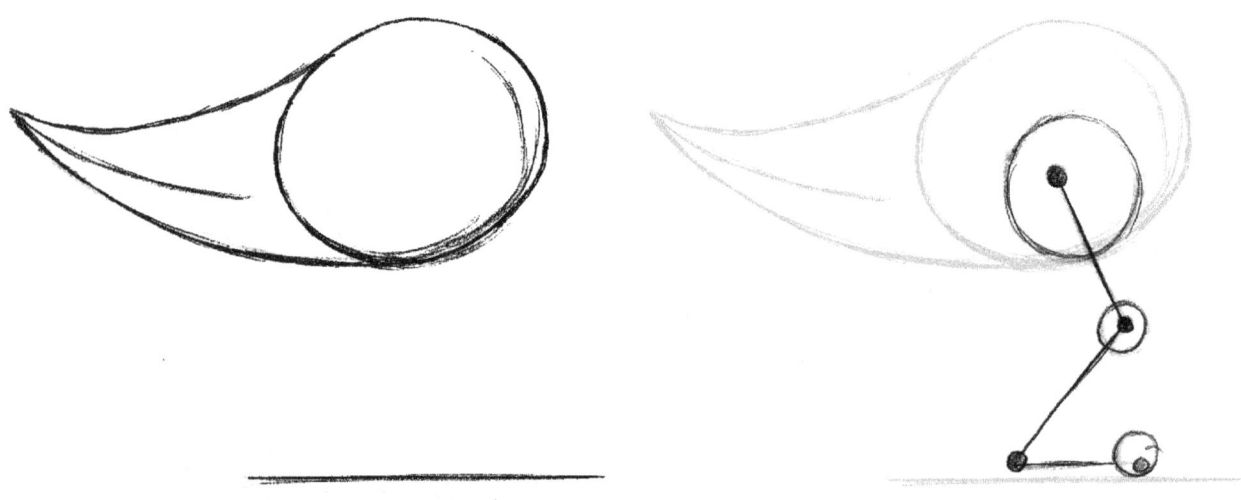

STep - #1

STep - #2

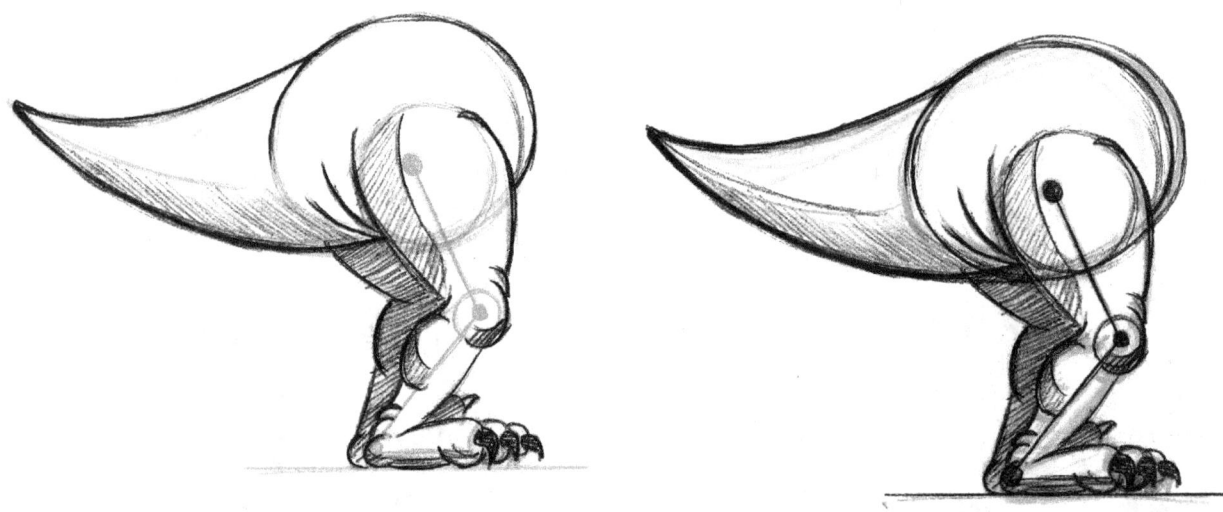

STep - #3

Toon sketch

4.

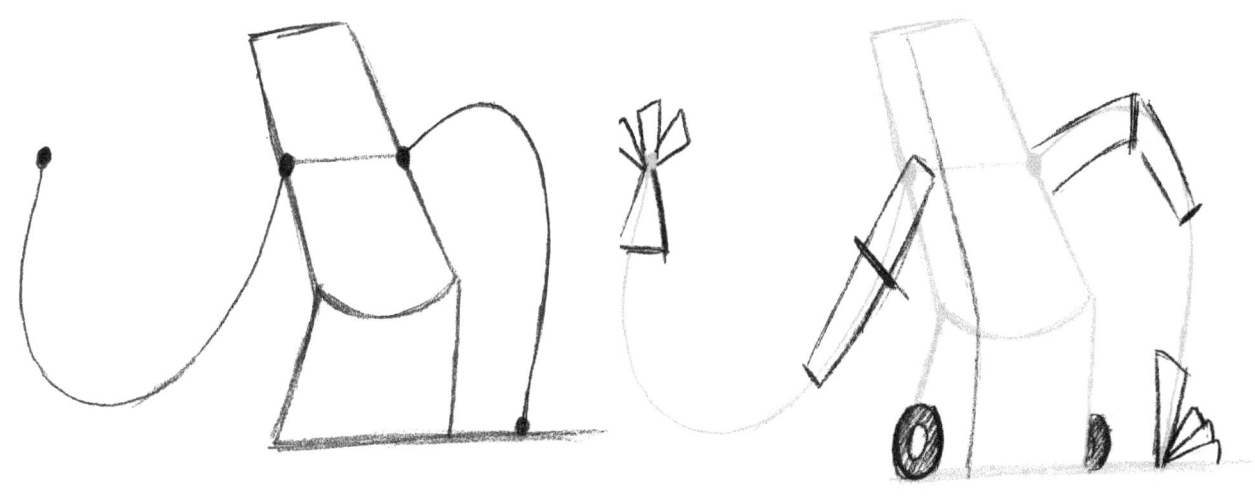

STep - #1

STep - #2

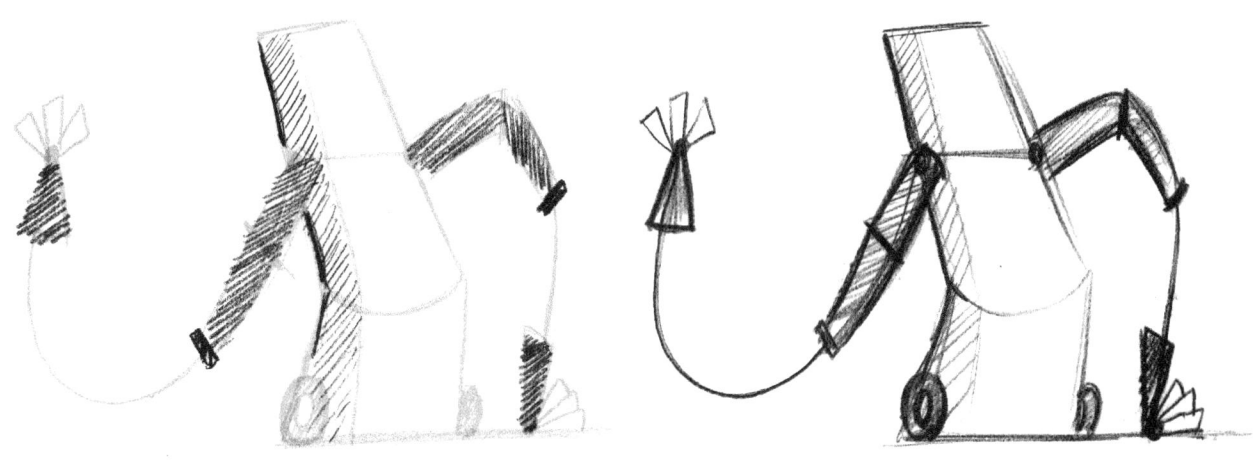

STep - #3

Toon sKeTch

5.

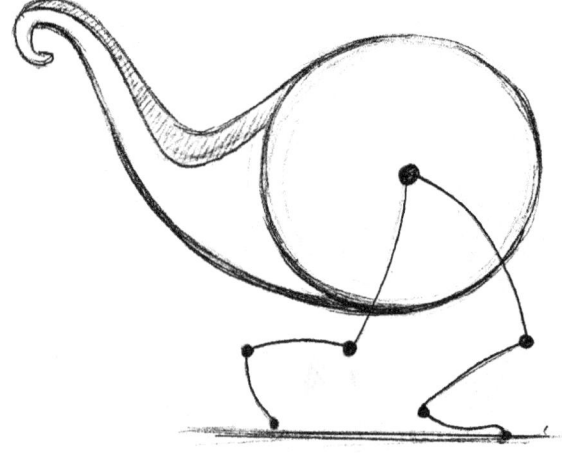

Step - #1

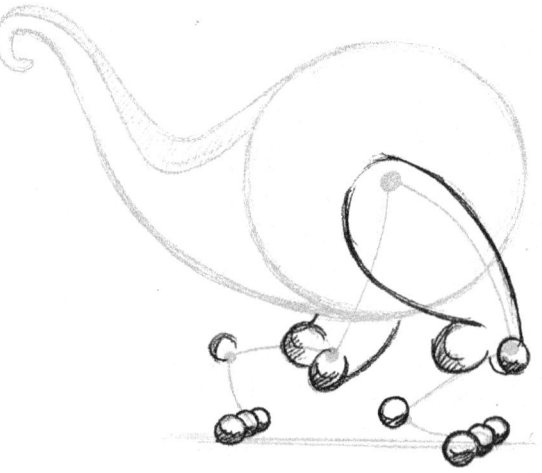

Step - #2

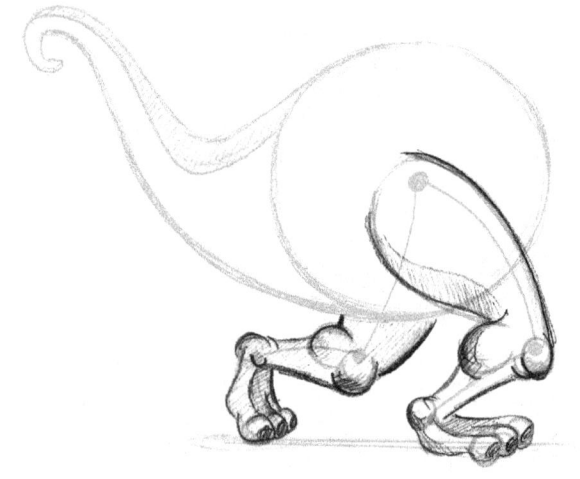

Step - #3

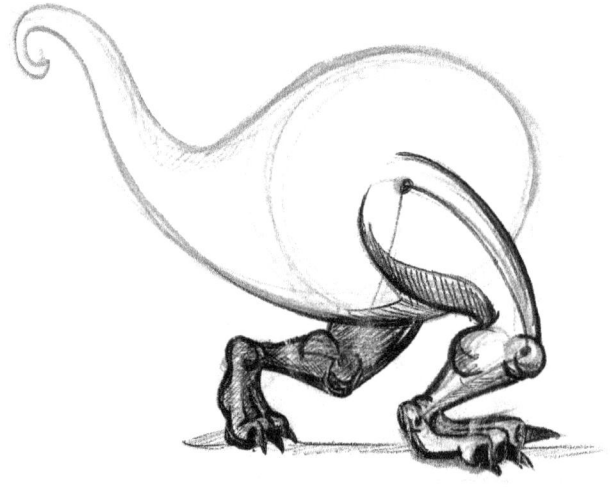

Toon sketch

6.

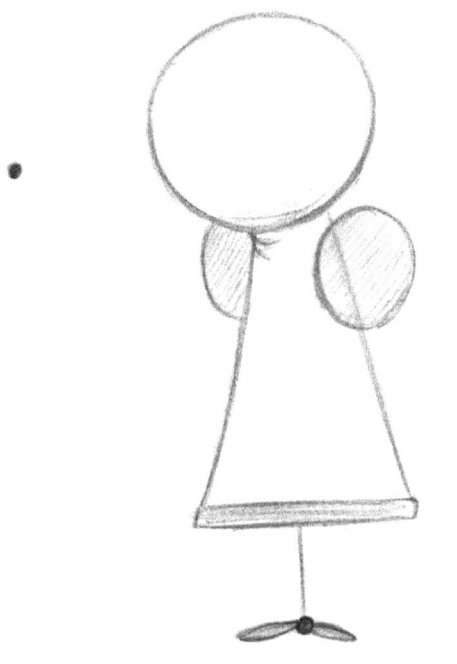

Step - #1

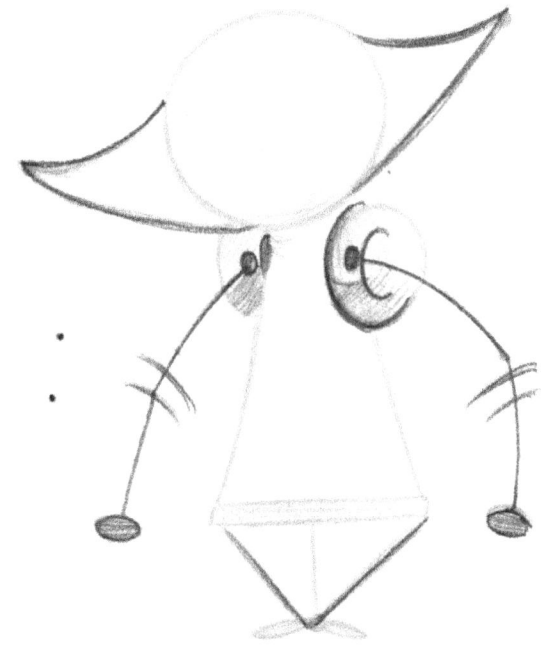

Step - #2

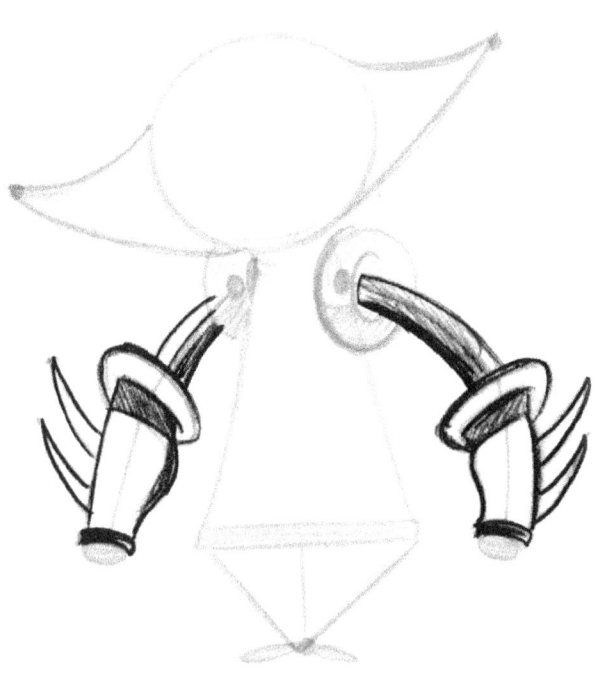

Step - #3

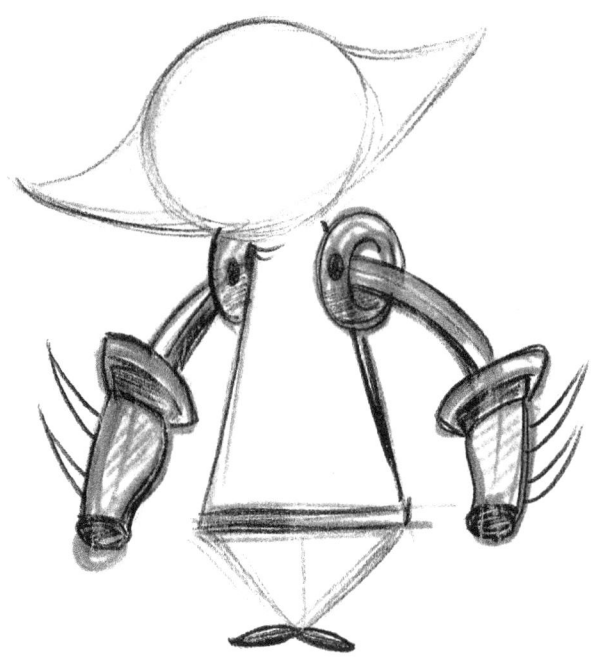

Toon sketch

7.

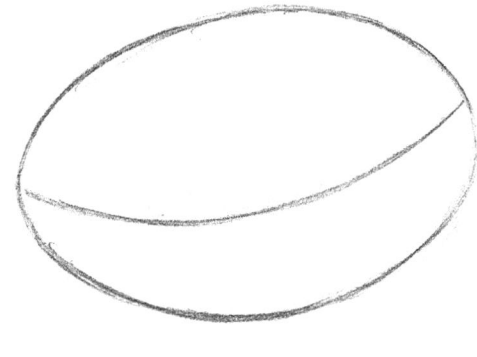

Step - #1

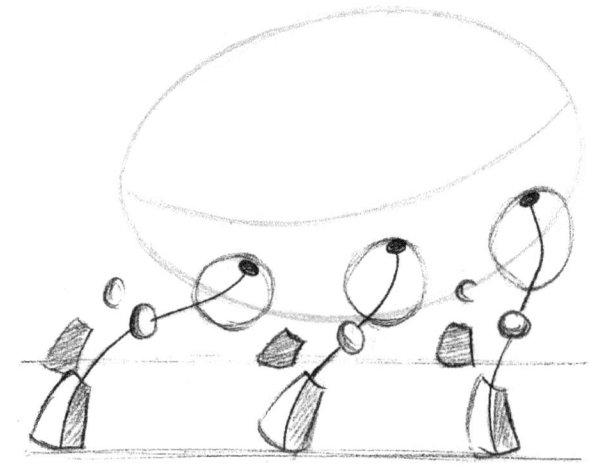

Step - #2

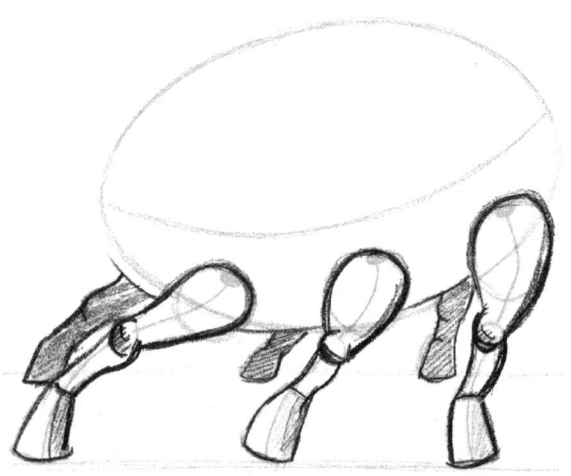

Step - #3

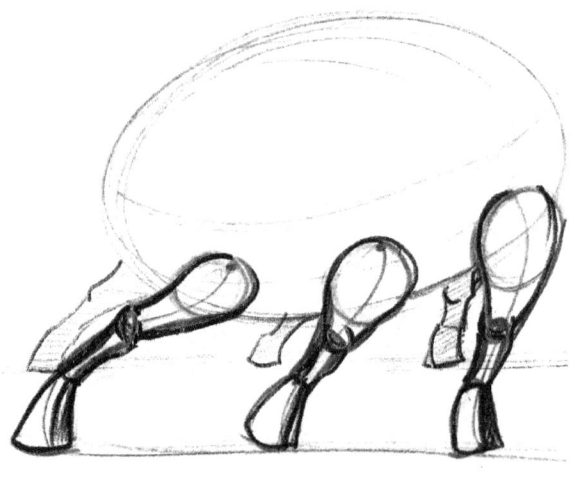

Toon sketch

8.

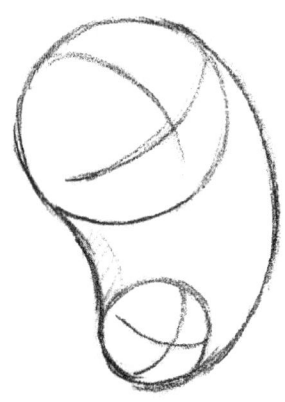

Step - #1

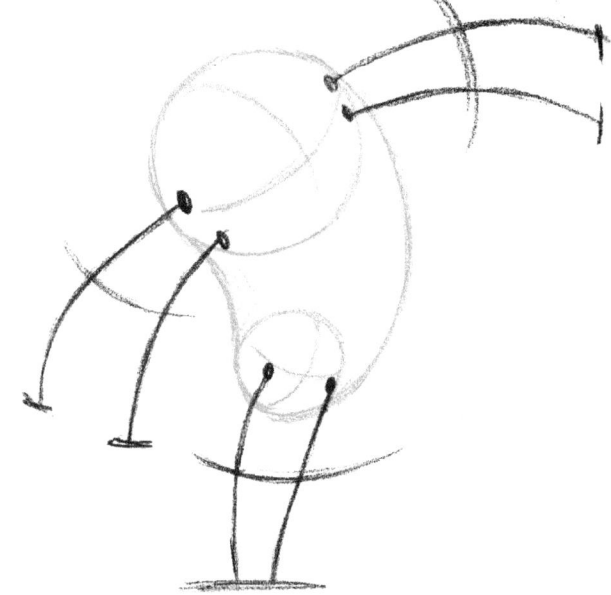

Step - #2

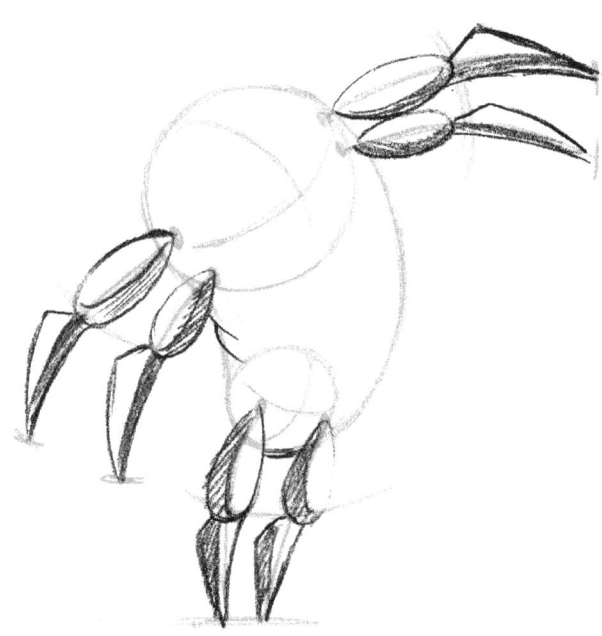

Step - #3

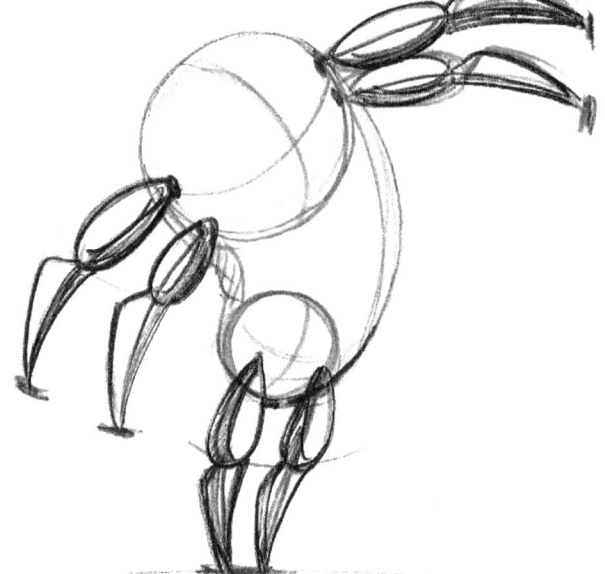

Toon Sketch

9

# Drawing Space

# Distorting and using The basic Shapes

Step 1. Make shapes as seen on samples
or explore with any desired shapes.

Step 2. Create secondary shapes or duplicate
The first shape. Try making The second shape
Larger, smaller or different Than The first shape.

Step 3. Unite both shapes with Lines and curves
or close The gaps between shapes by using
more shapes or solid planes.

## Basic Shapes And Points

Step 1. Draw basic shape or Shapes and cool clusters.

Step 2. Add a secondary shape or points around The initial shape.

Step 3. Add Lines, points and close The shape clusters To
ILLustrate one whole distorted shape. (Shaded sections are optional )

# Basic Shapes Lesson 1

STep - #1

STep - #2

STep - #3

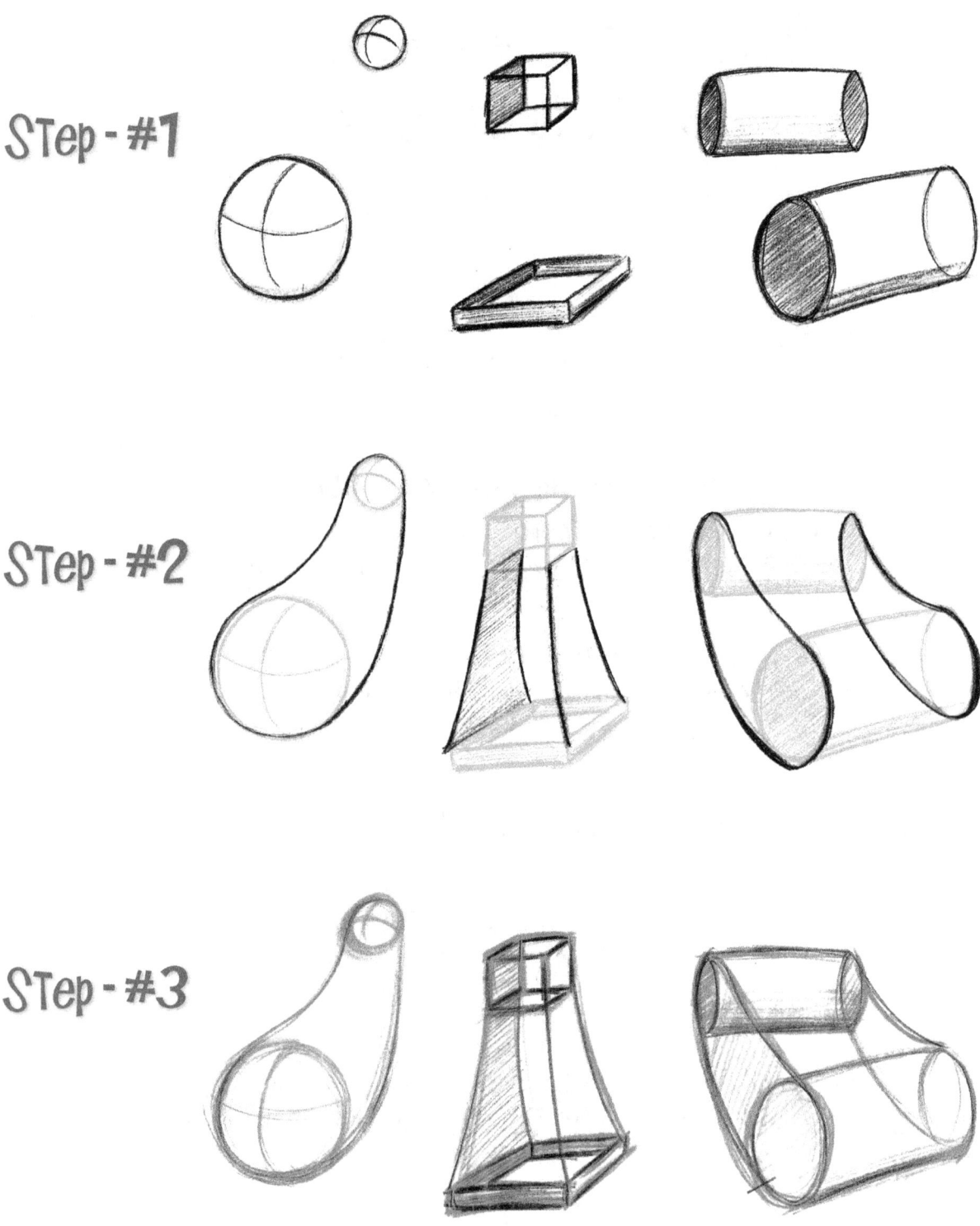

# Basic Shapes Lesson 2

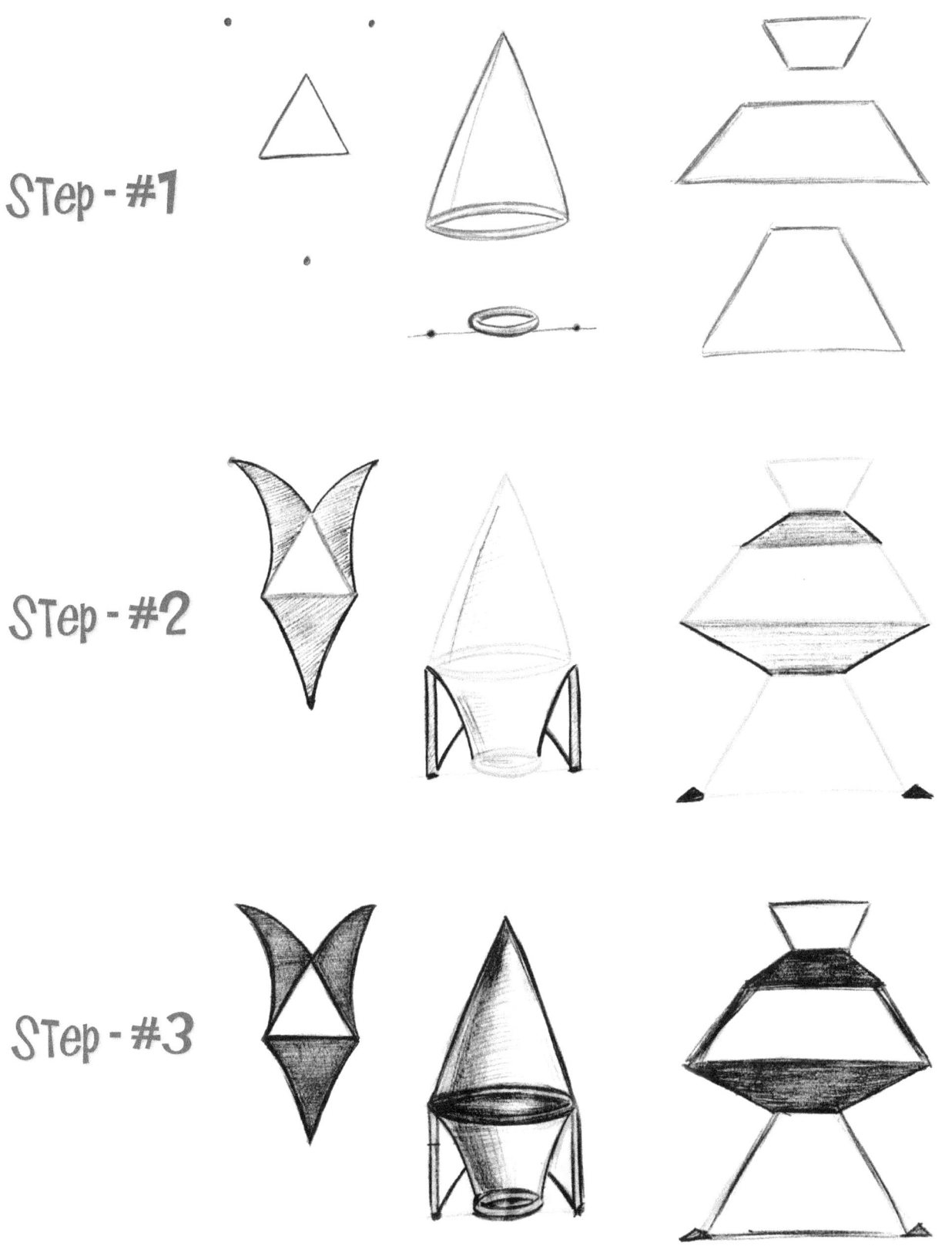

STep - #1

STep - #2

STep - #3

13.

# Drawing Space

# Character Face Definition
# Center Axis & Feature Lines

STep 1. create your overall face shape with circles Squares and other Shapes.

STep 2. Add your center-axis of The face and feature Lines for mouth, eyes, nose and ears.

STep 3. GeT creative by filling in The feature shapes aLong with other defying facial deTaiLs and hair shapes.

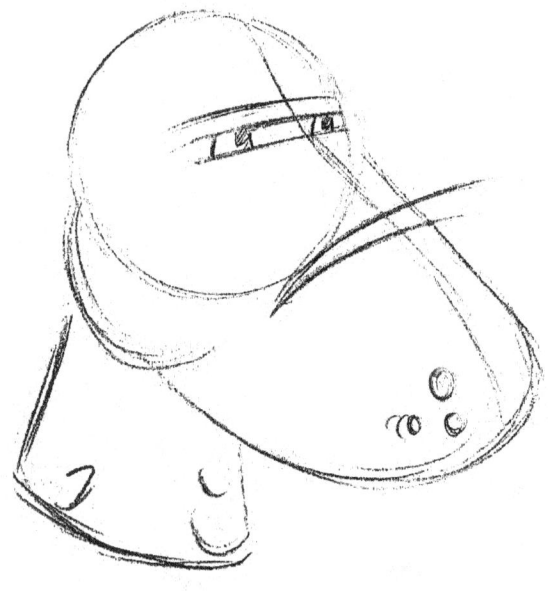

Step - #1

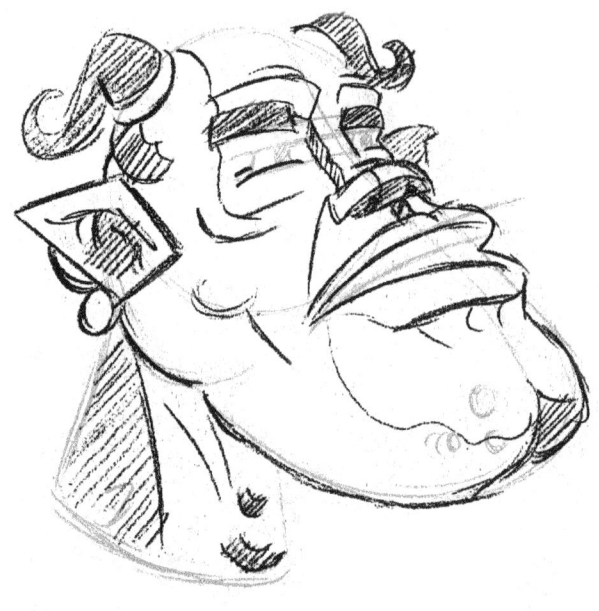

Step - #2

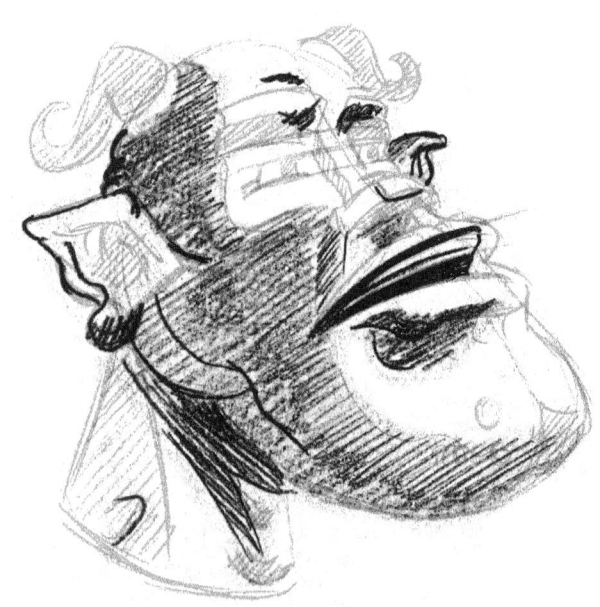

Step - #3

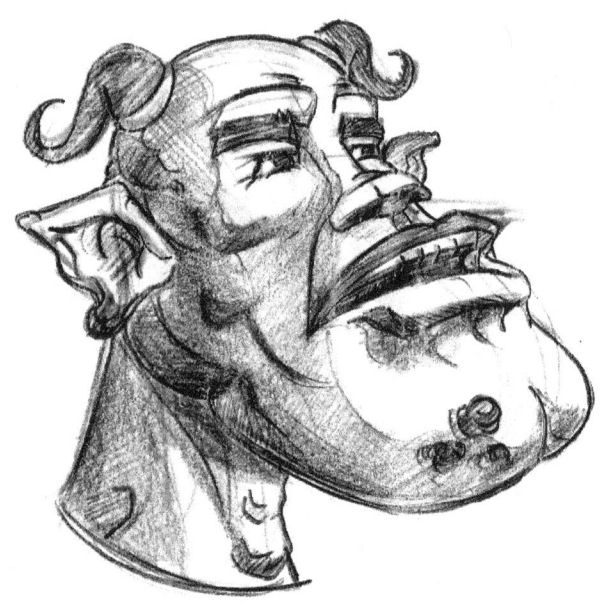

Toon sketch

16.

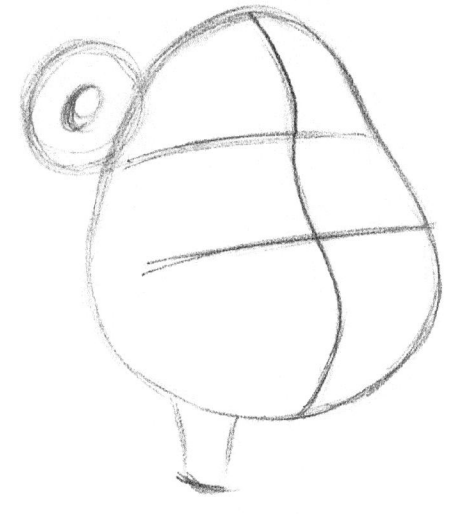

STep - #1

STep - #2

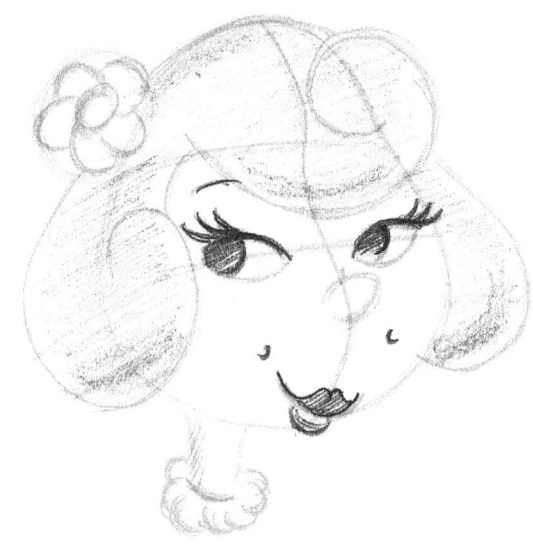

STep - #3

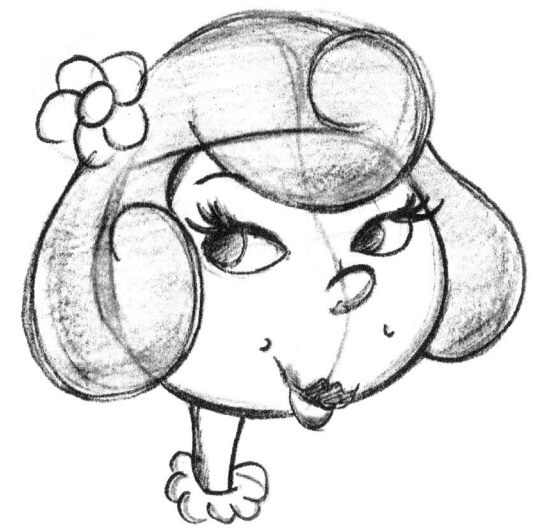

Toon skeTch

17.

STep - #3

STep - #2

STep - #1

18.

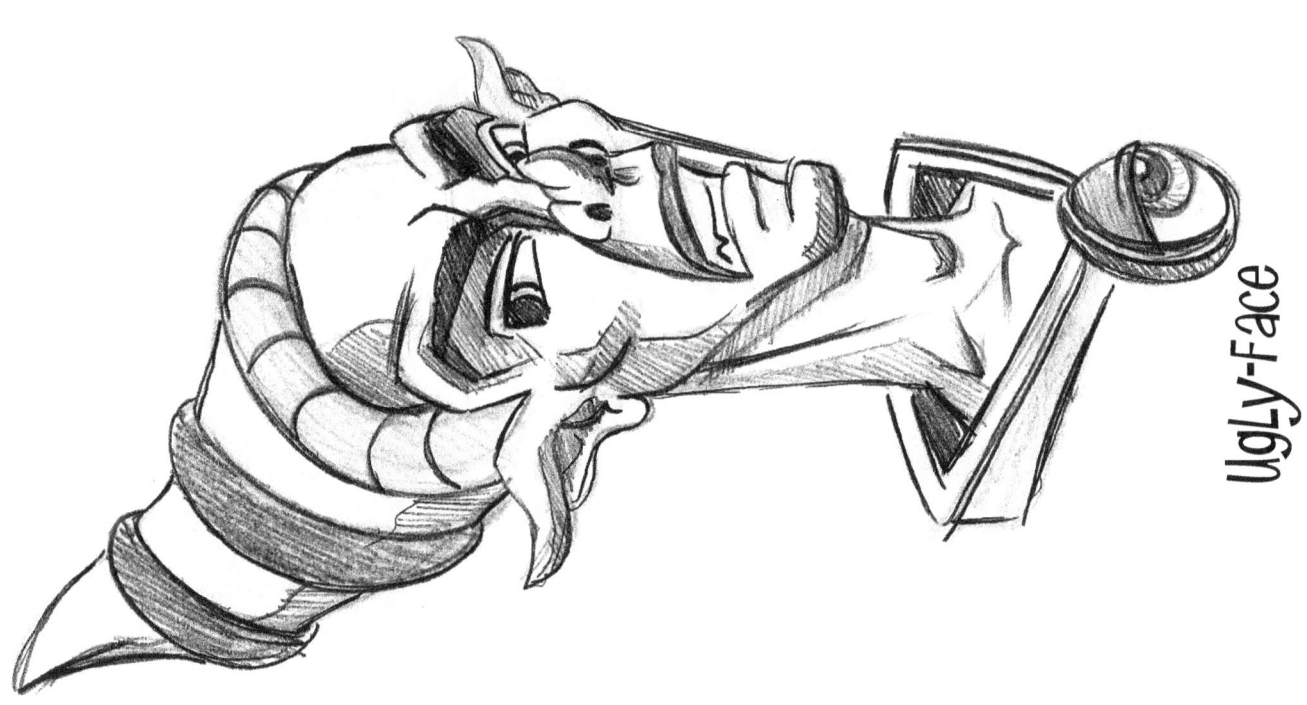

UgLy-Face

19.

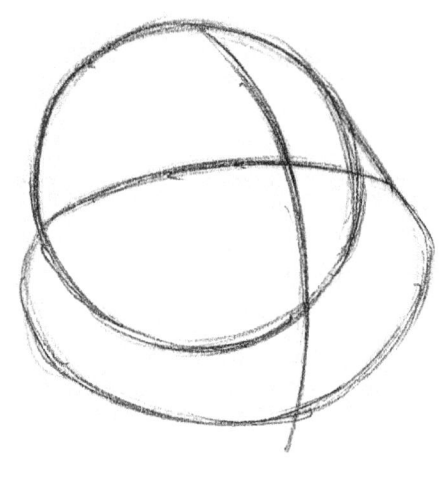

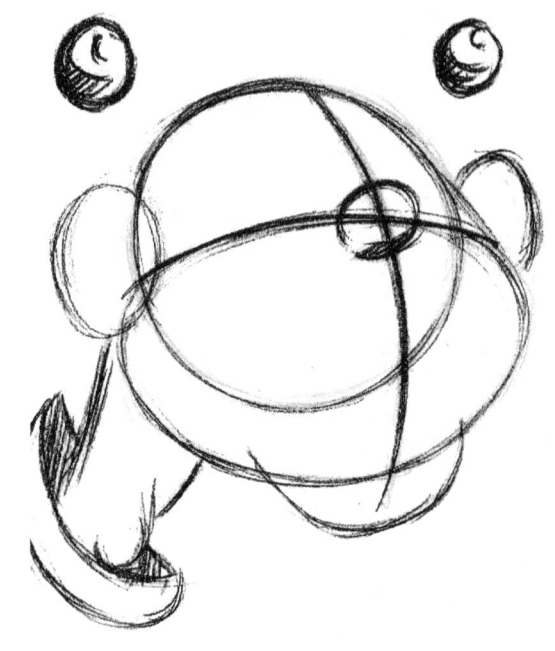

Step - #1

Step - #2

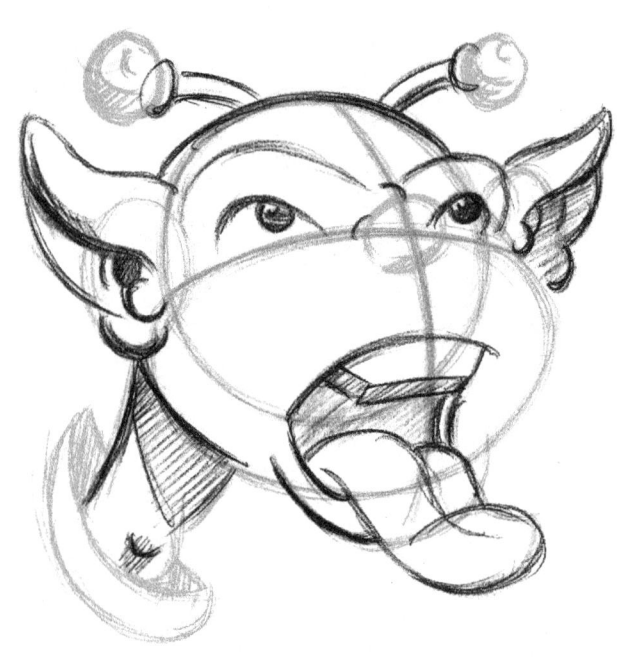

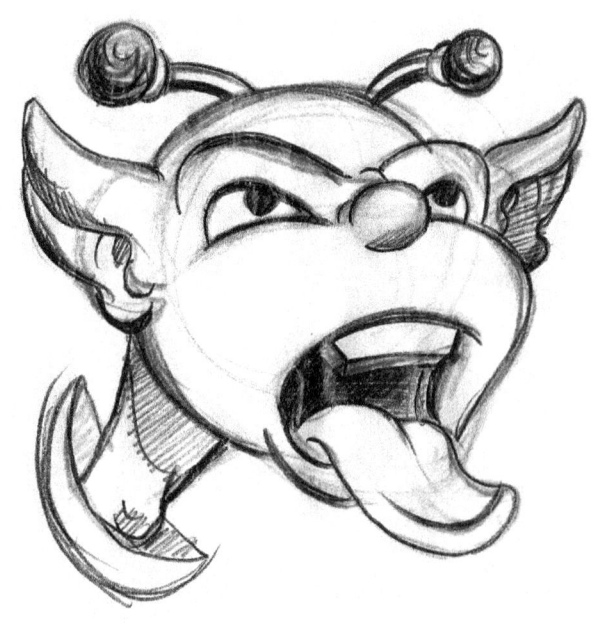

Step - #3

Toon sketch

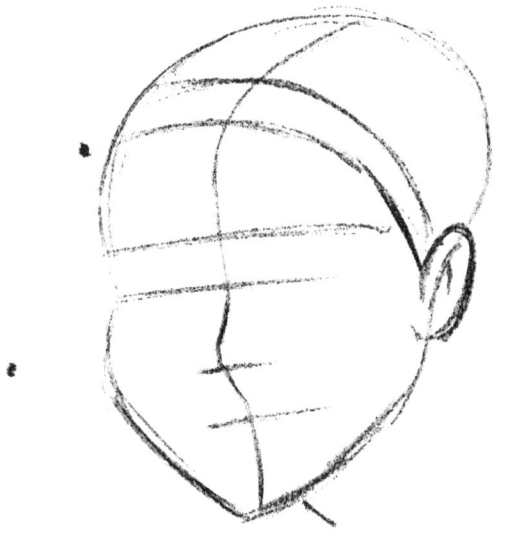

STep - #1

STep - #2

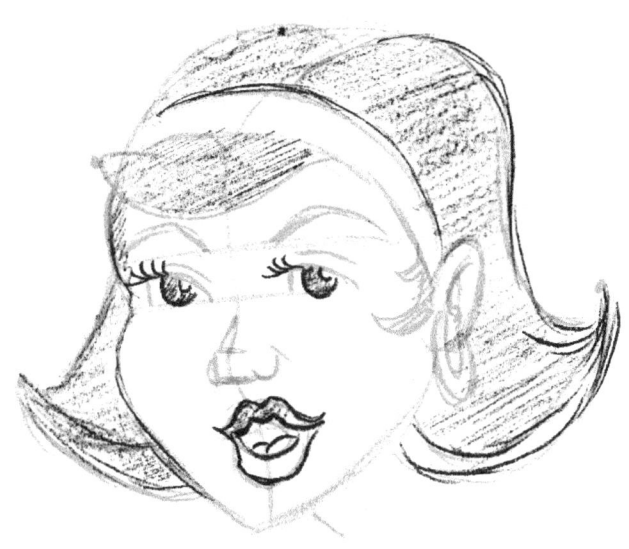

STep - #3

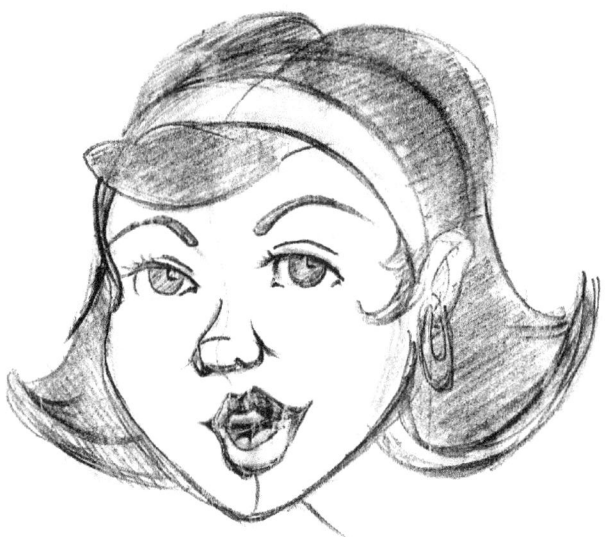

Toon sKeTch

21.

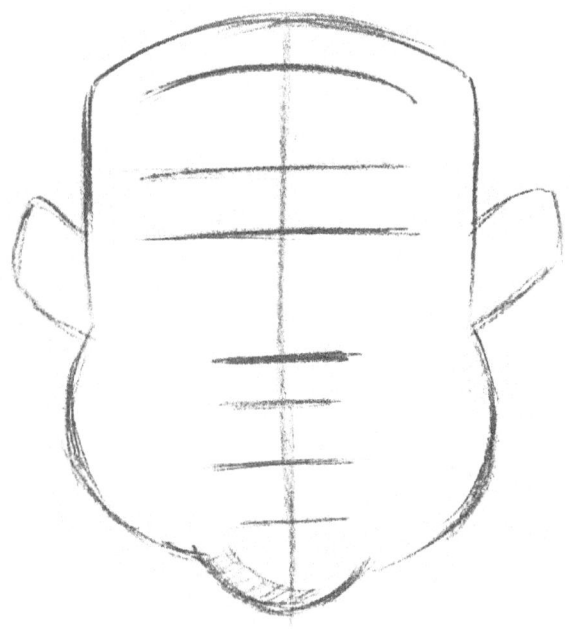

STep - #1

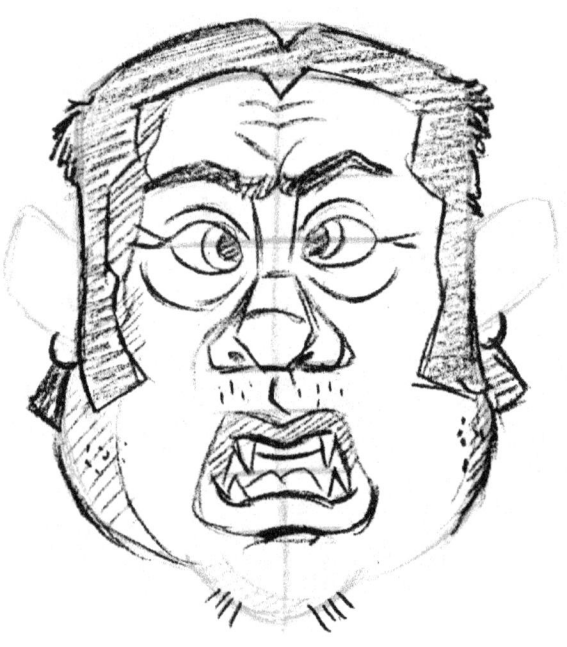

STep - #2

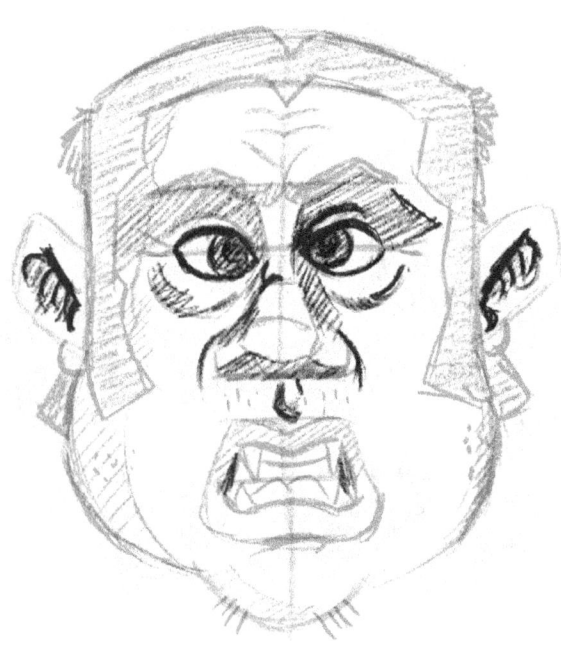

STep - #3

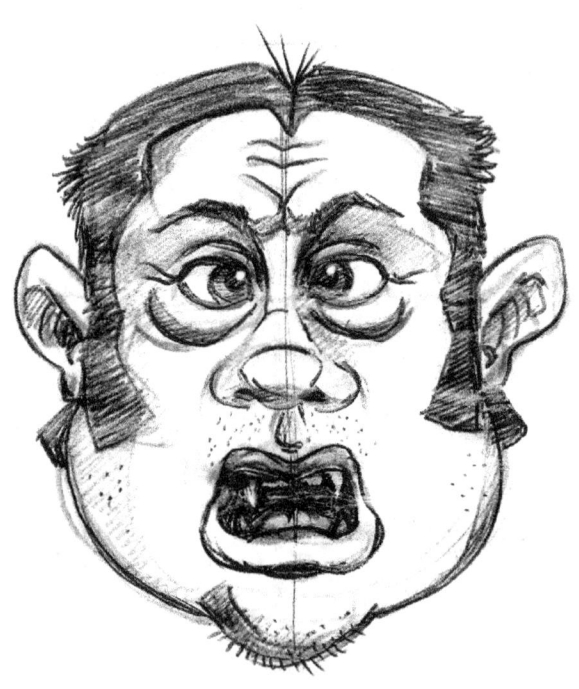

Toon sketch

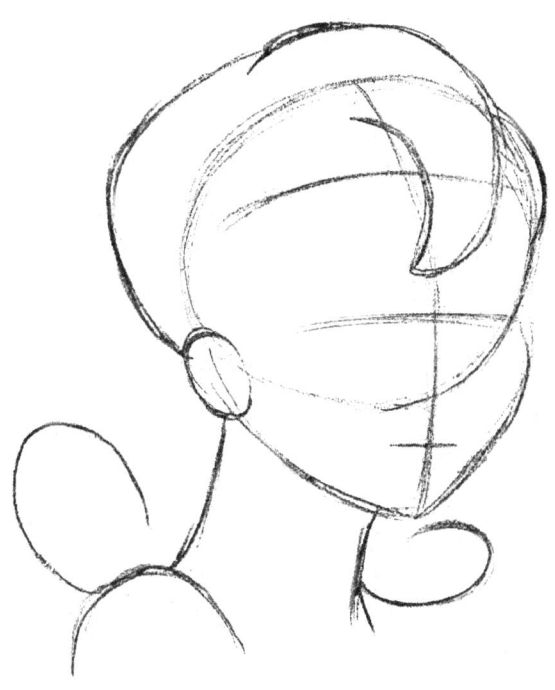

Step - #1

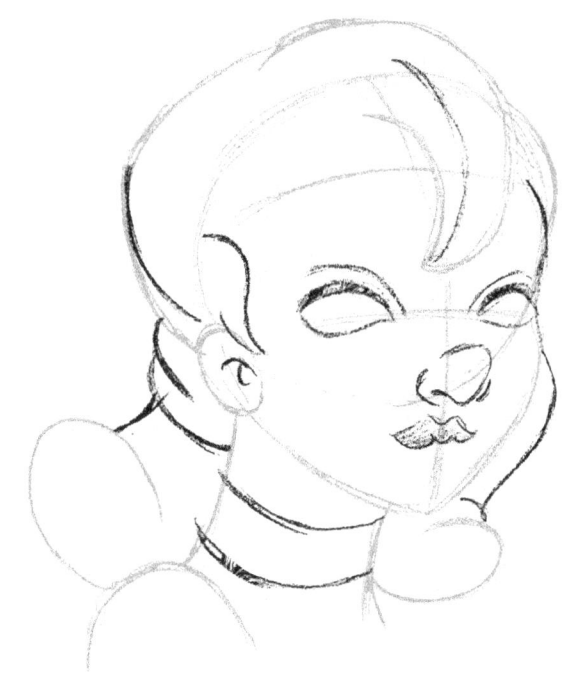

Step - #2

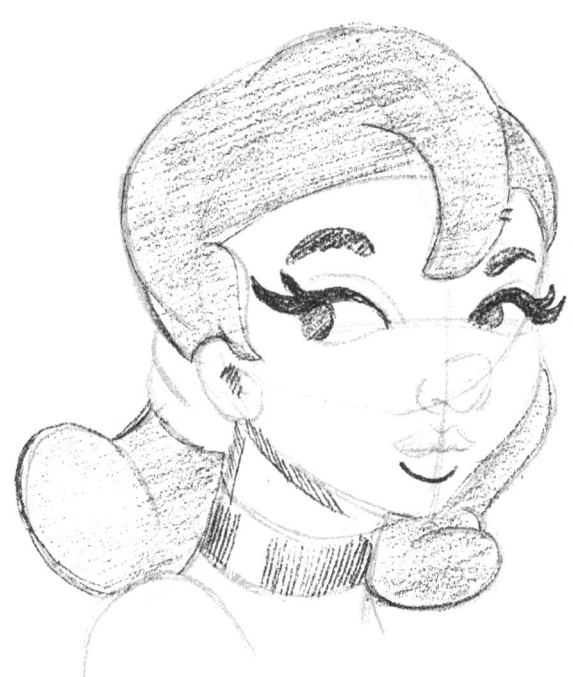

Step - #3

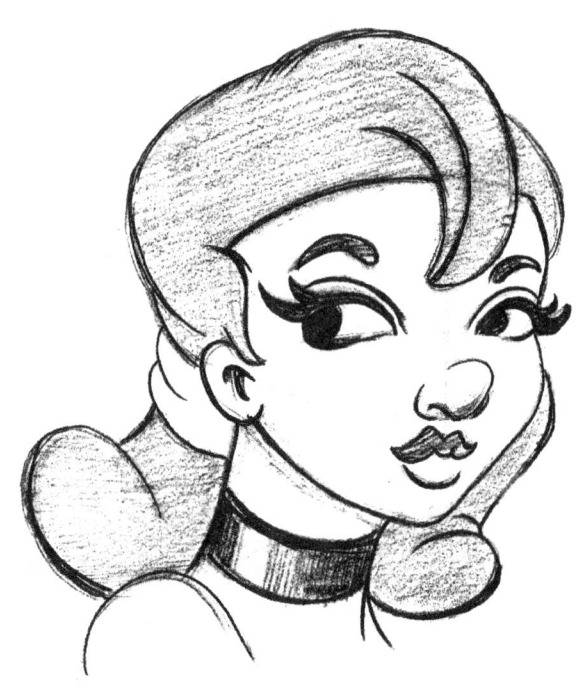

Toon sketch

23

# Drawing Space

# Three Steps in developing cartoon hands

Step 1. Block out your overall hand with blocks, shapes or circles. Then make your finger suggestions with planes distorted squares or curves.

Step 2. Create knuckles with shapes and use curved lines drawn in a sweeping motion. Add spheres, blocks or masses to indicate bones knuckles and hand shapes.

Step 3. Connect your fingers and other hand parts by adding lines from shape to shape towards the finger tips. Fully develop the hand by distorting blocks and spheres as needed. Lastly, to finalize hands render the finished construction lines.

ALien Hands

STep - #1

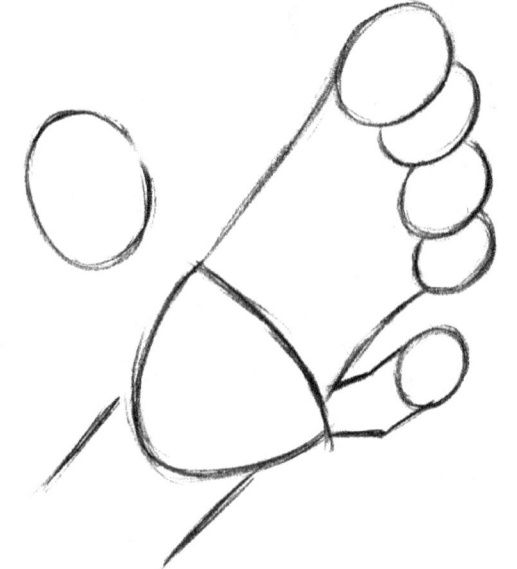
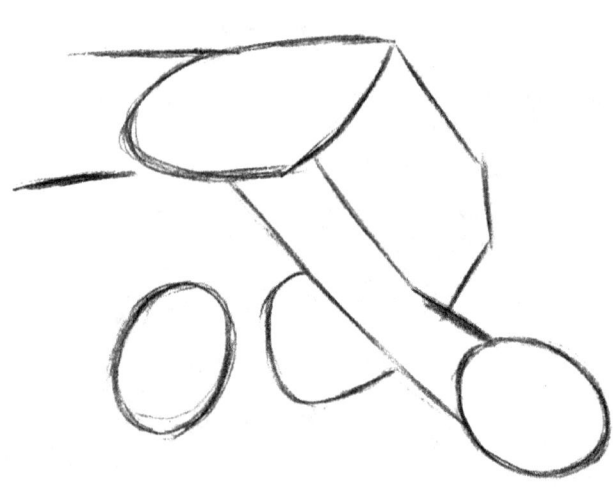

STep - #2

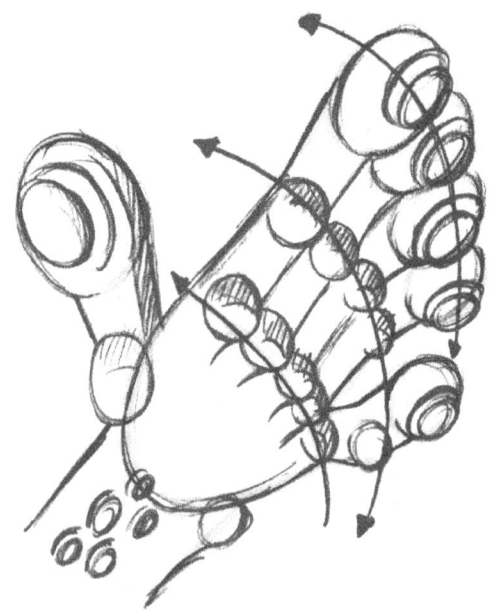
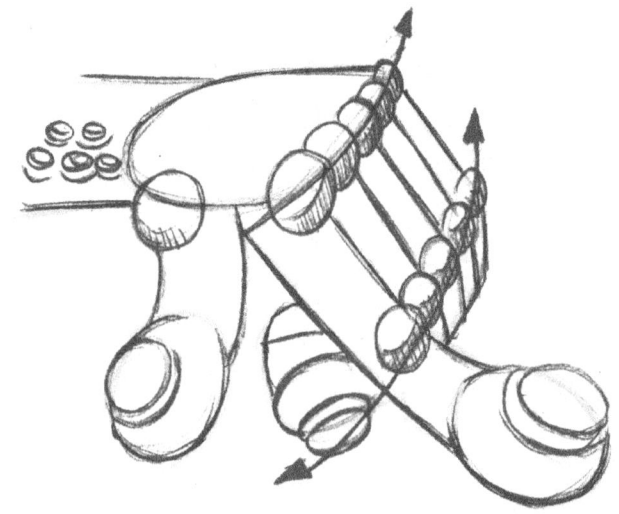

# STep - #3

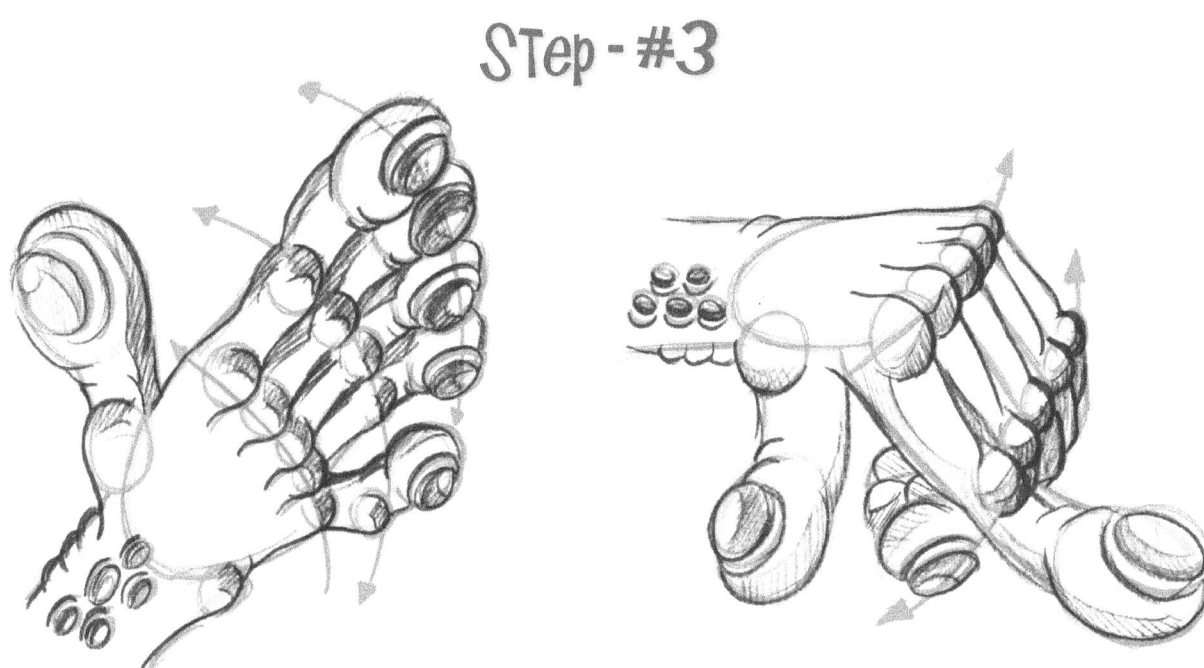

# Toon sketch

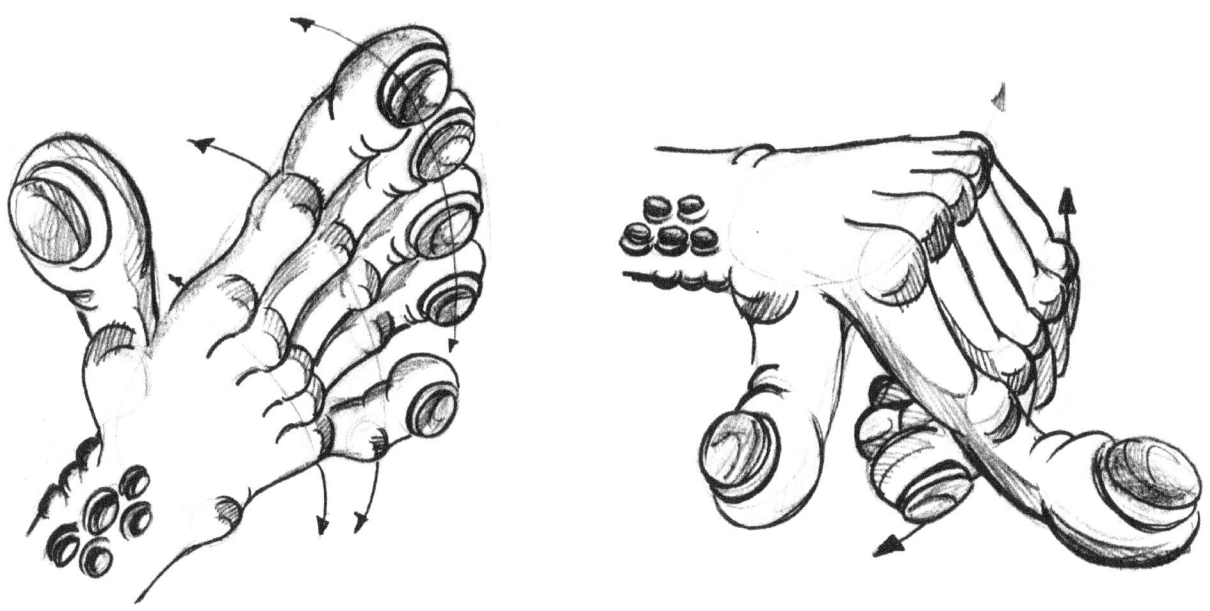

27

# Robotic Hands

## Step - #1

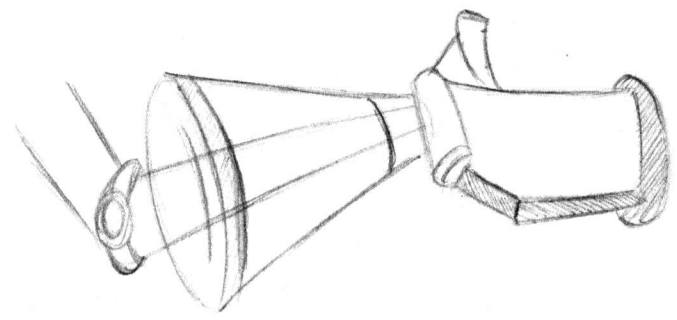
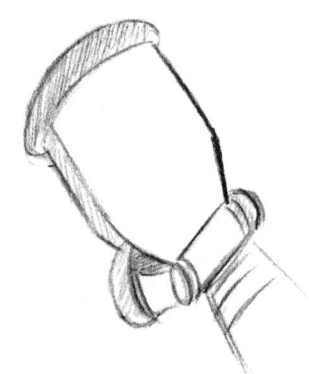

## Step - #2

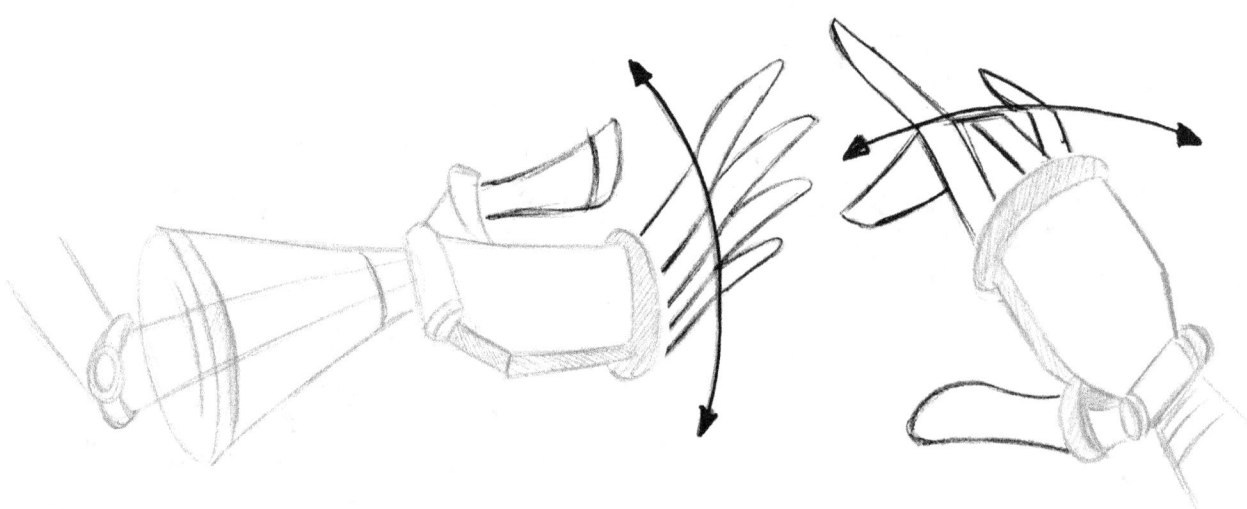

# STep - #3

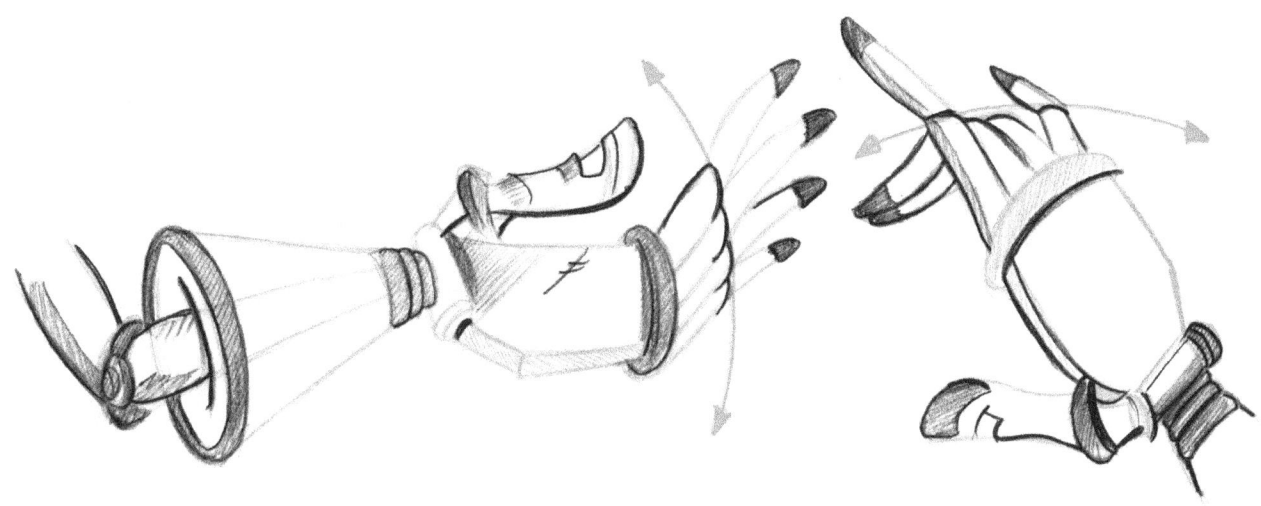

# Toon sketch

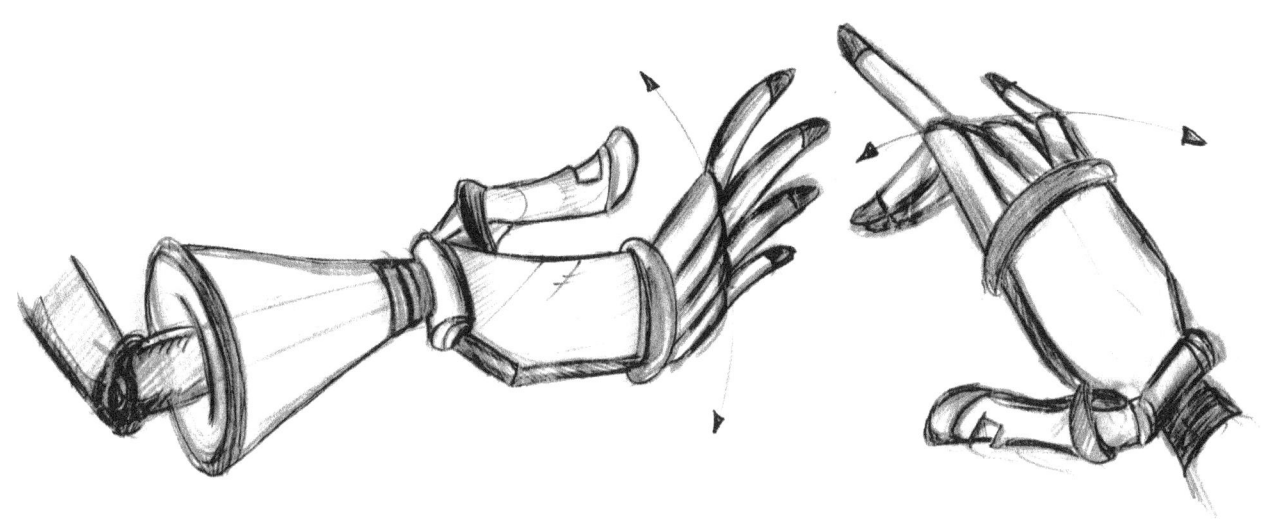

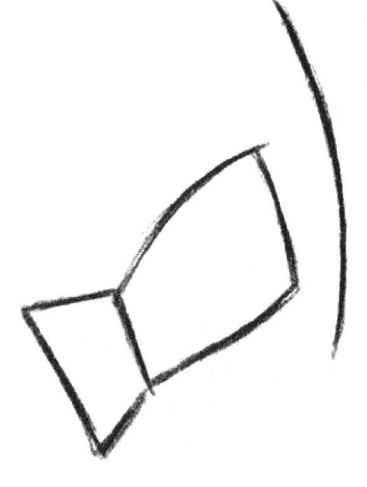

STep - #1

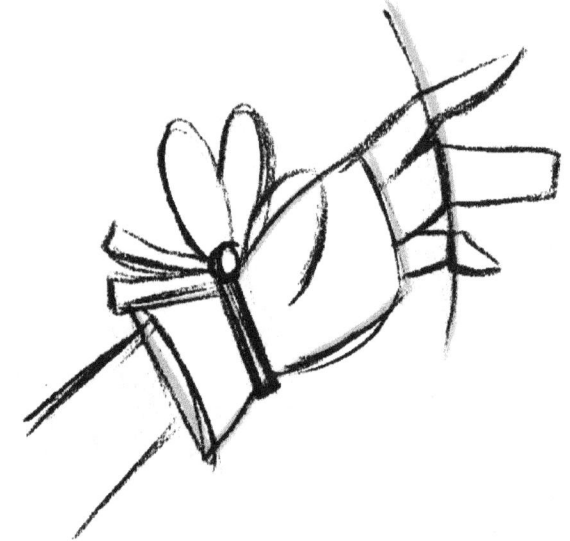

STep - #2

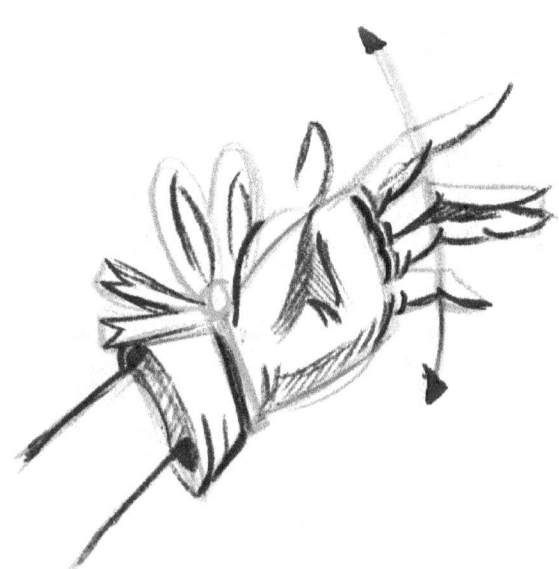

STep - #3

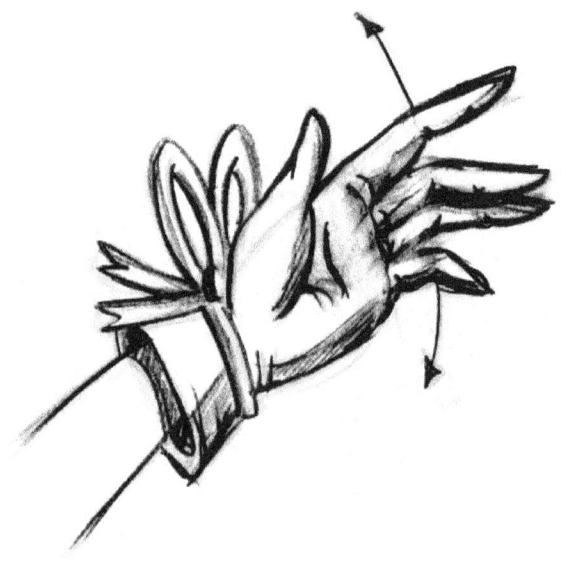

Toon sketch

30.

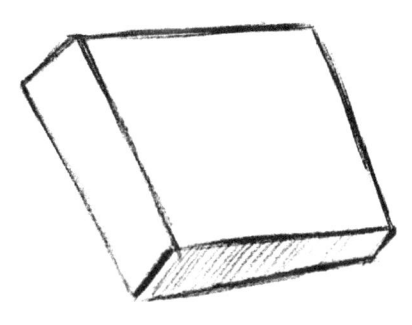

Step - #1

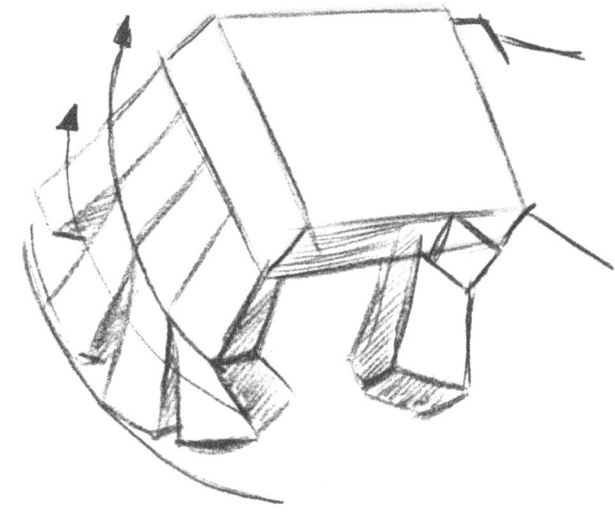

Step - #2

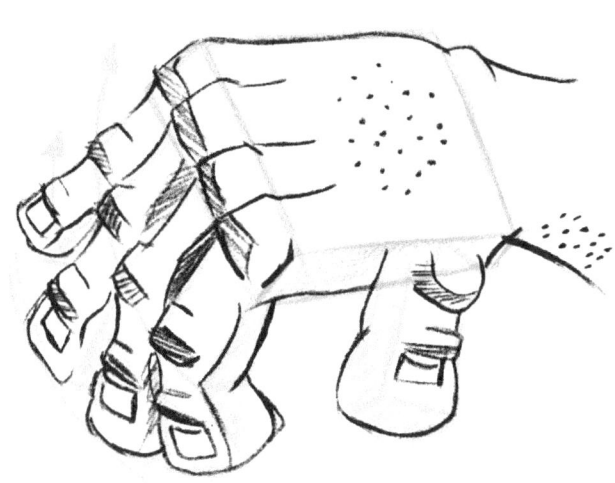

Step - #3

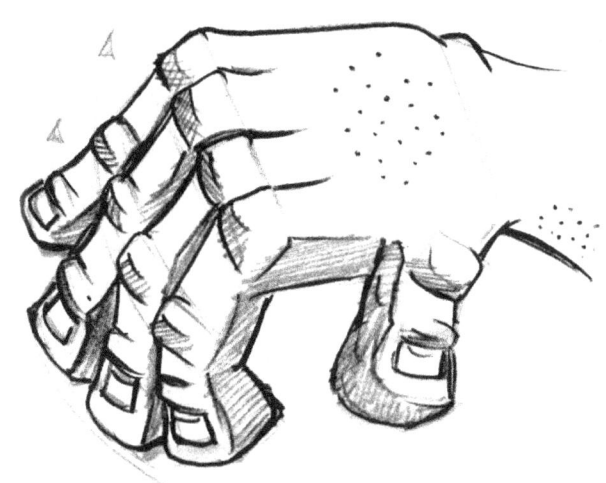

Toon sketch

# Drawing Space

# Chapter 2 Drawing Robots

## Five Robots with Combinations of Shapes

Step 1. Start with Laying out The body by combining variations of unique designs or shapes. Explore your own ways to build The following robots, and feel free To change The shapes To create completely different robots

Step 2. Then add secondary shapes such as Hand Shapes, Feet Wheels or any other fun features The character will have.

Step 3. Add all your detail and be creative with Lines To make The characters appear to be robots.

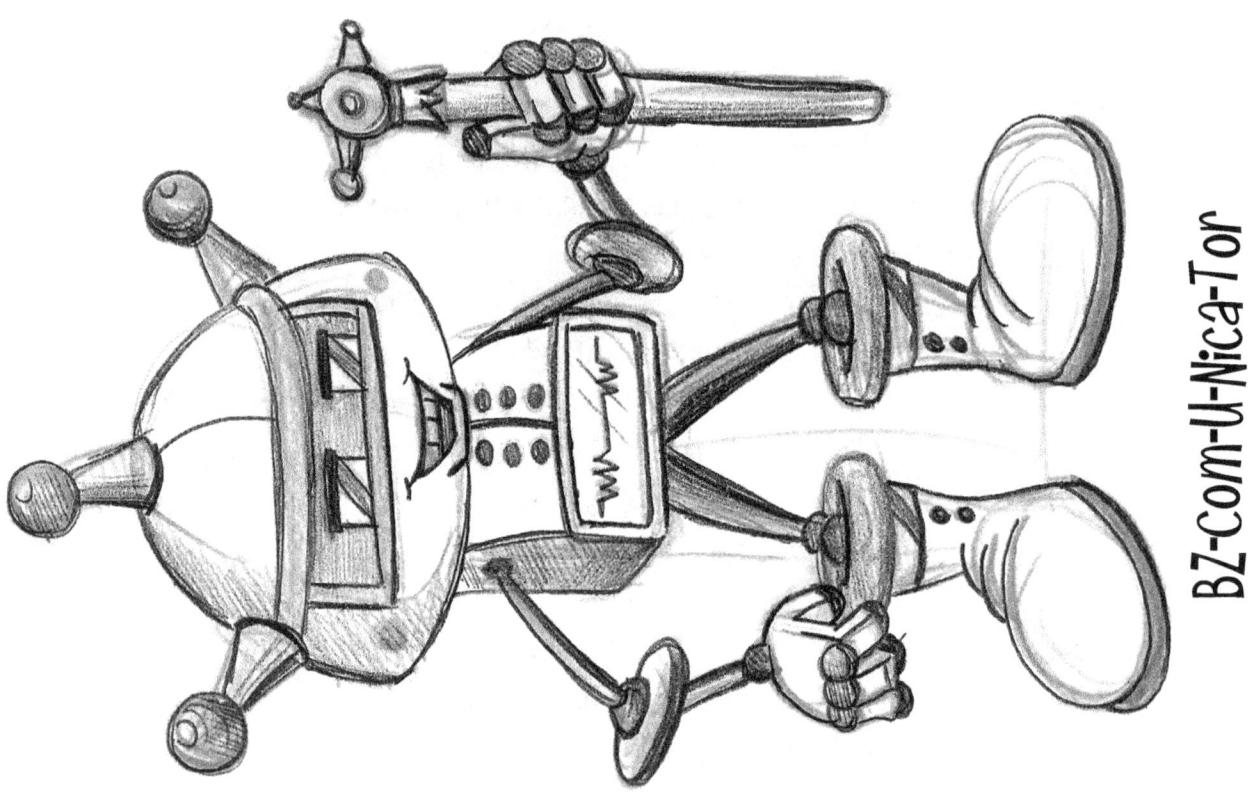

BZ-Com-U-Nica-Tor

STep - #3

STep - #2

STep - #1

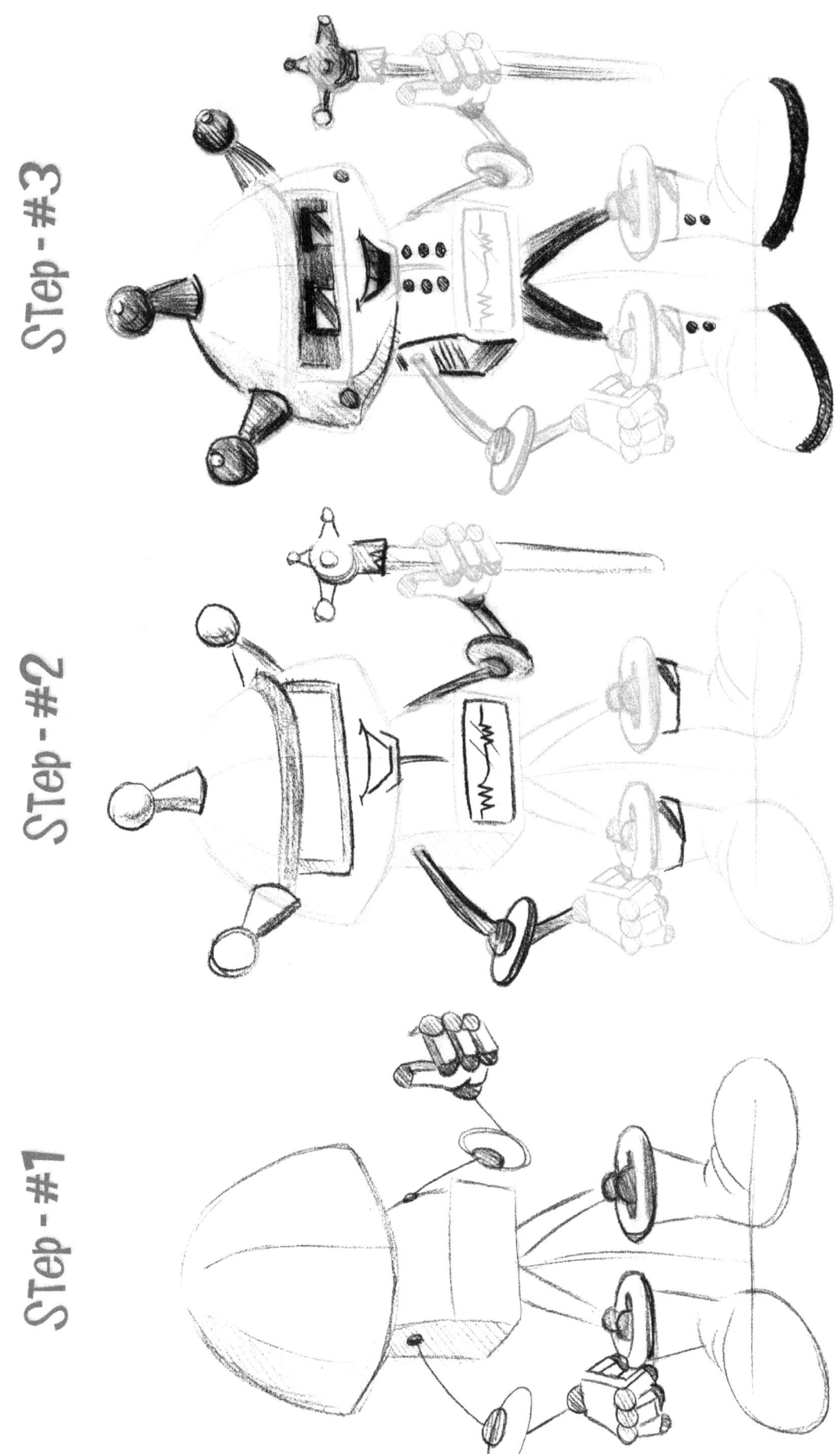

35

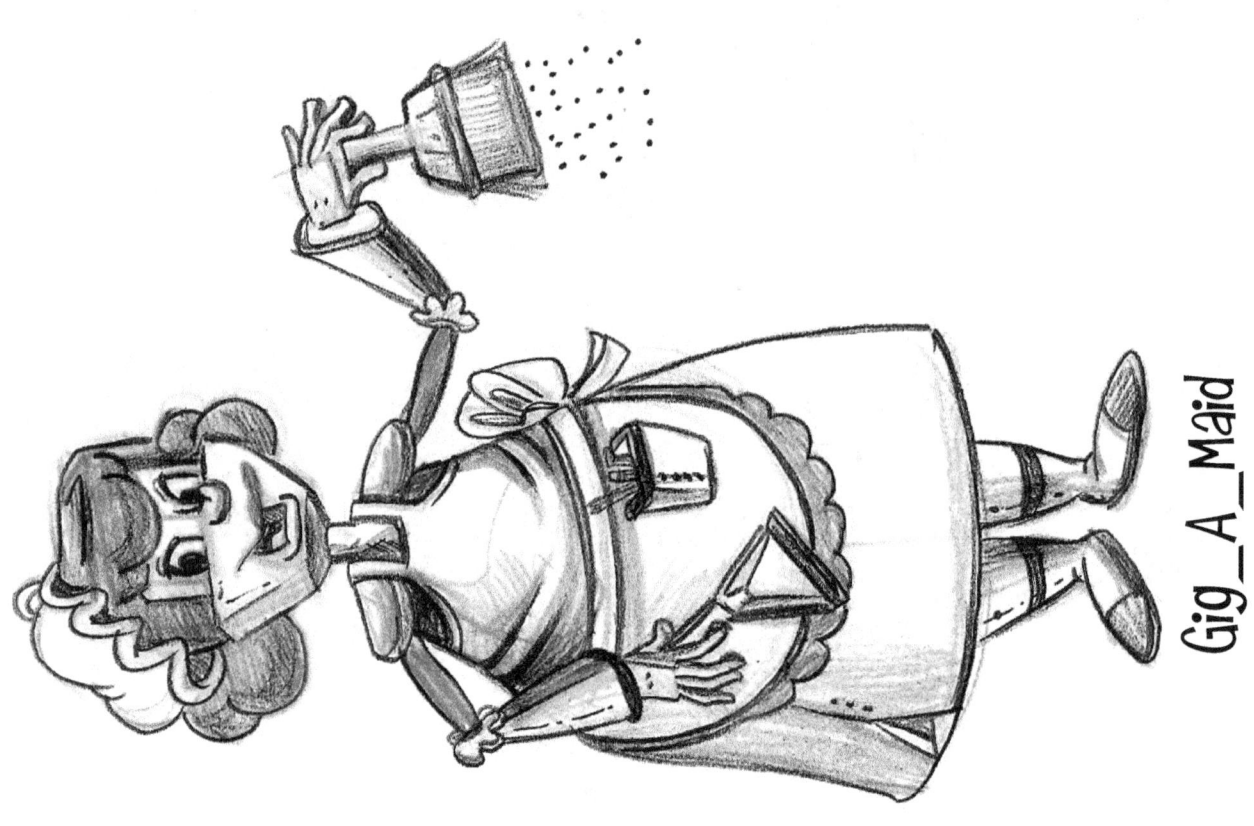

Gig_A_Maid

36.

STep - #3

STep - #2

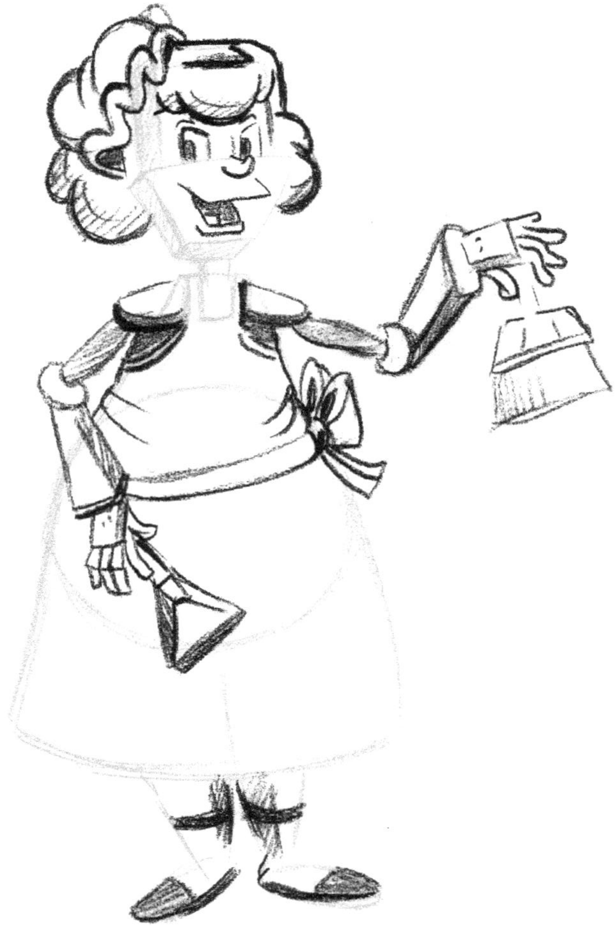

STep - #1

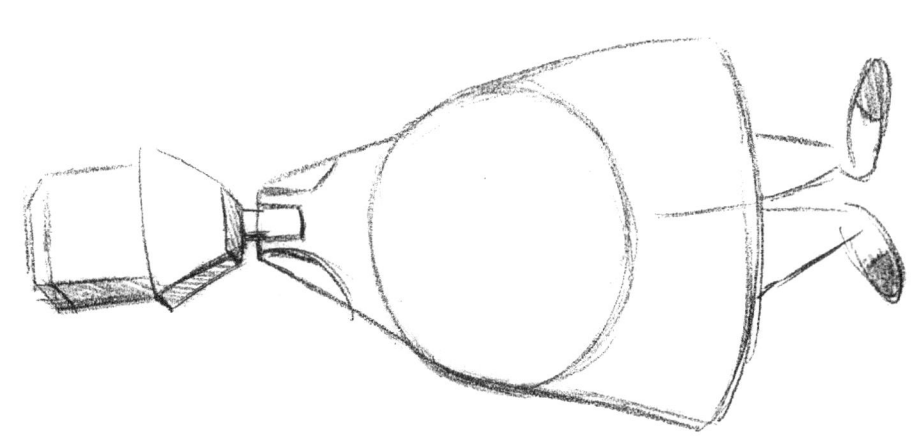

37

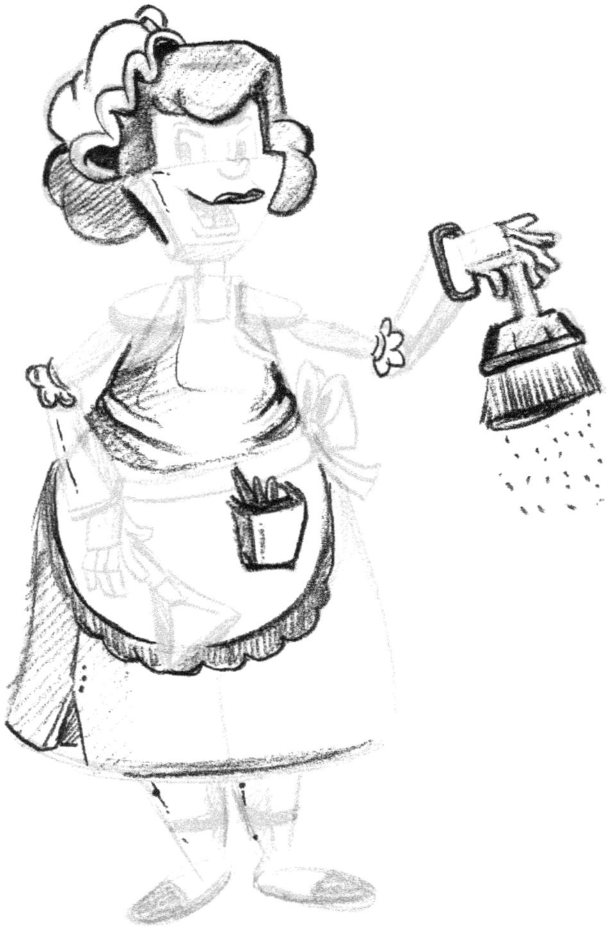

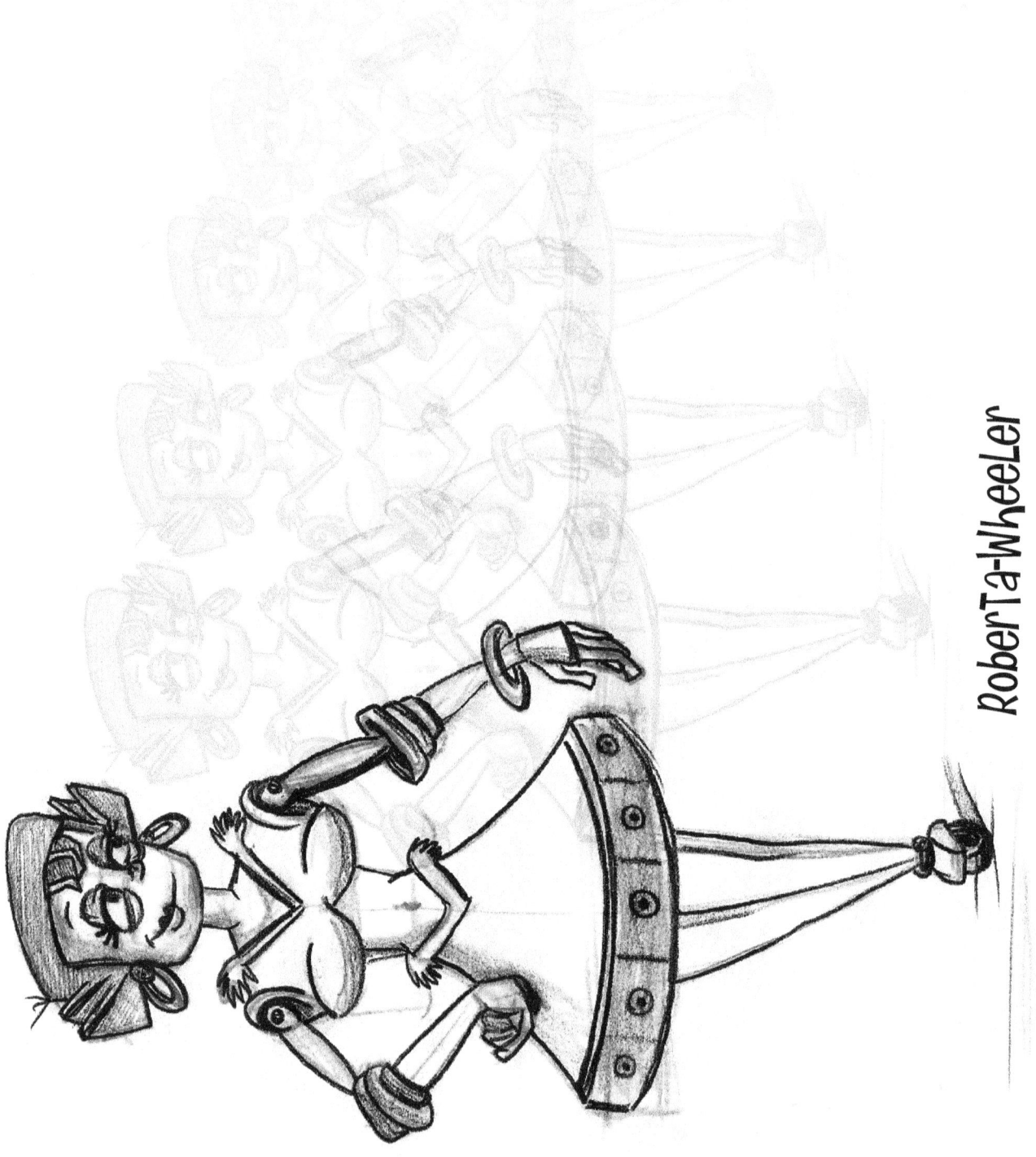

Roberta-Wheeler

STep-#1

STep-#2

STep-#3

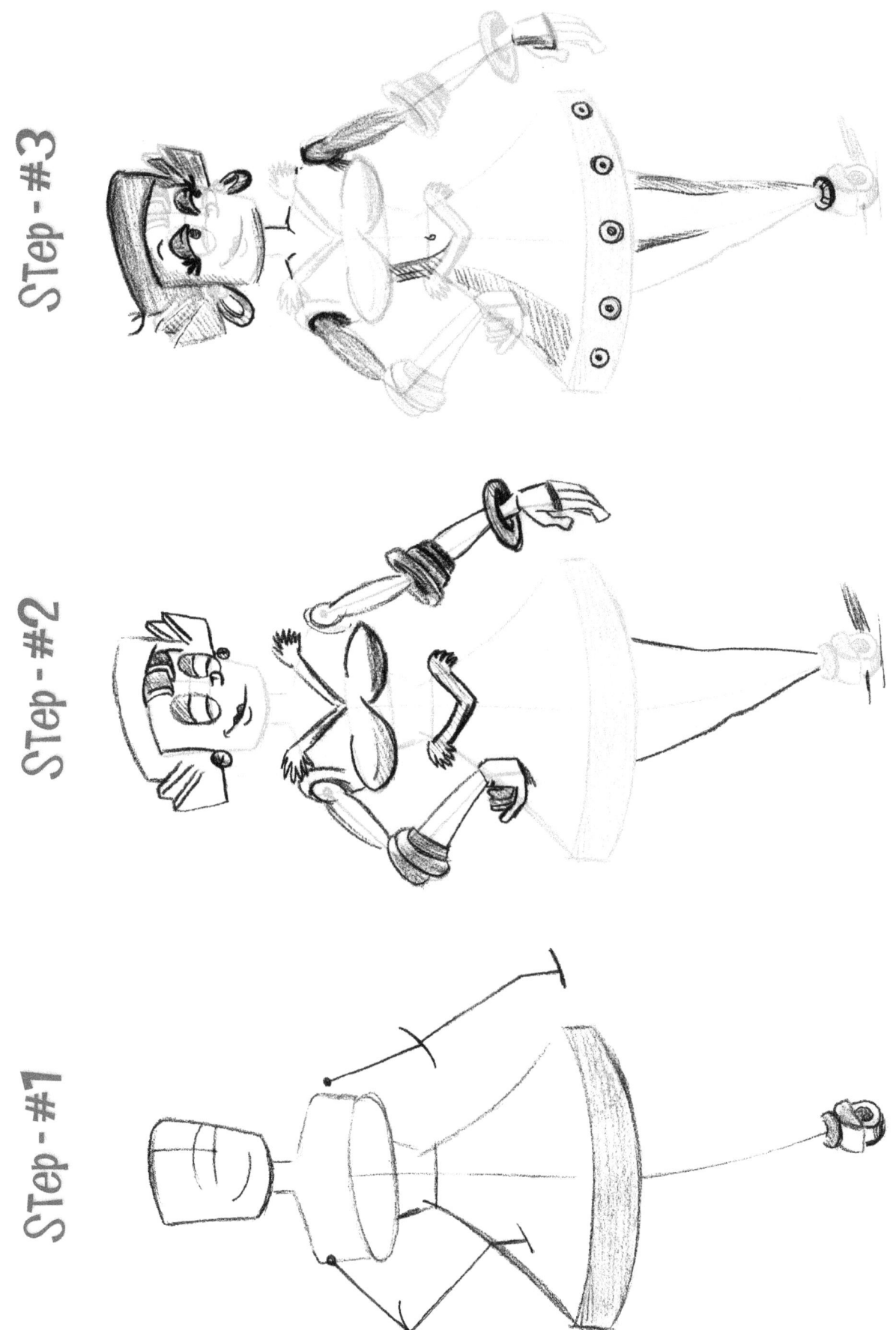

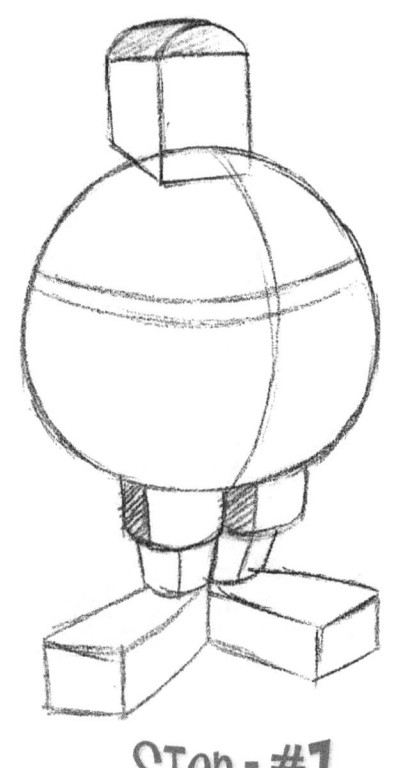

Step - #1

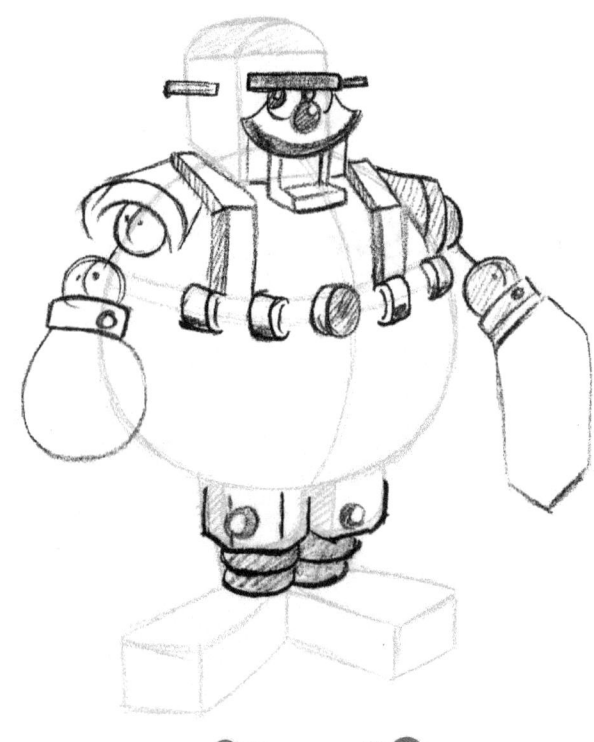

Step - #2

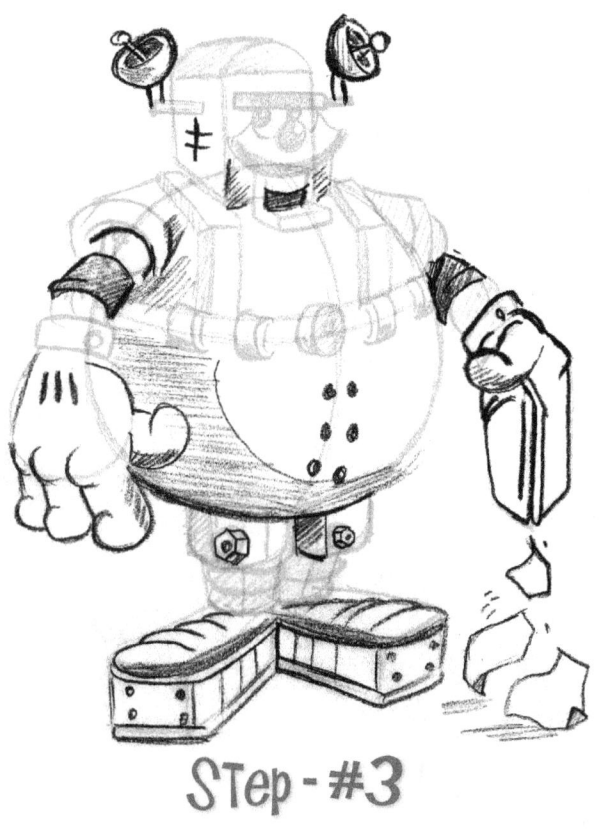

Step - #3

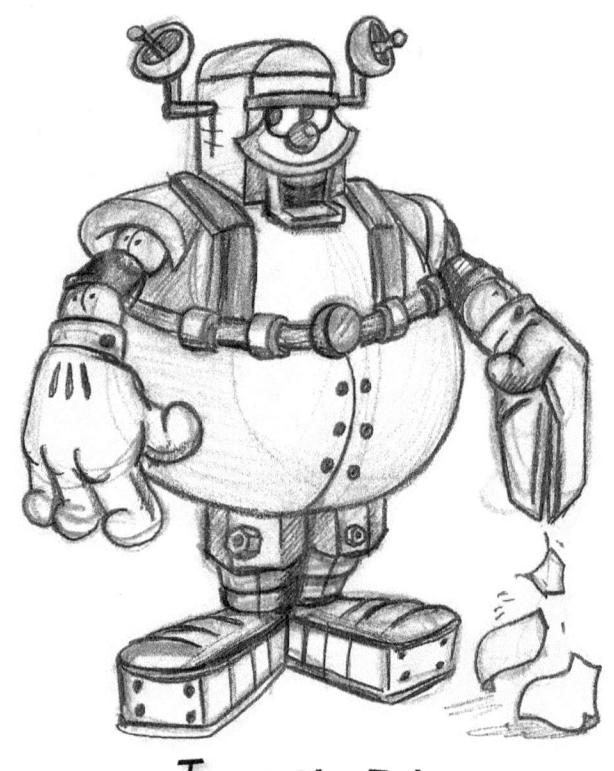

Toon sketch

40.

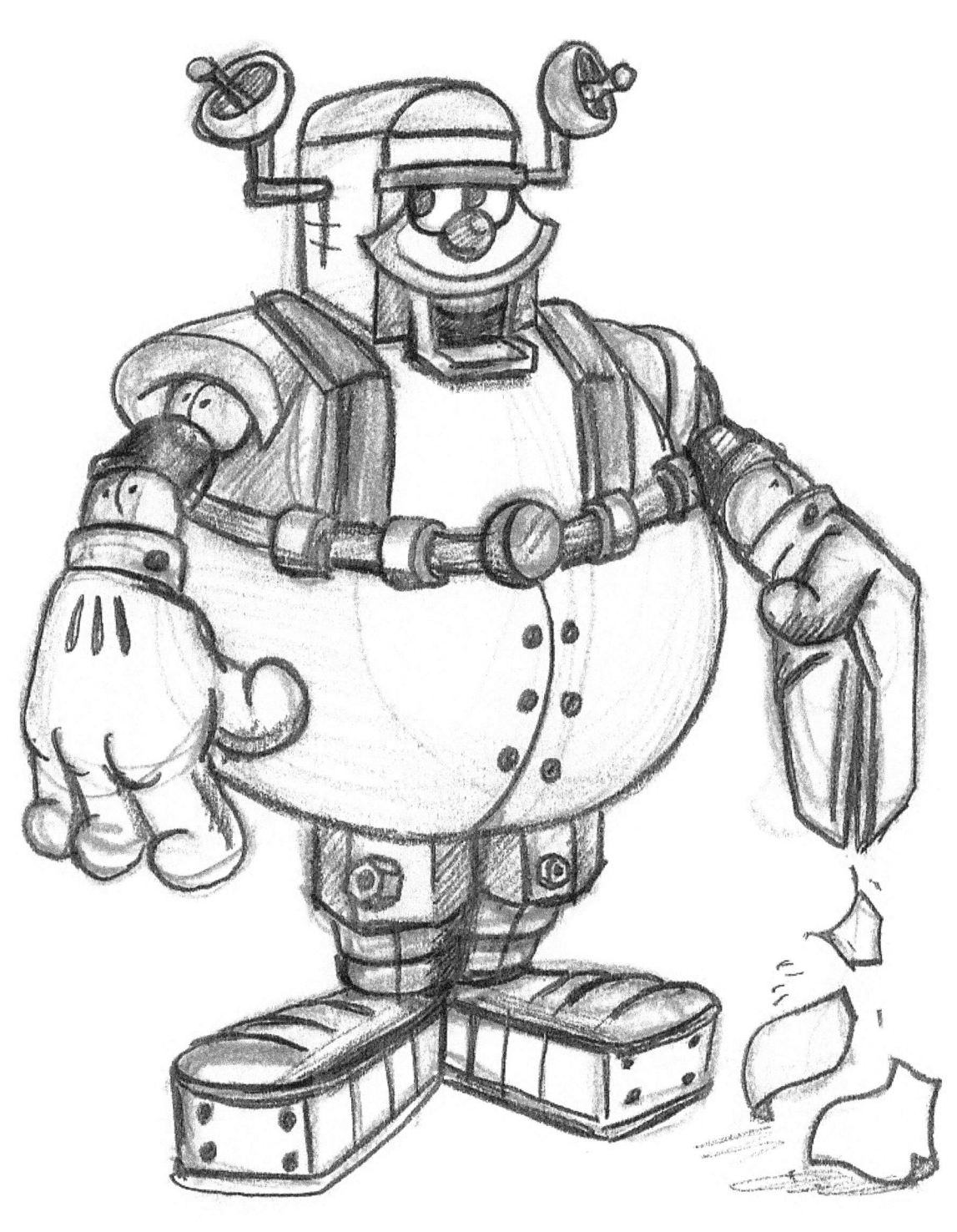

PAr-Tee-BoT- ModeL # f.u.n

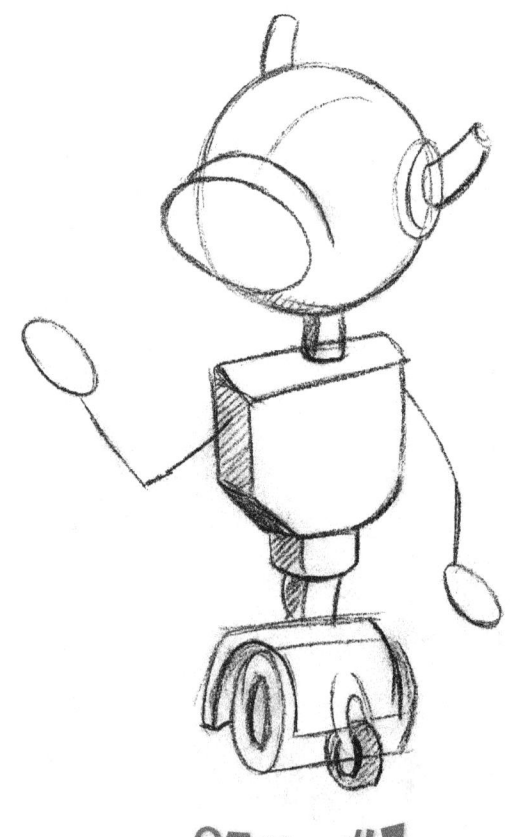

**STep - #1**

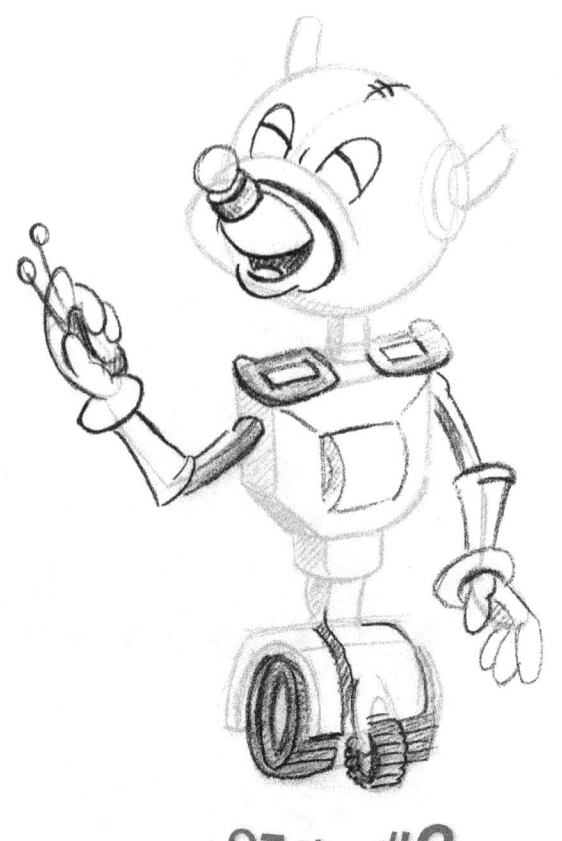

**STep - #2**

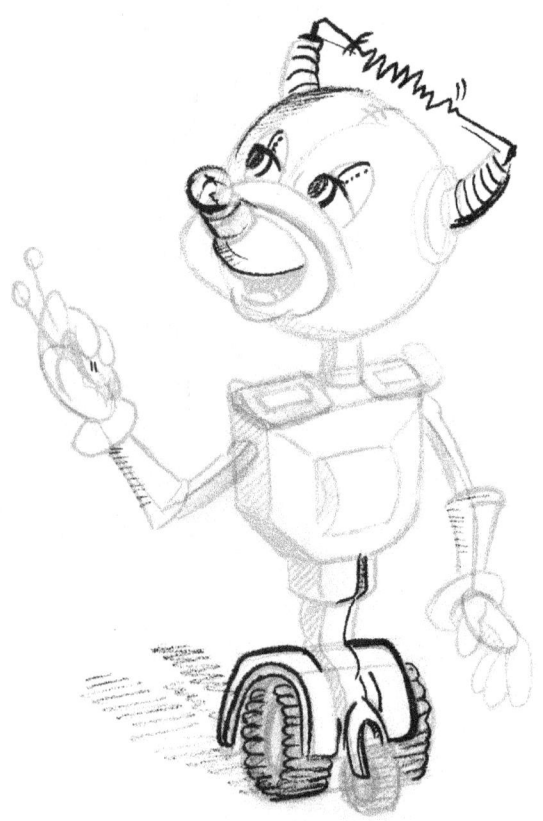

**STep - #3**

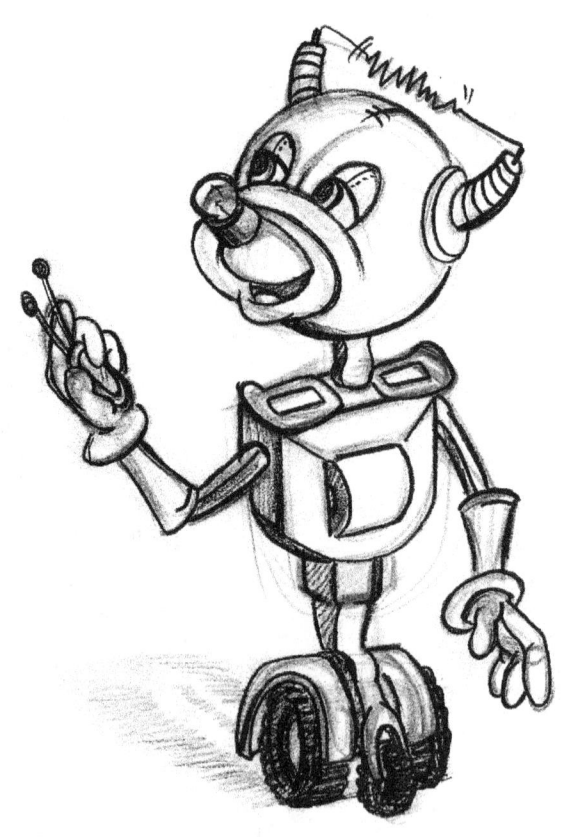

**Toon skeTch**

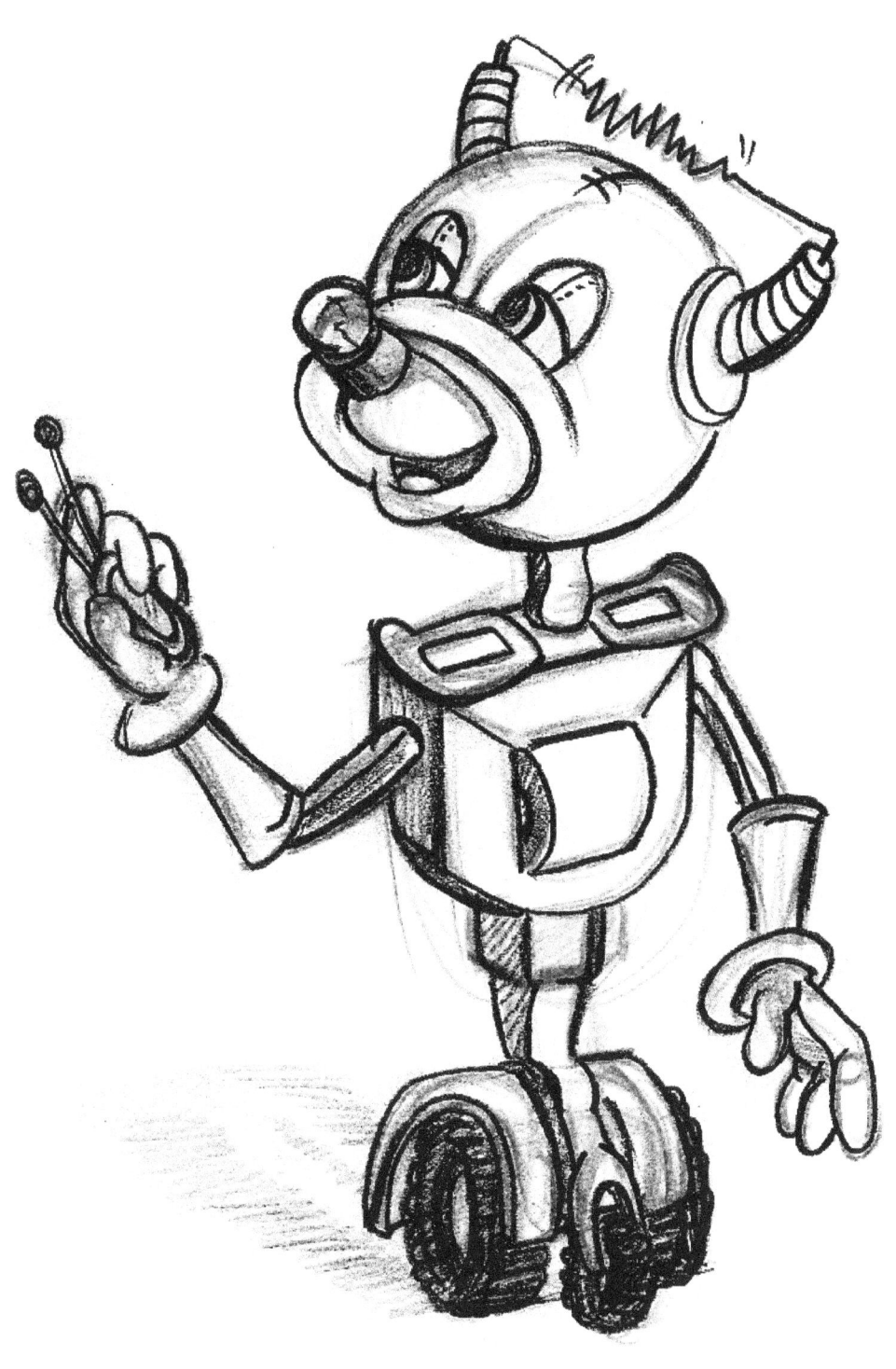

RoTT-WheeL-R

# Drawing Space

# Ten Robots with Distorted Boxes and cubes

Step 1. These robots will all be constructed
with basic squares and block shape types. Make interesting
styles of boxes to make body components and parts.

Step 2. Maintain the same types of shapes throughout
the entire character composition, and make the blocks
work proportionately for a better and more
solid character finish.

Step 3. Apply all your detail and shade sections that might
face away from the light. Always consider the front
of the character where the light source will bounce.
Cross hatches and Angled lines are
brilliant on Robots.

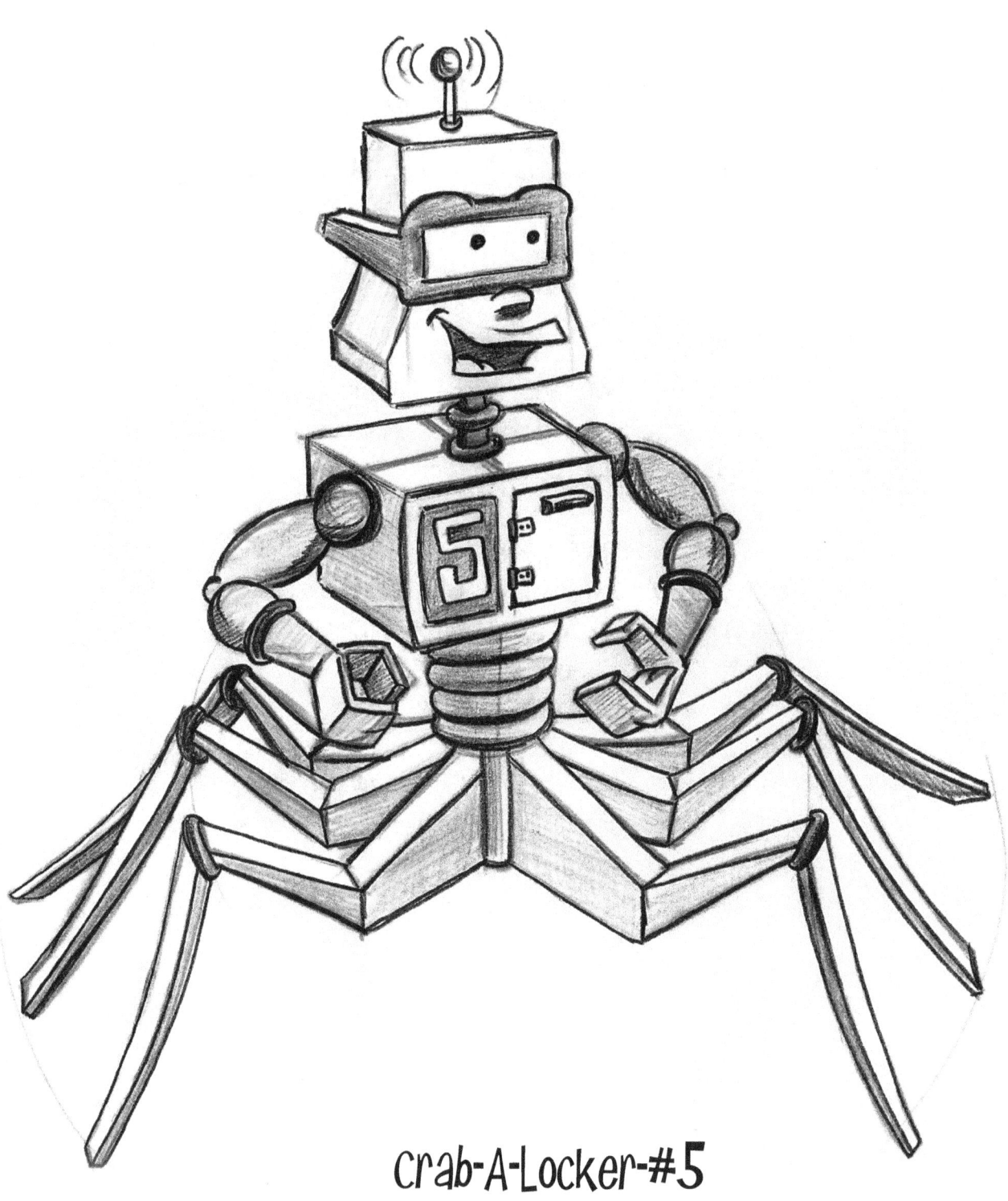

crab-A-Locker-#5

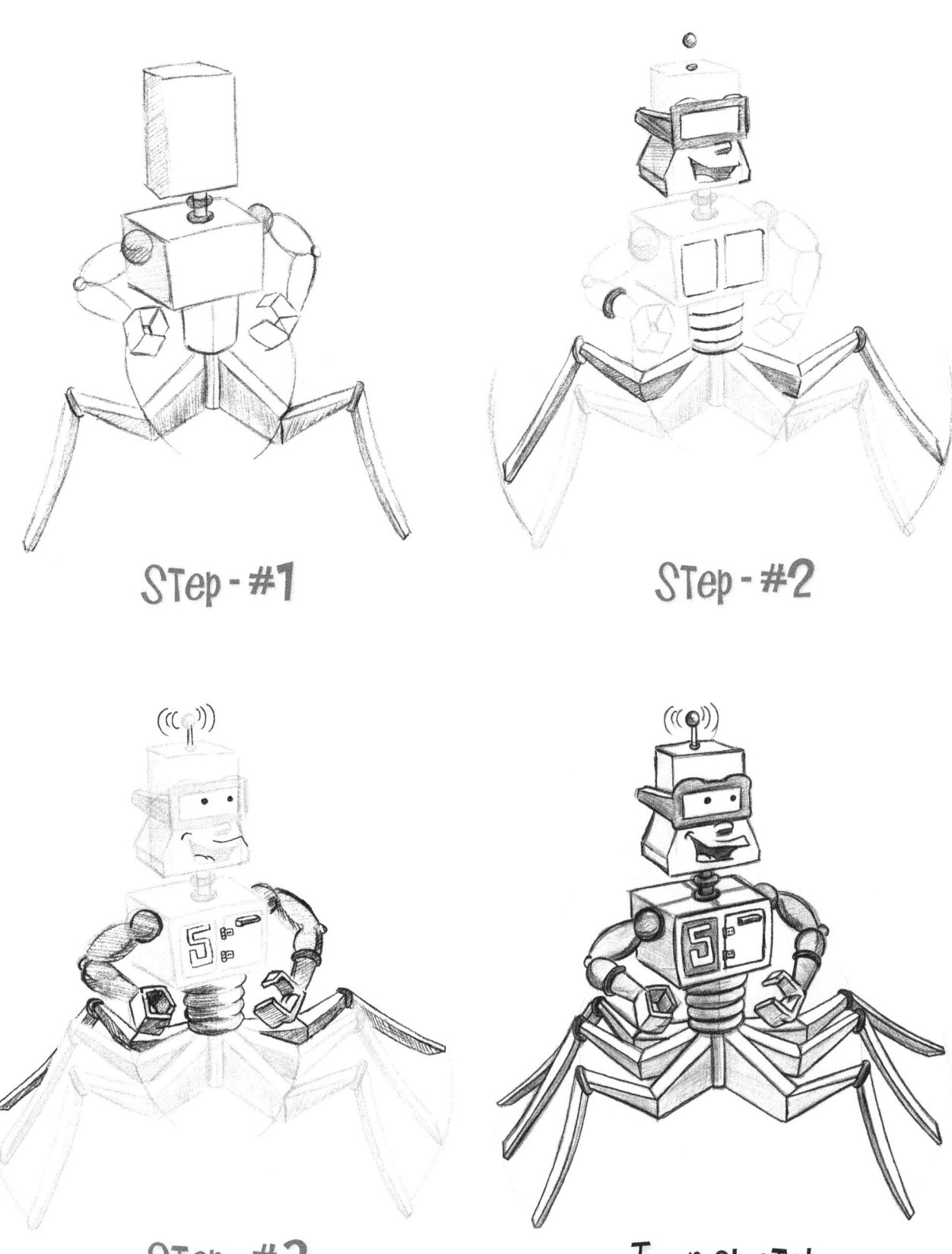

Step - #1

Step - #2

Step - #3

Toon sketch

47.

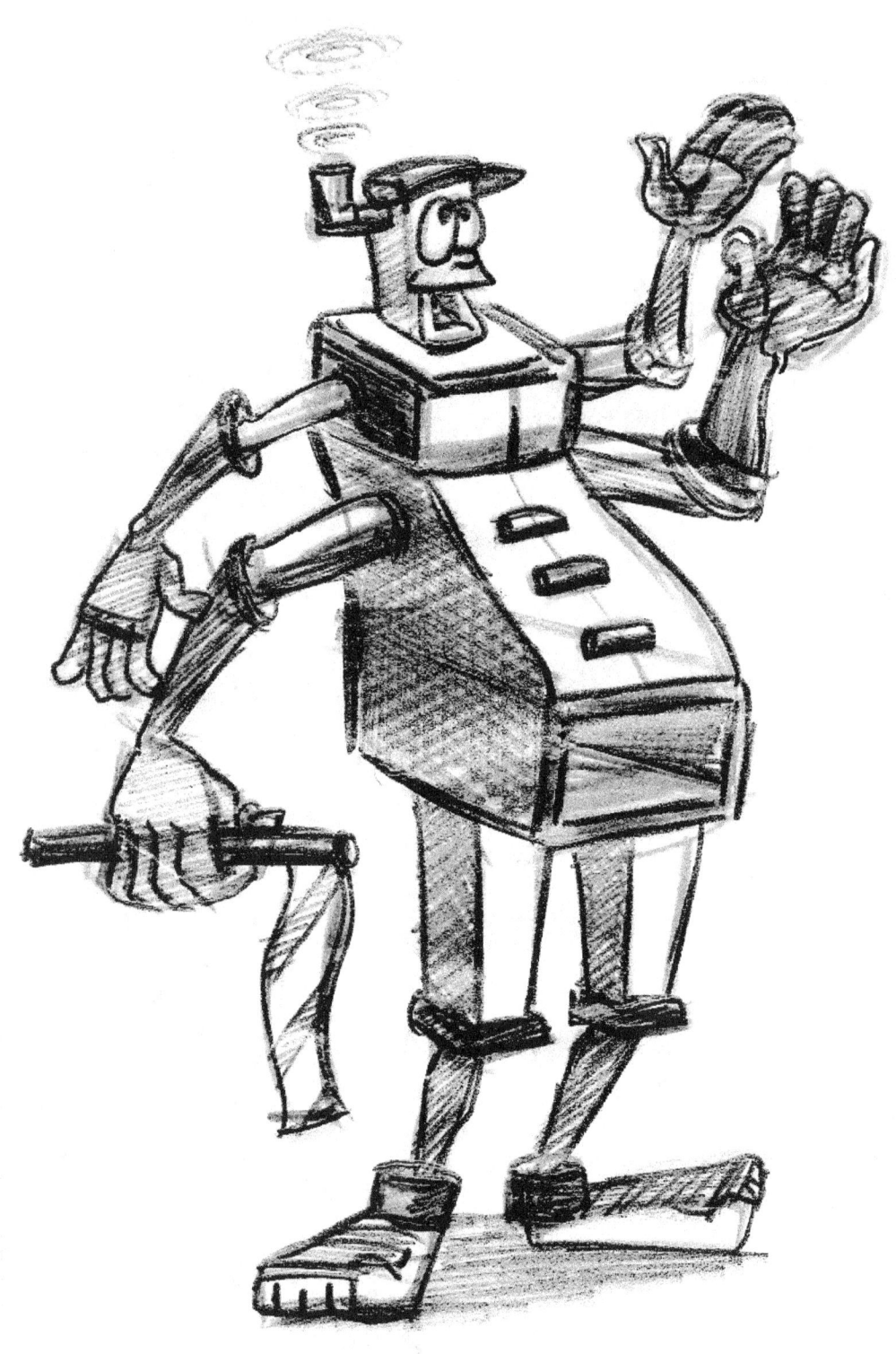

Dr. Robo-Guy-Der

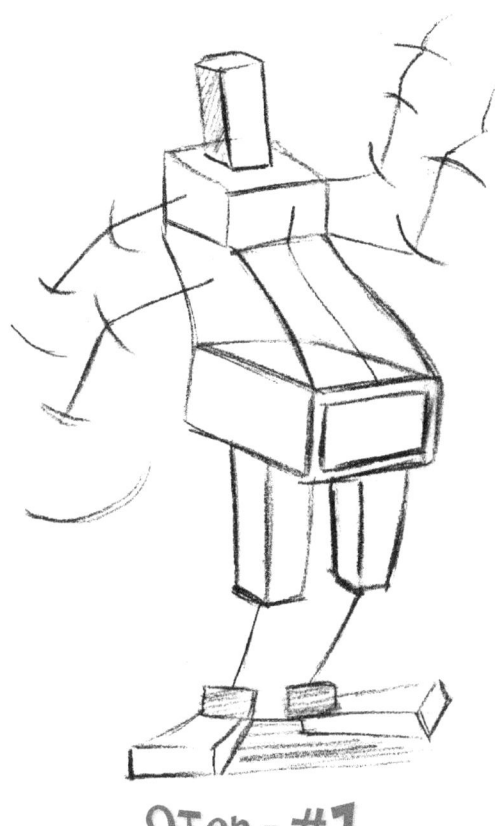

STep - #1

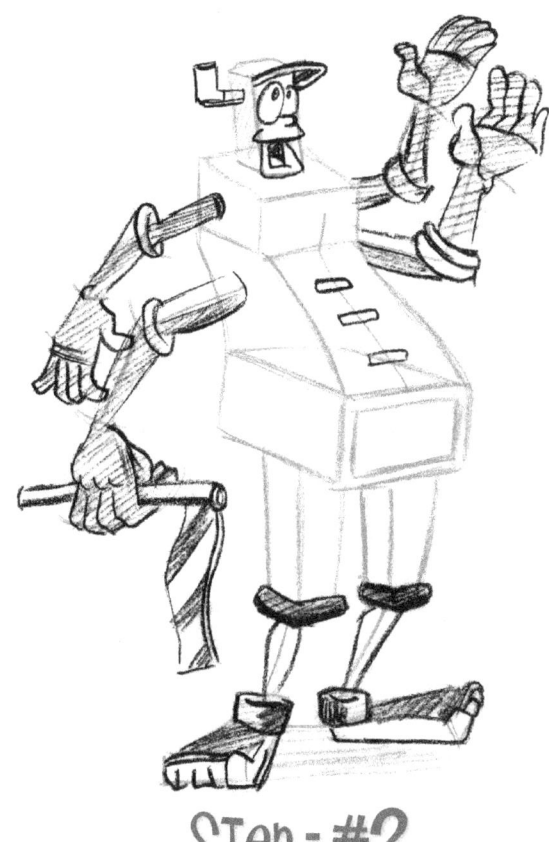

STep - #2

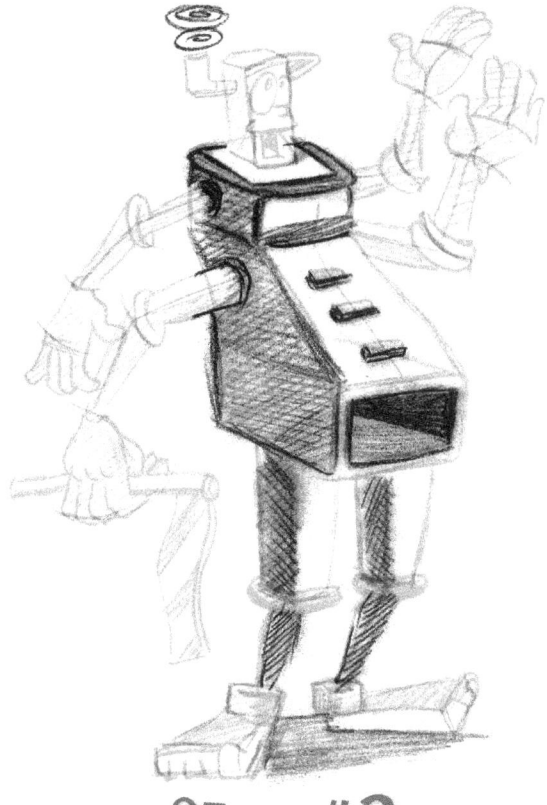

STep - #3

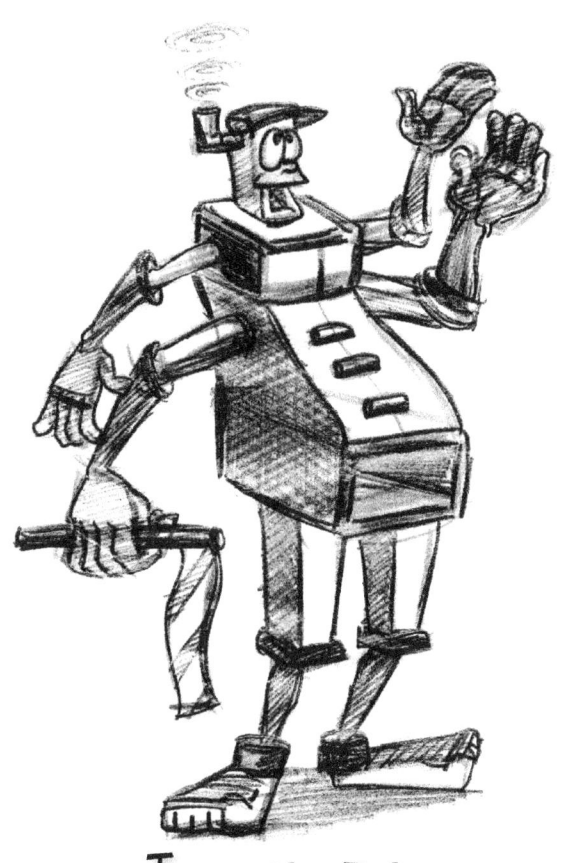

Toon sketch

49.

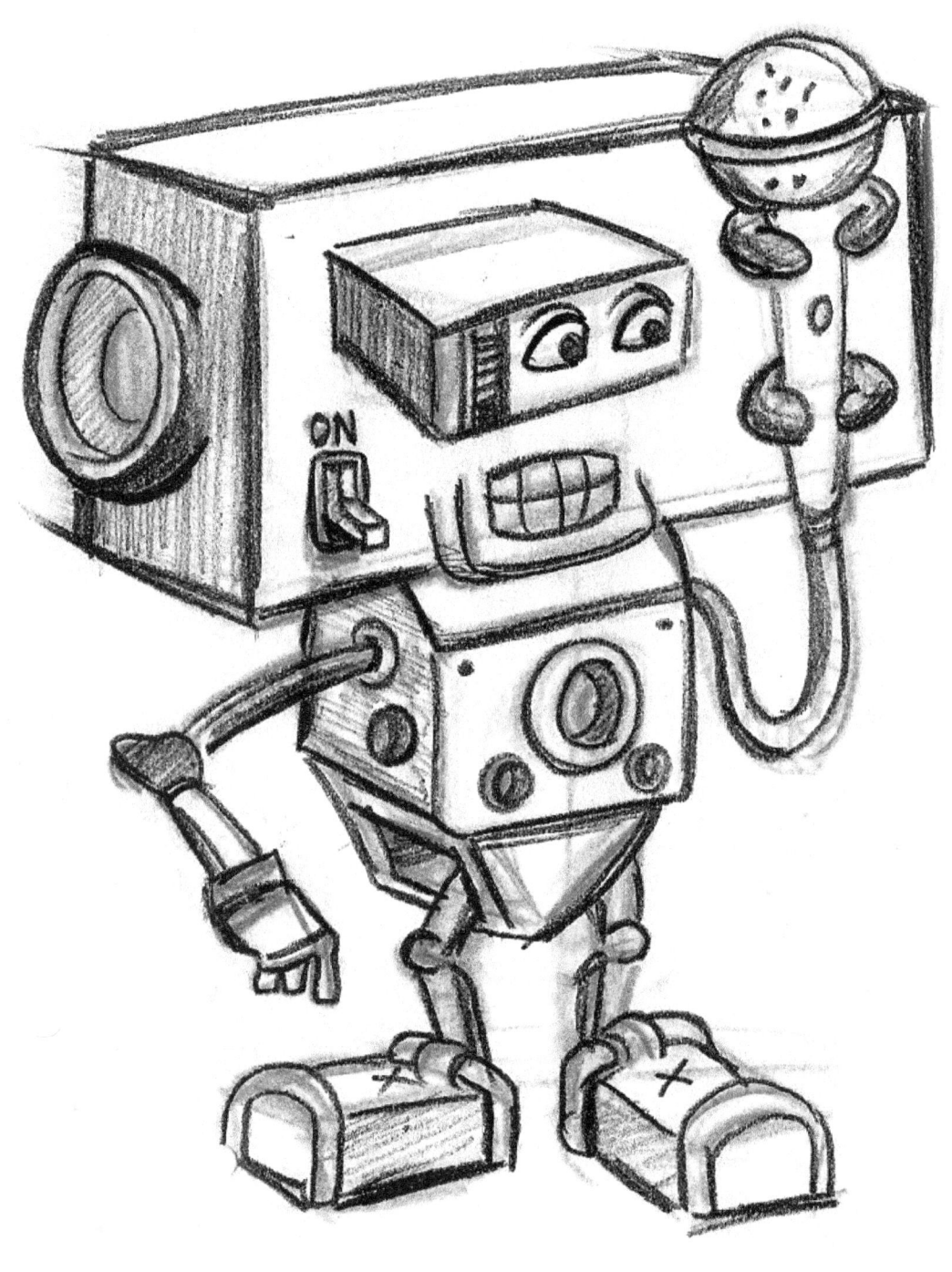

Kara-O-Key-Tron

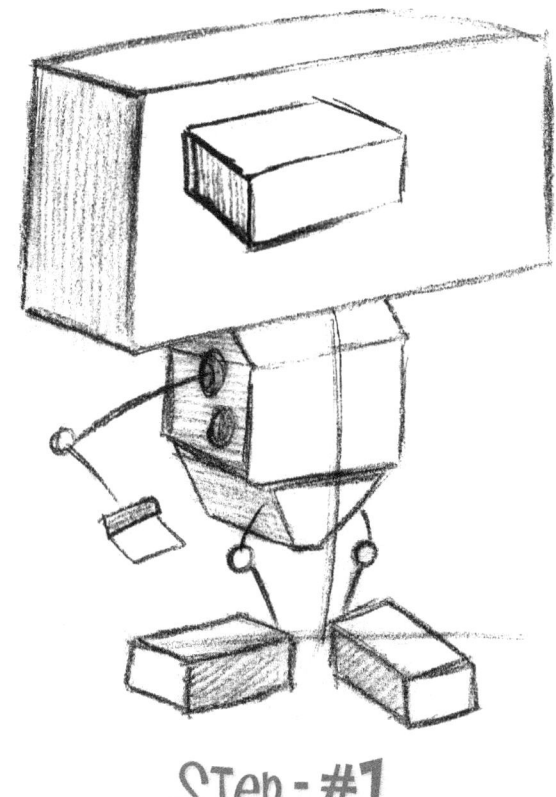

STep - #1

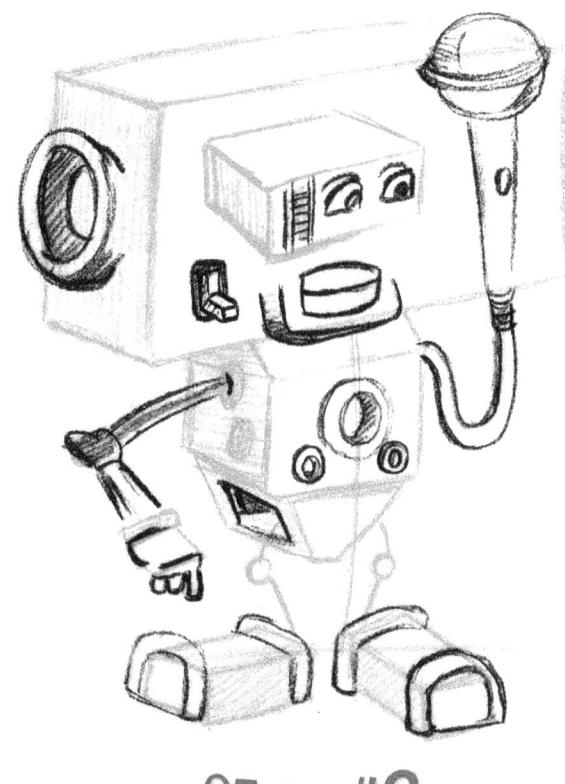

STep - #2

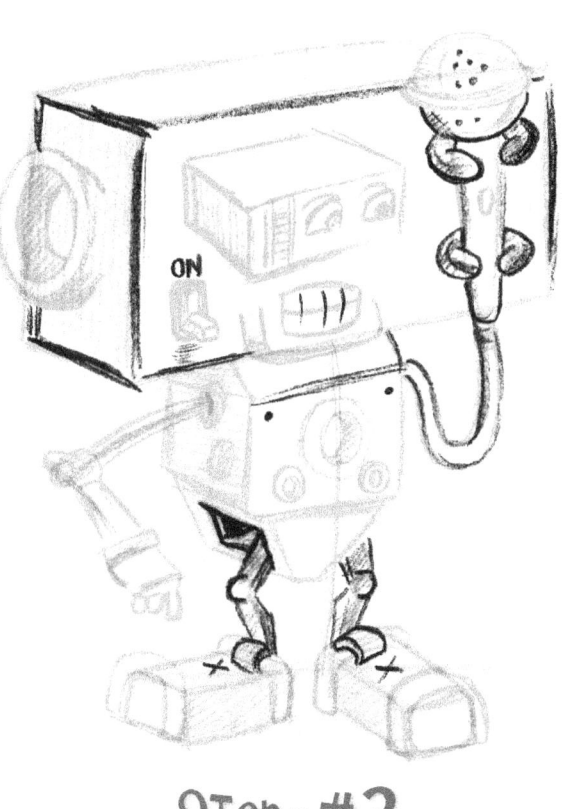

STep - #3

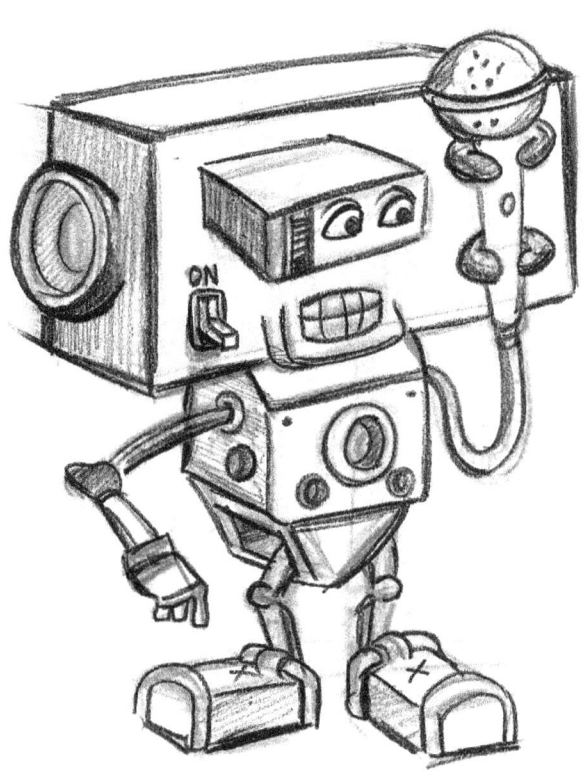

Toon sketch

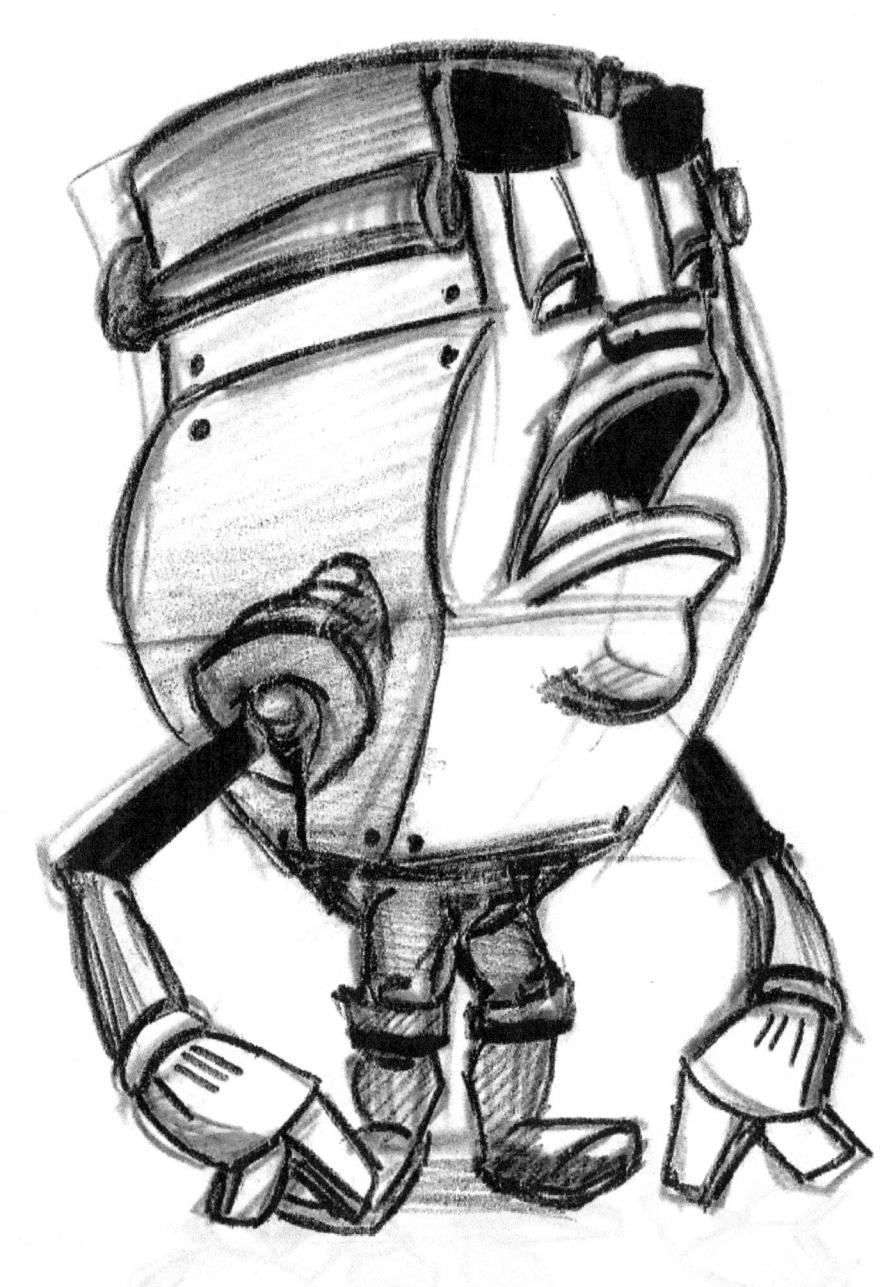

Mega-Disposer-613

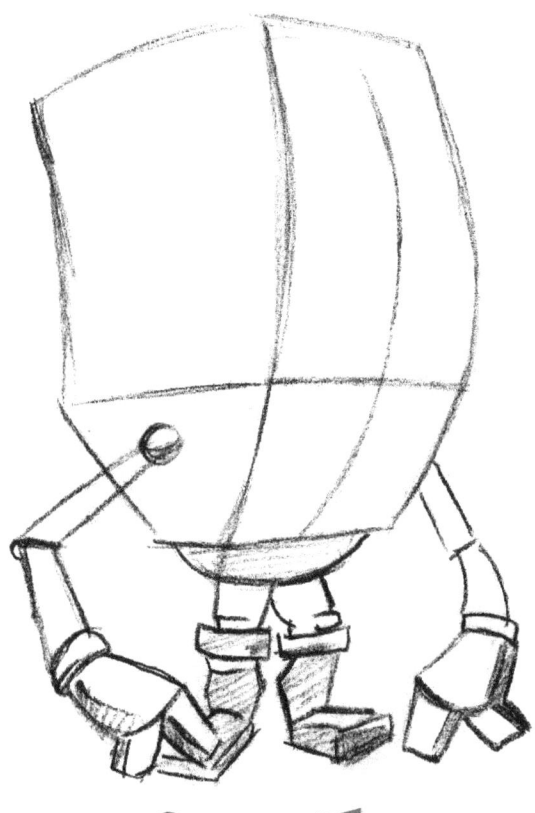

Step - #1

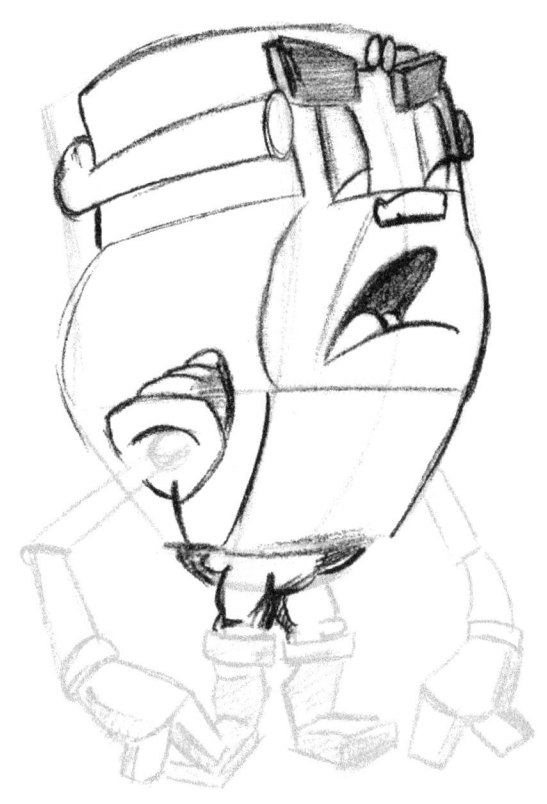

Step - #2

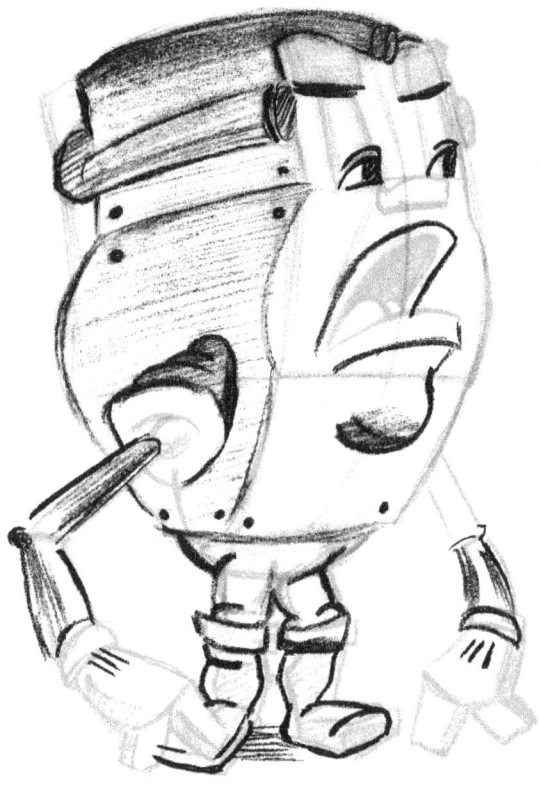

Step - #3

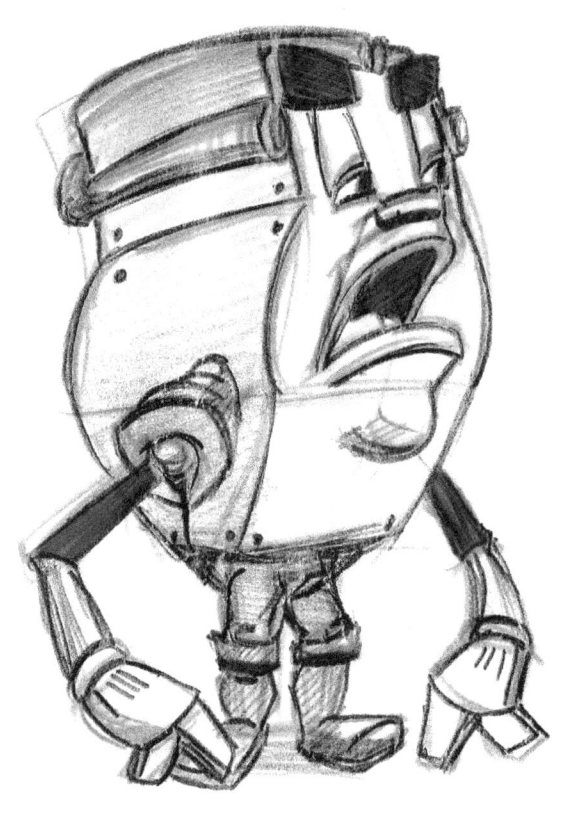

Toon Sketch

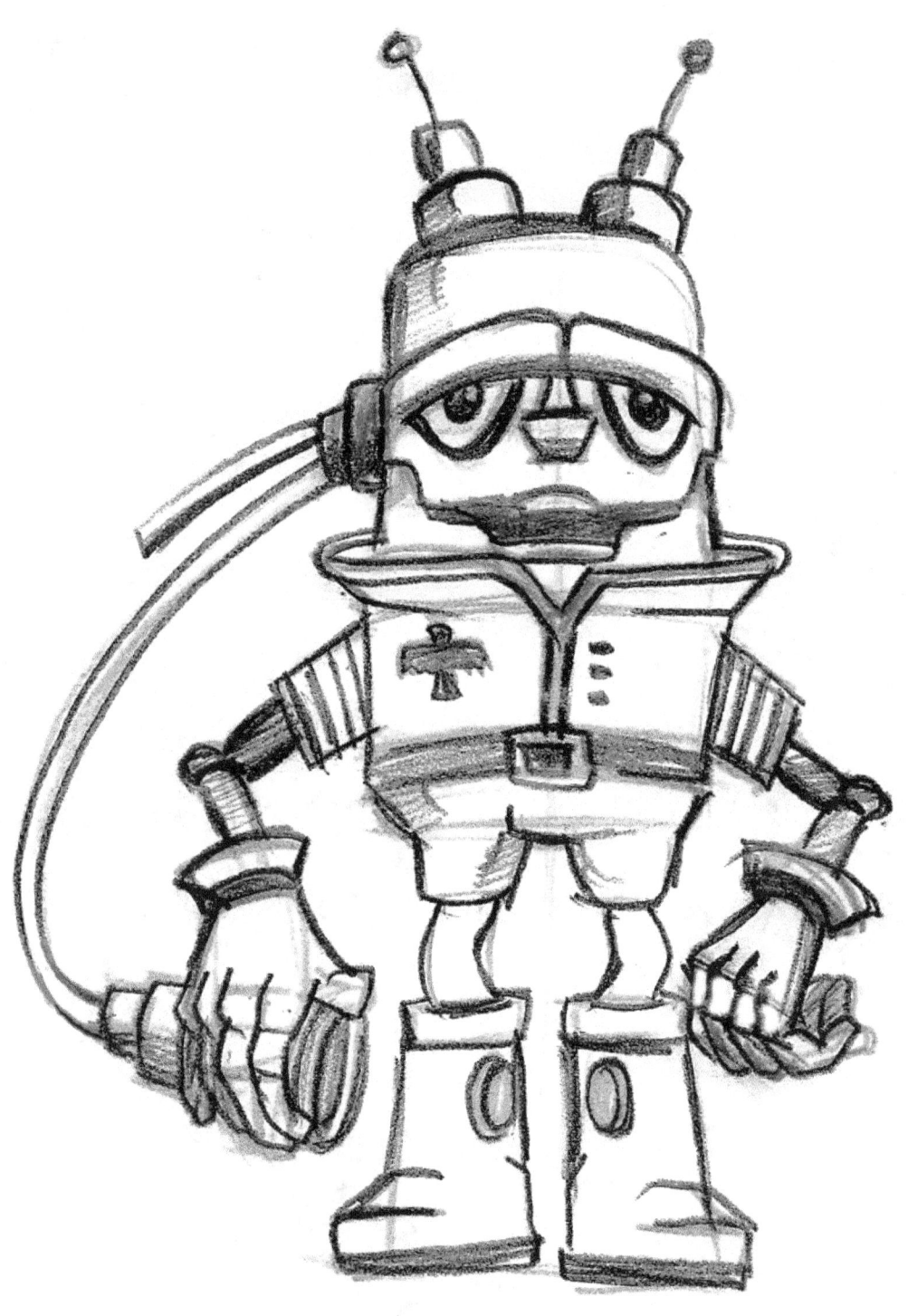

Officer Space-McMoon

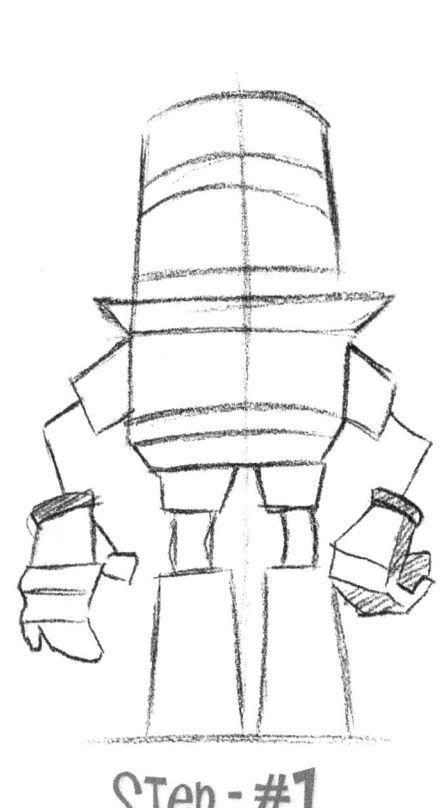

STep - #1

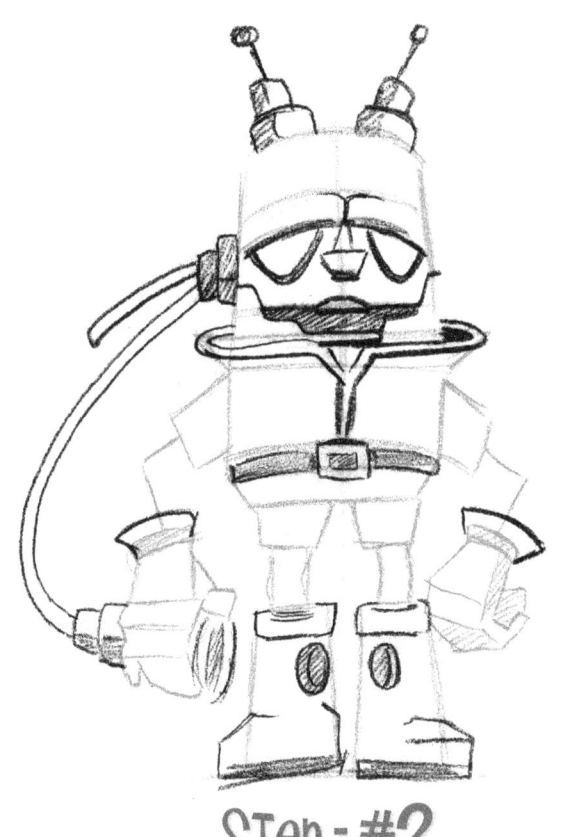

STep - #2

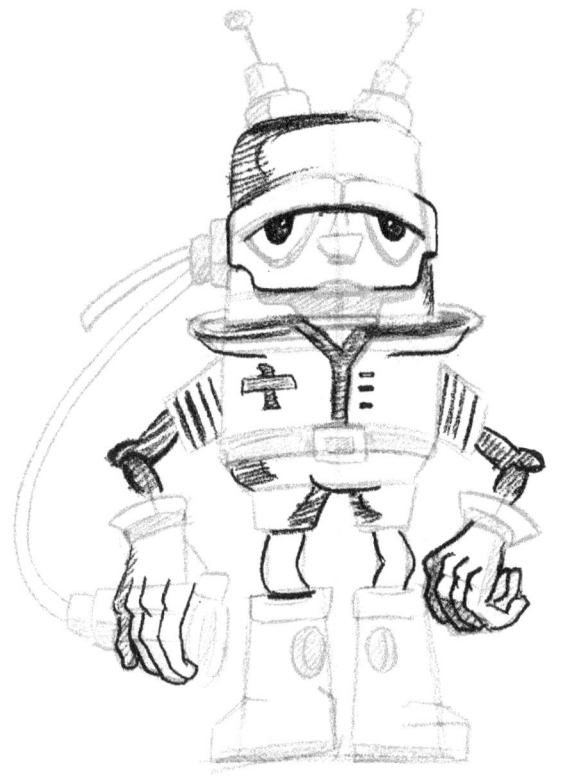

STep - #3

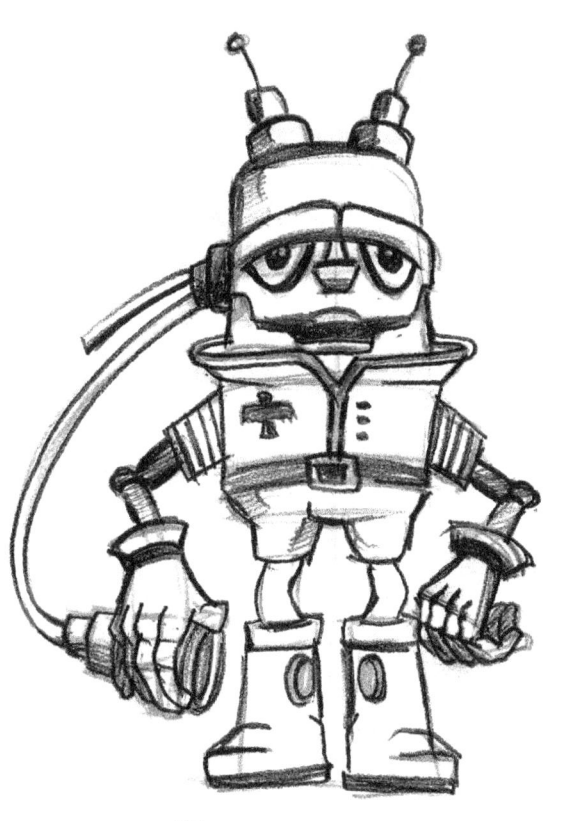

Toon sketch

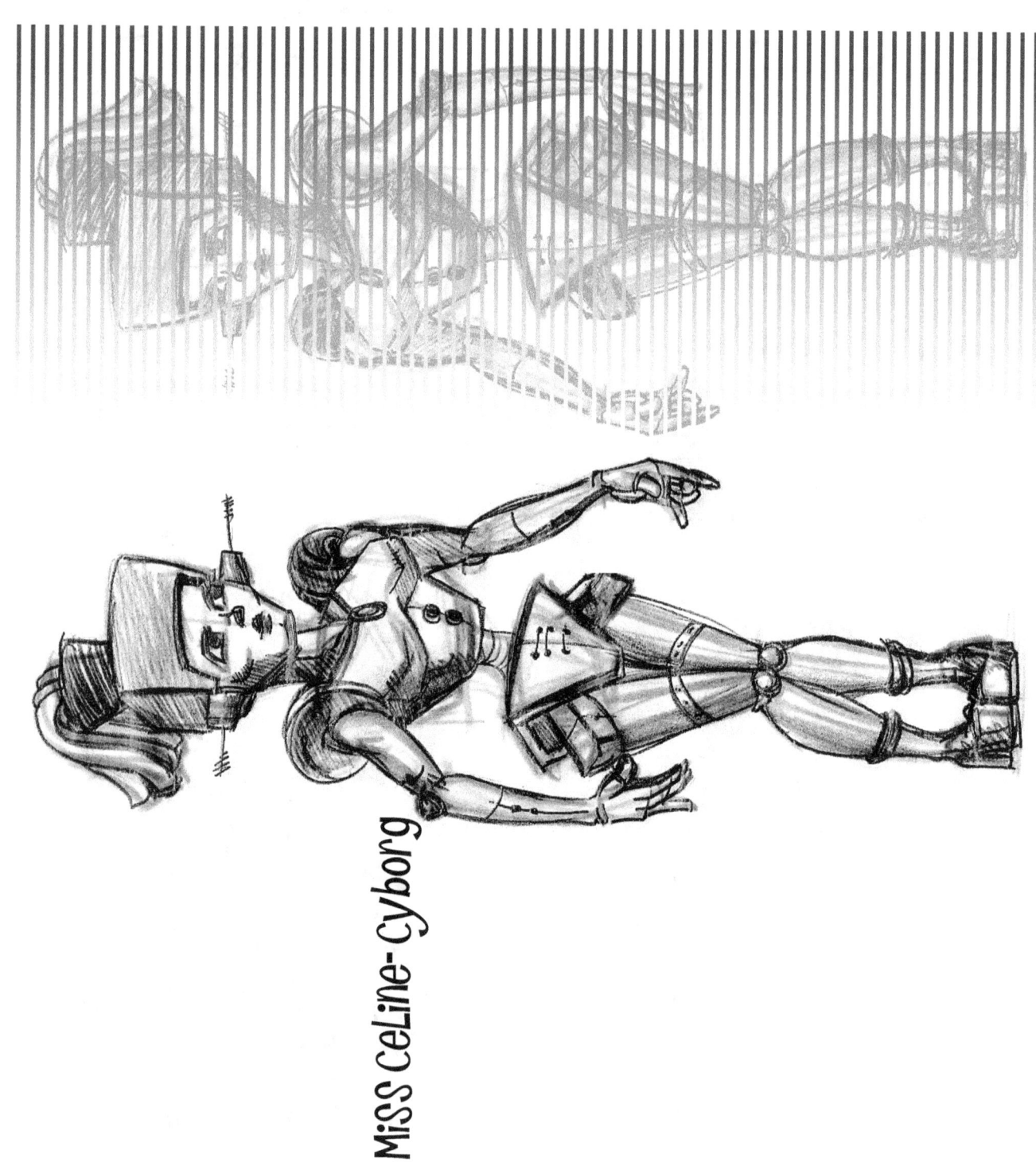

MiSS CeLine- Cyborg

56.

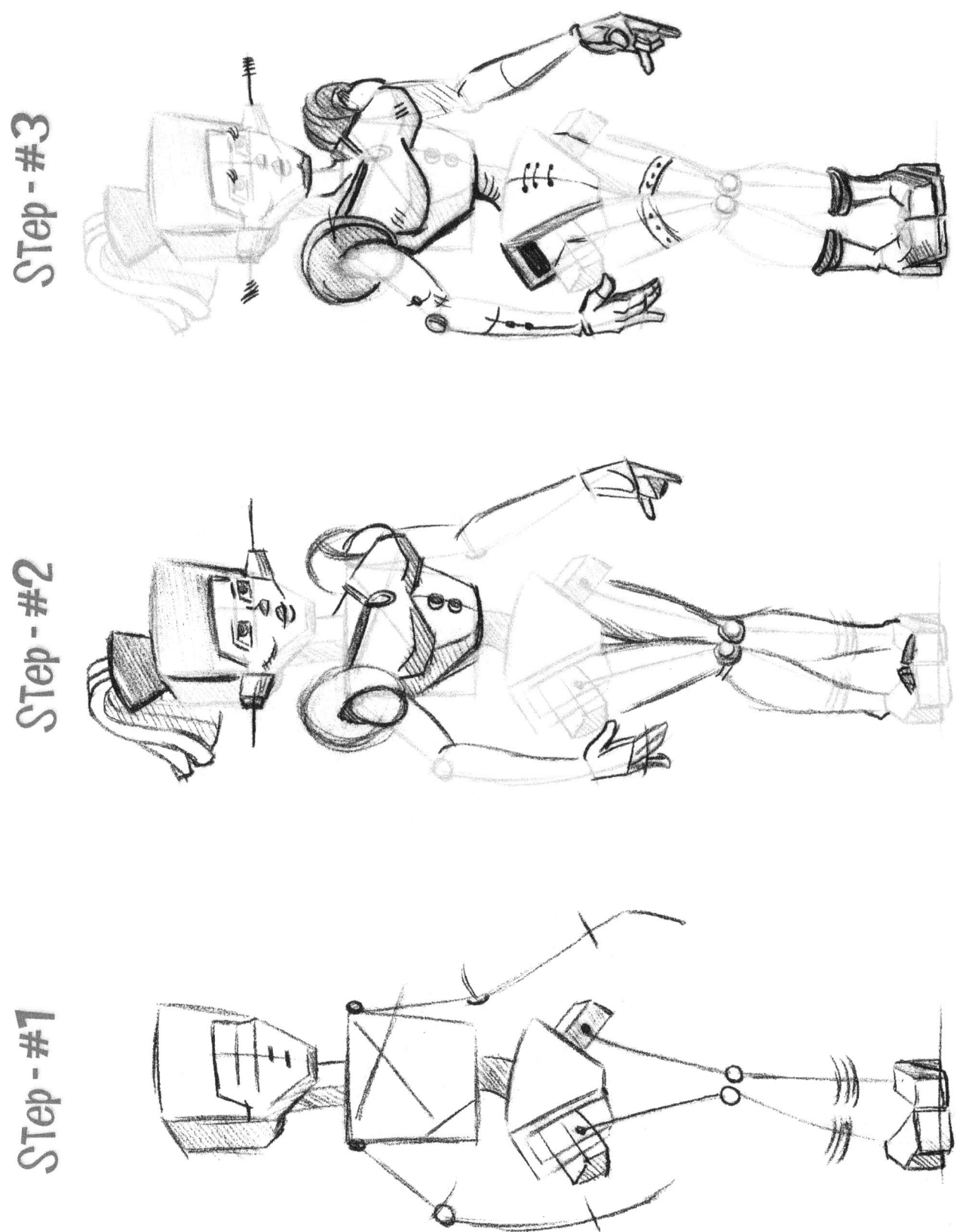

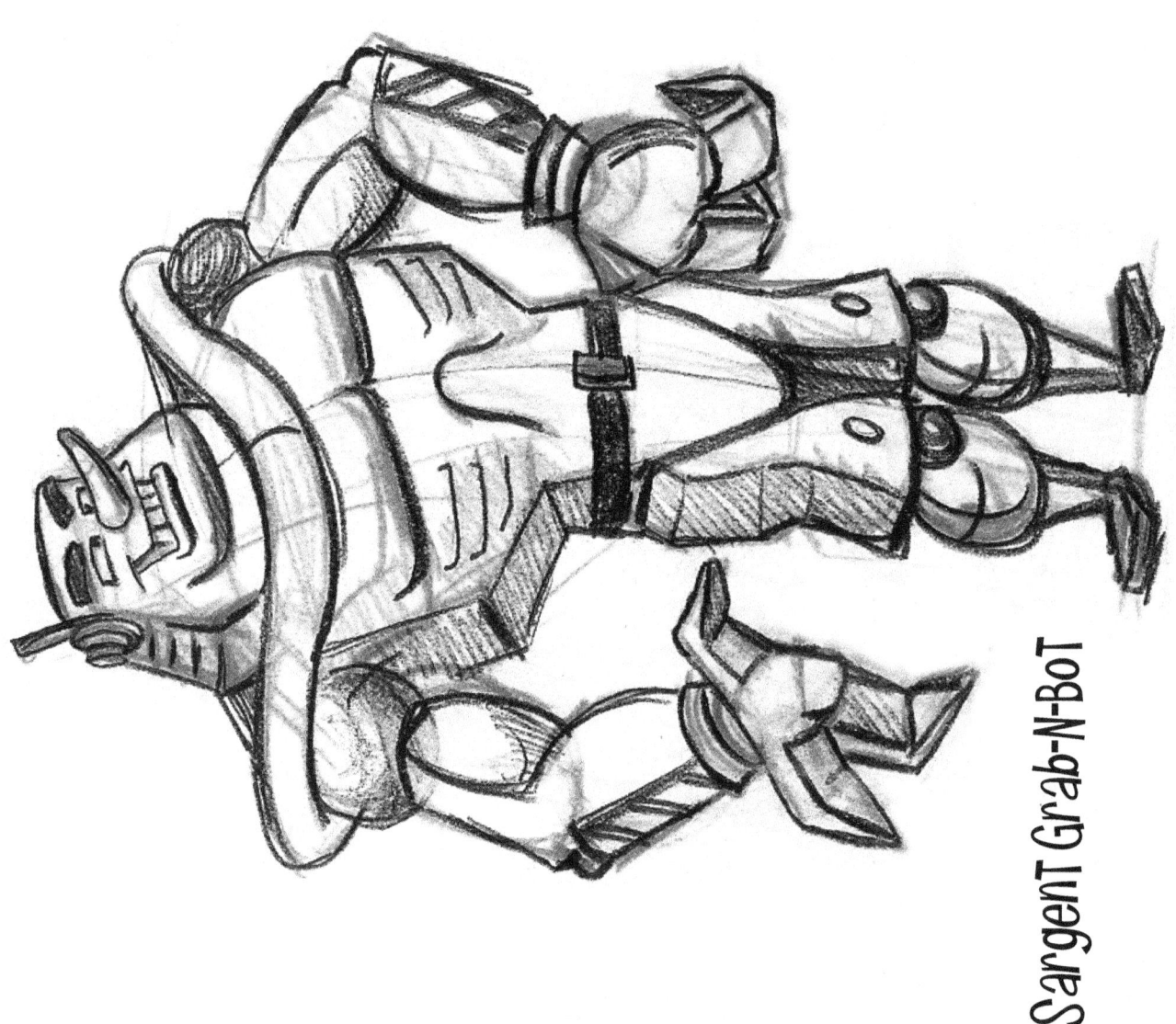

Sargent Grab-N-BoT

STep - #1

STep - #2

STep - #3

59

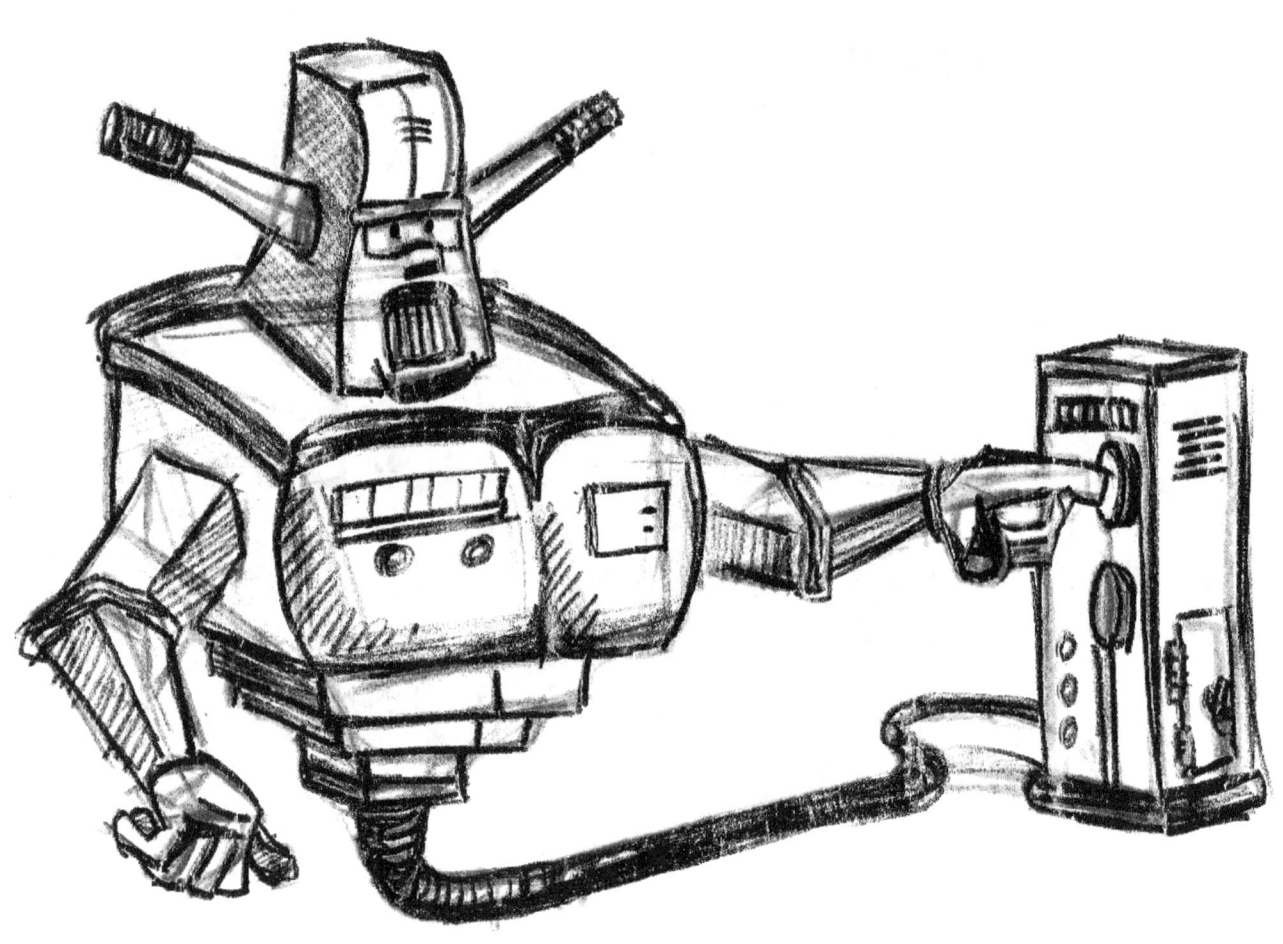

X-10-Tionator

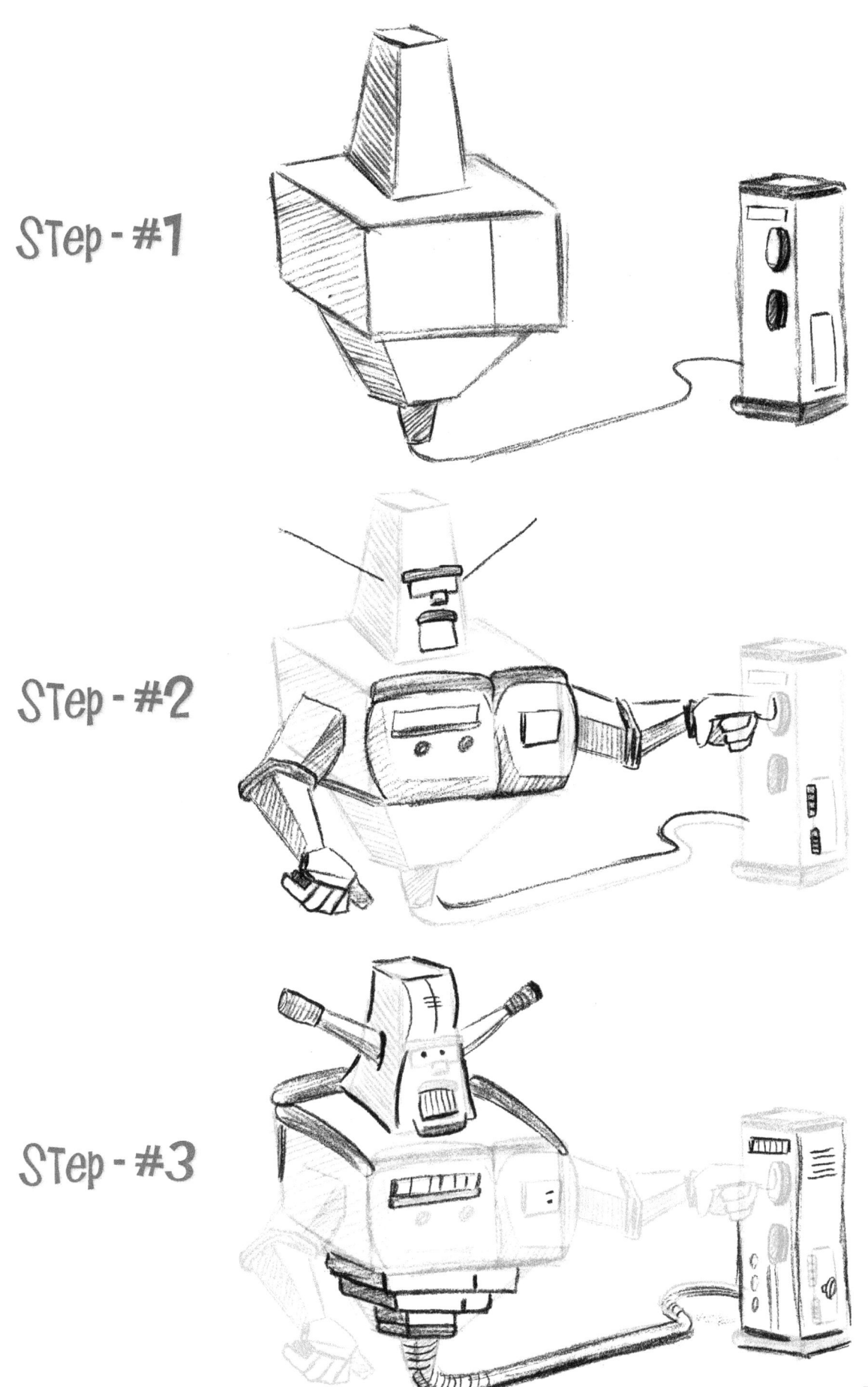

STep - #1

STep - #2

STep - #3

61.

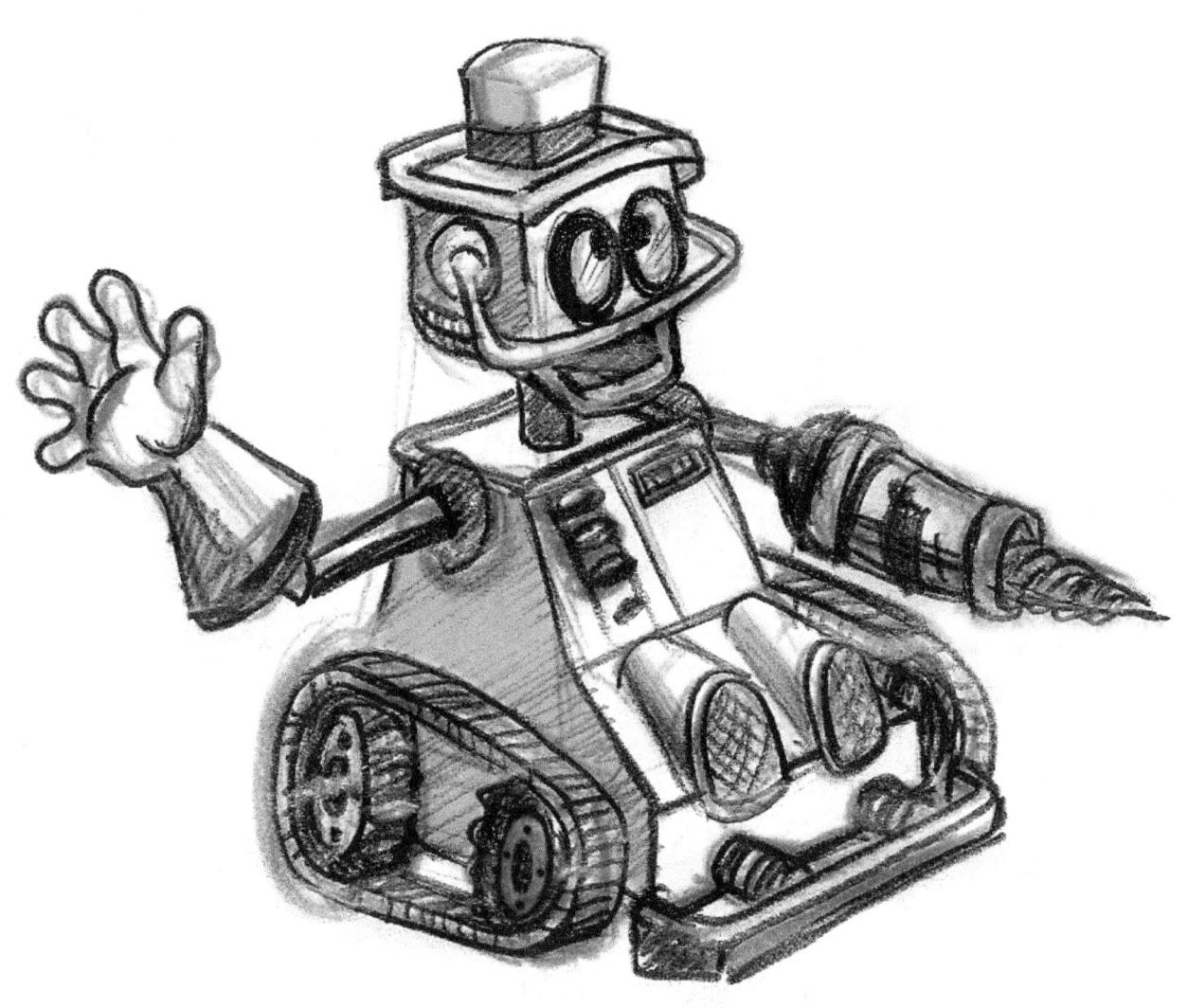

Mr. DriLL-D-Trax-Tor

STep - #1

STep - #2

STep - #3

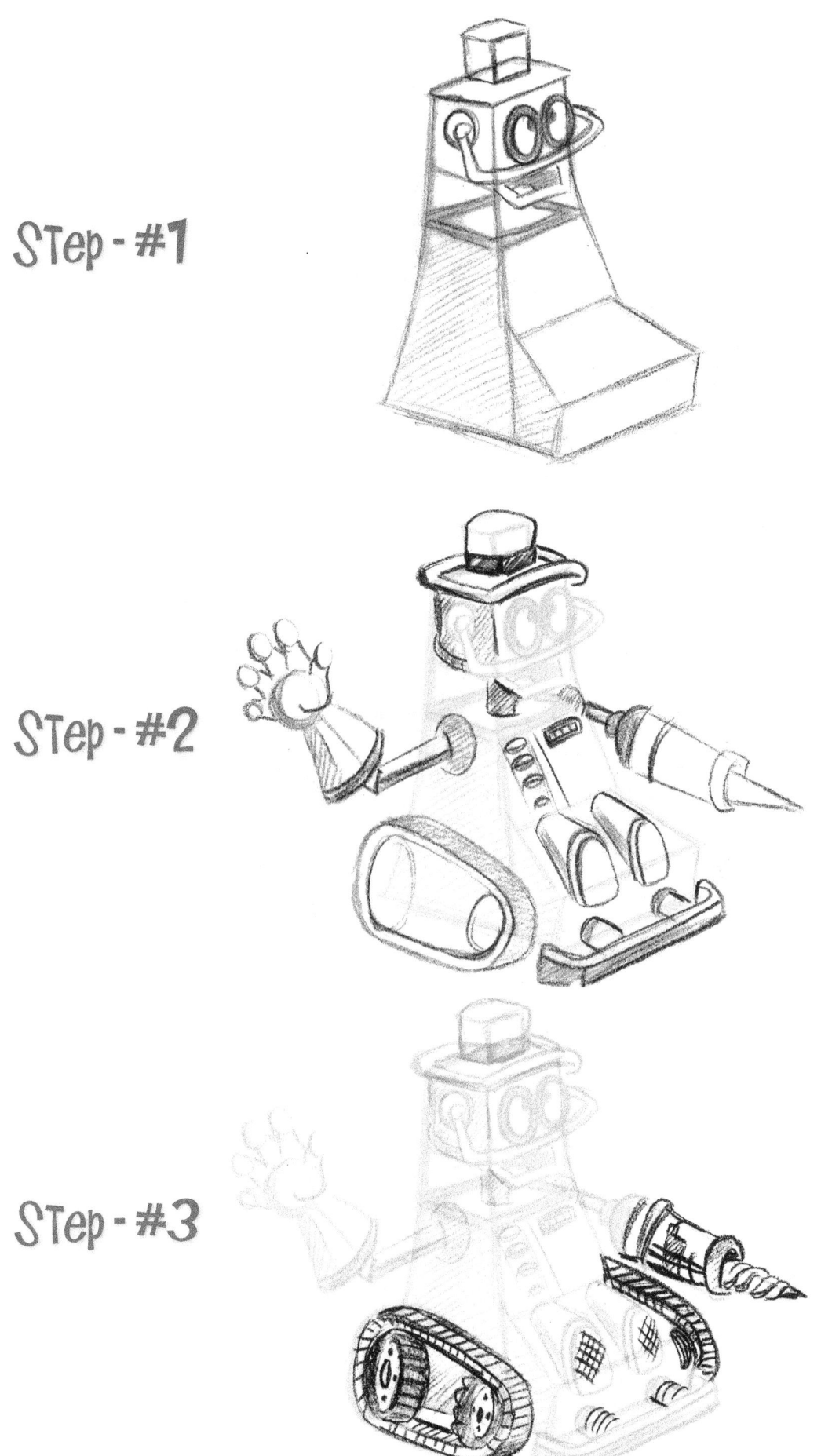

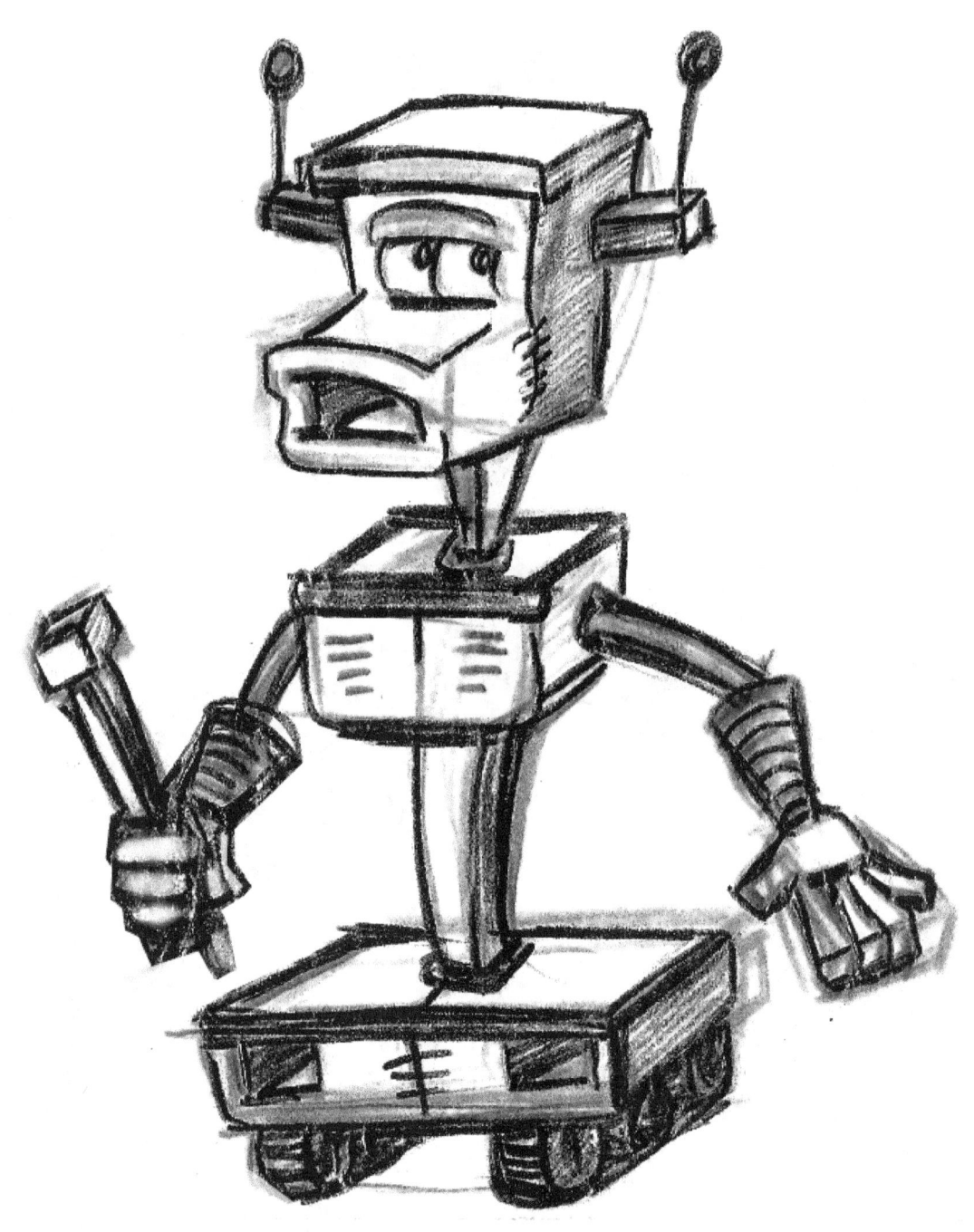

Row-Lee

64.

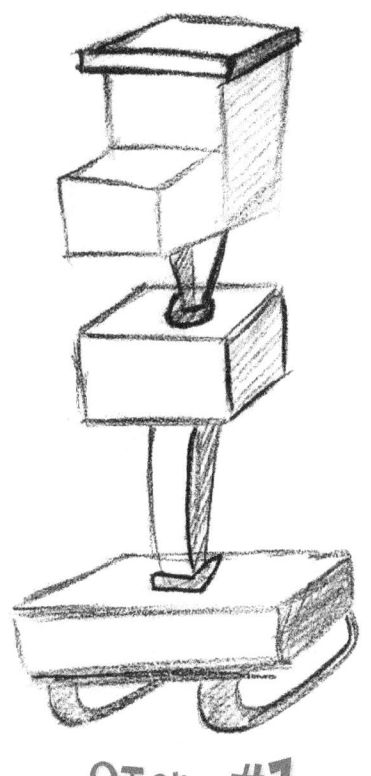

STep - #1

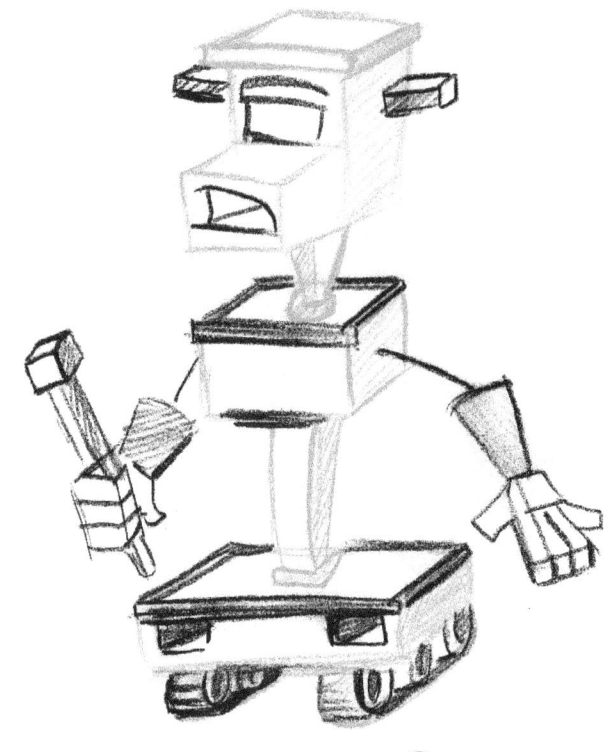

STep - #2

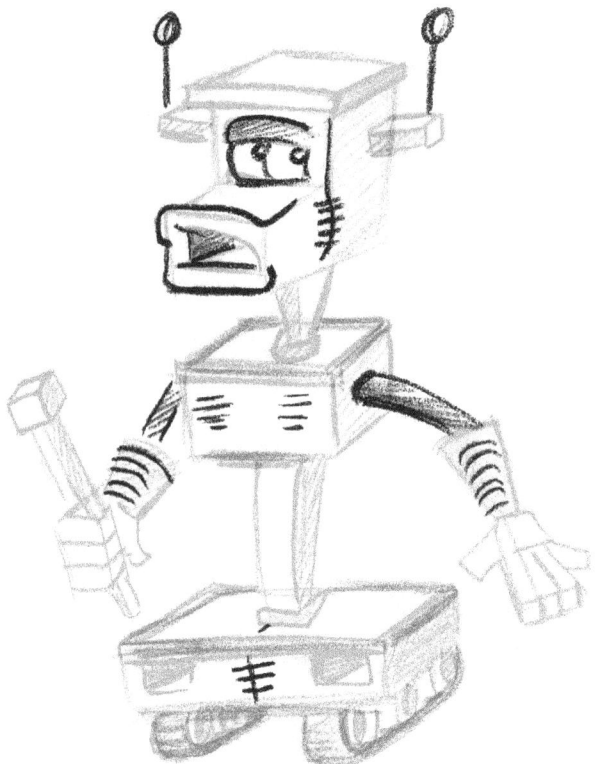

STep - #3

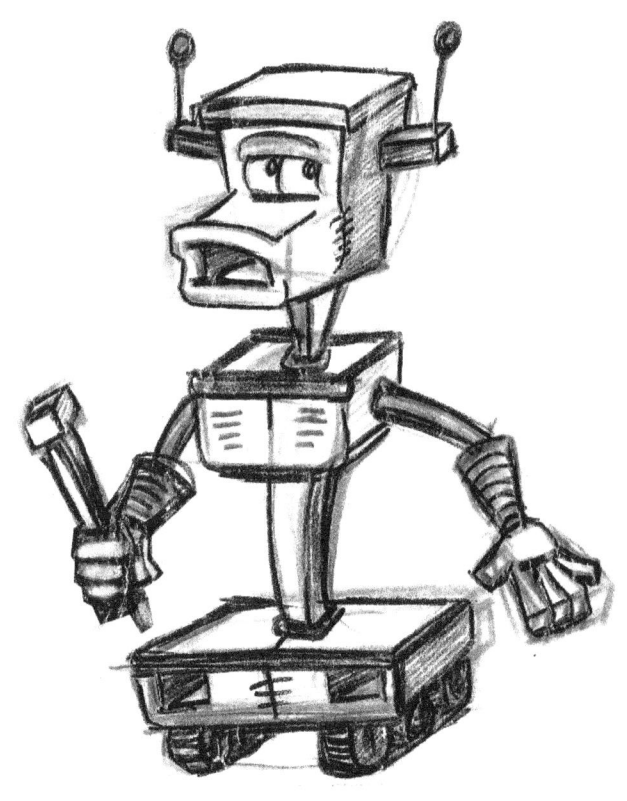

Toon skeTch

65.

# Drawing Space

# Chapter 3 Drawing Monsters

## Five monsters with
## exaggerated center axis

STep 1. The center Line of The following characters
will be expressed in a Long or curved formation.
This allows you To make your characters a Lot
more exaggerated.

STep 2. Once you have placed your center
axis, you will practice applying solid shapes
for The construction of your Toons along The Line.

STep 3. Detail and Shade your character shapes
by exaggerating The Shapes you have applied over The
center axis. Don't Limit yourself and get creative by
exaggerating Them To your Liking.

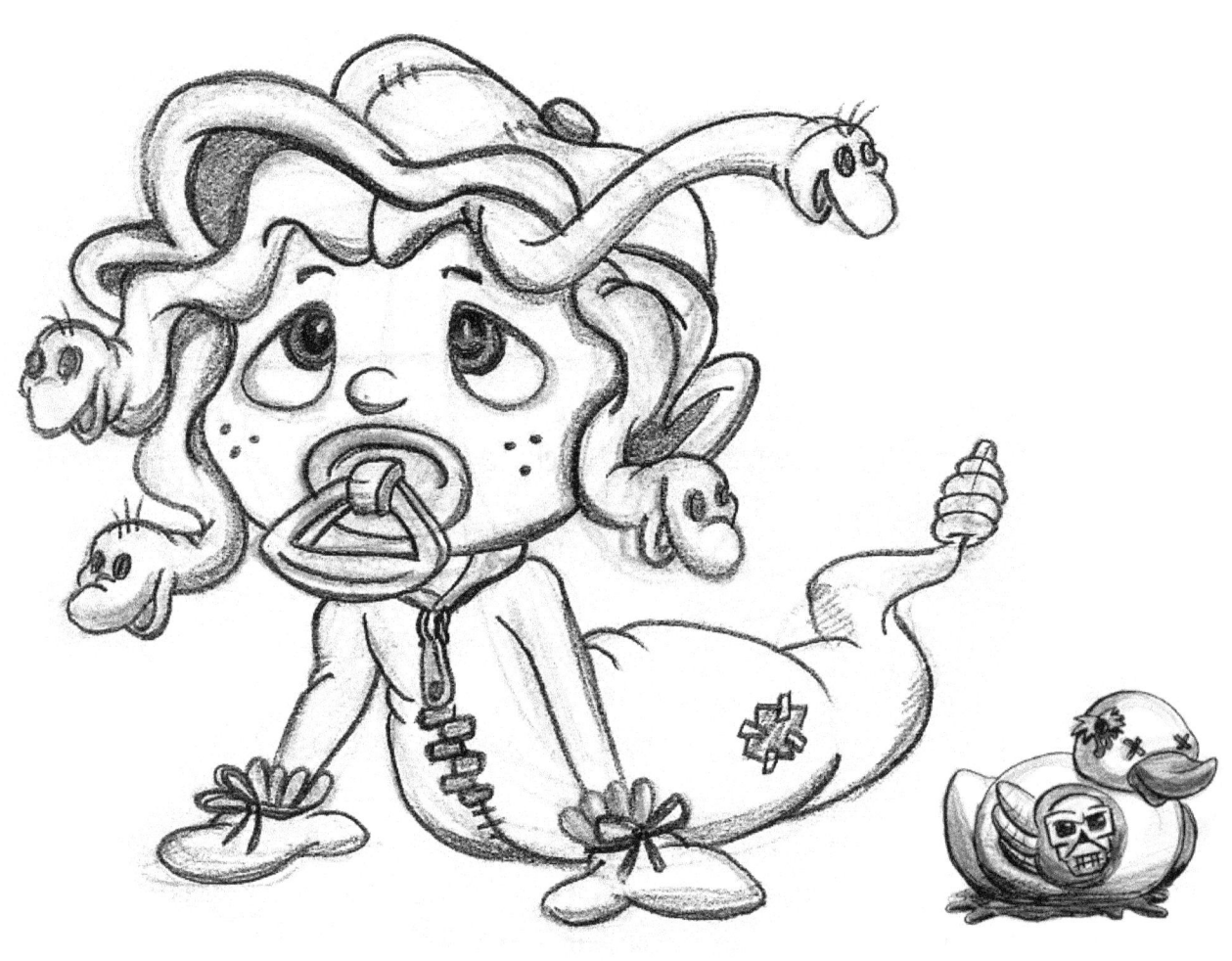

Bay-Bie-Medussa

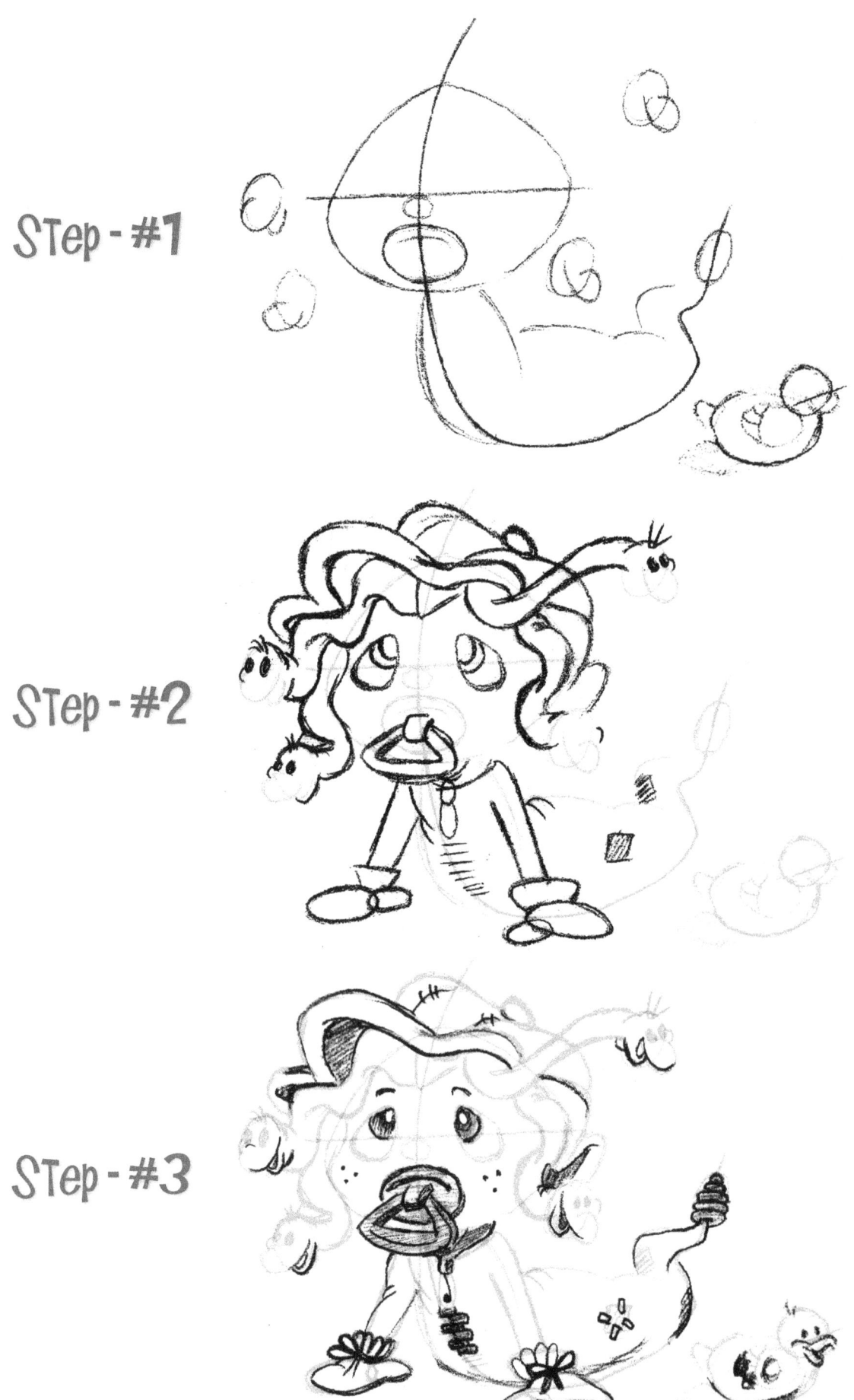

STep - #1

STep - #2

STep - #3

69.

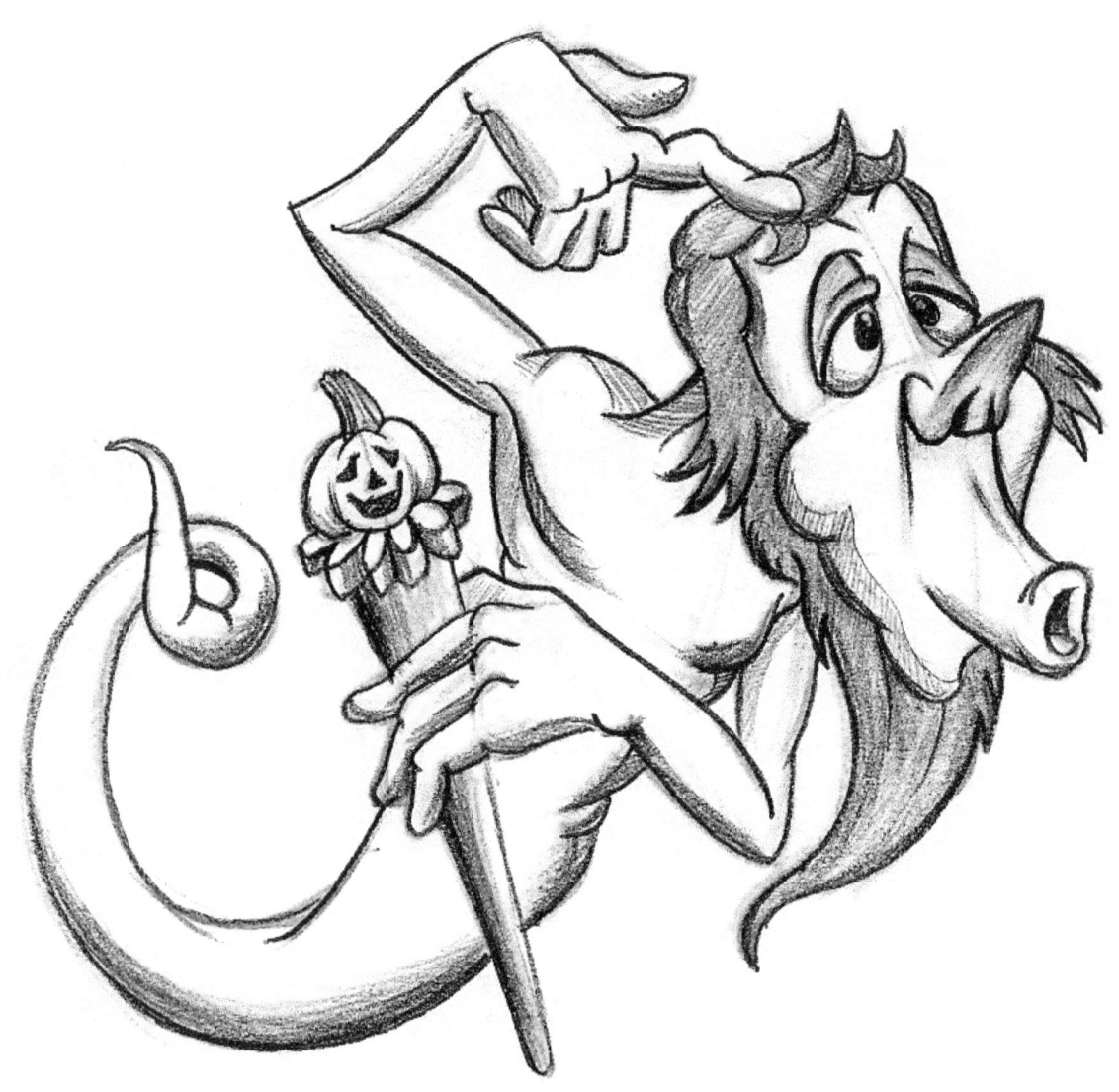

Boog-A-Loo

STep - #1

STep - #2

STep - #3

Slimmy-Slumper

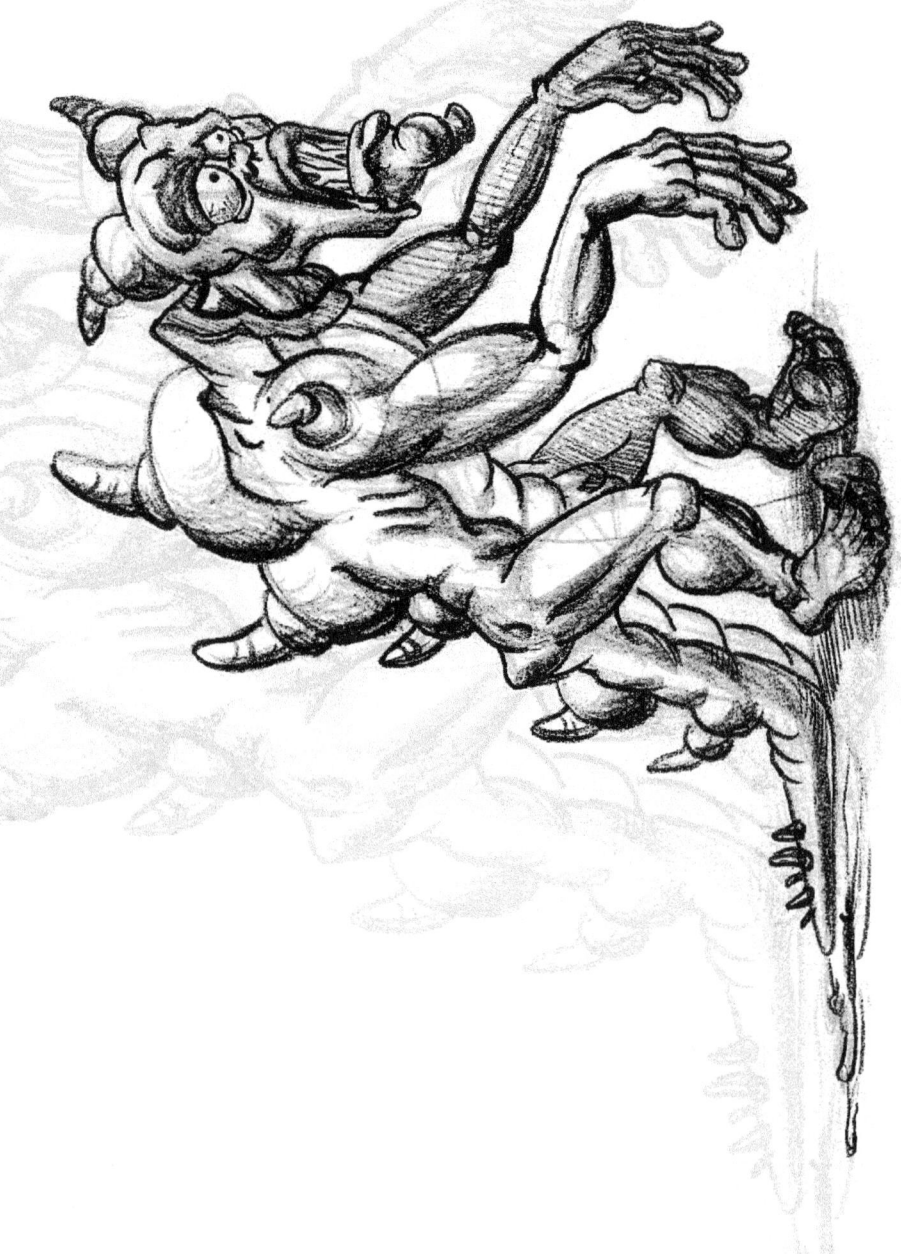

Step - #1

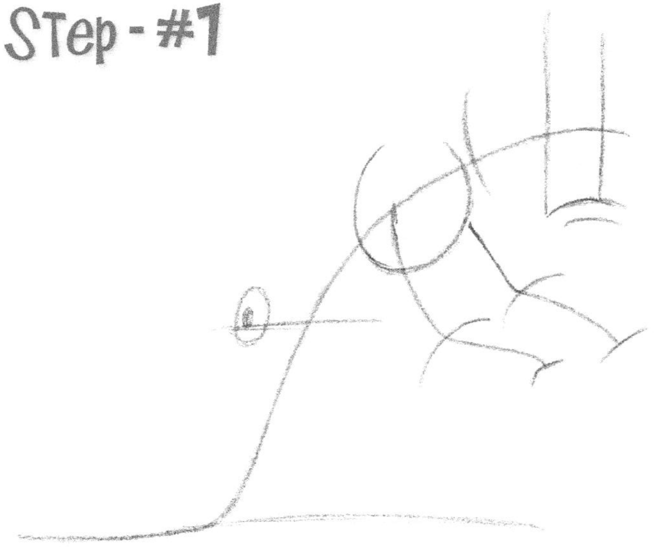

Step - #2

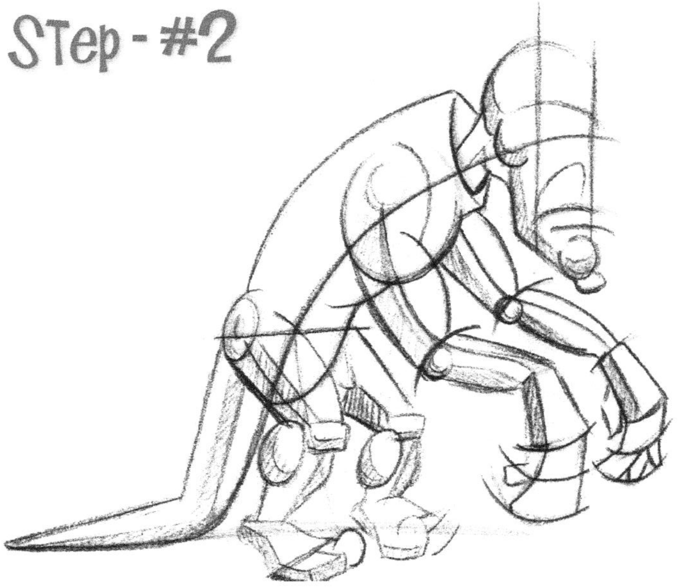

Step - #3

Toon sketch

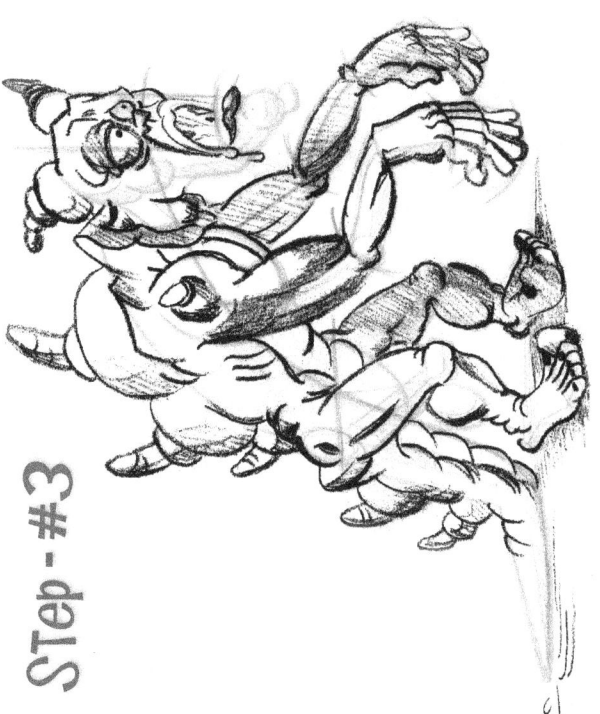

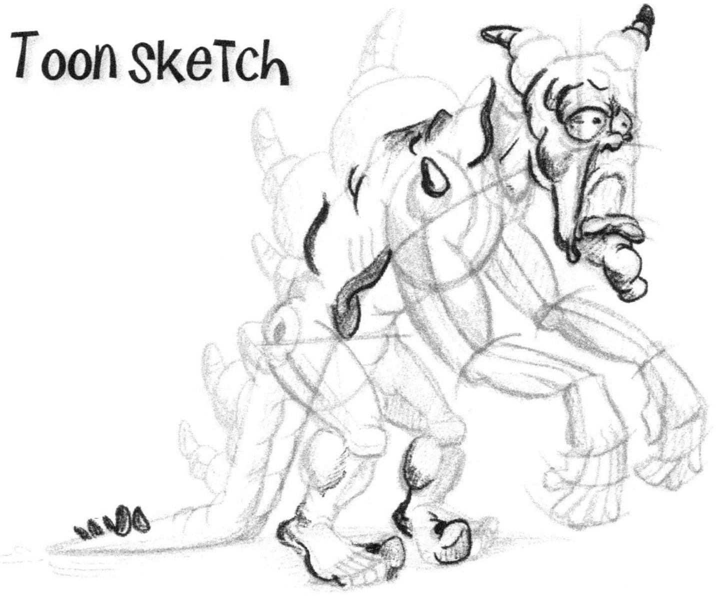

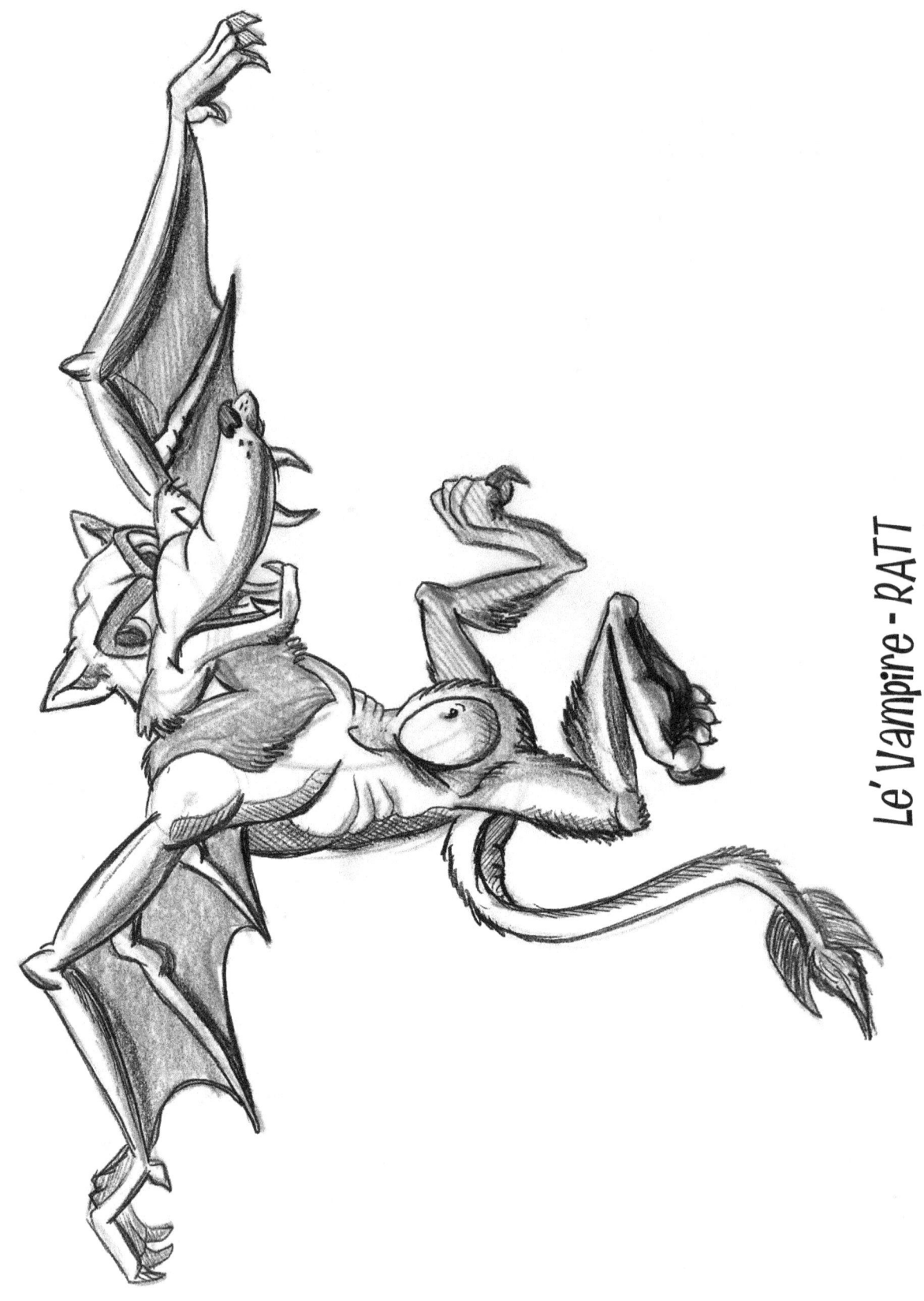

Le'Vampire - RATT

74.

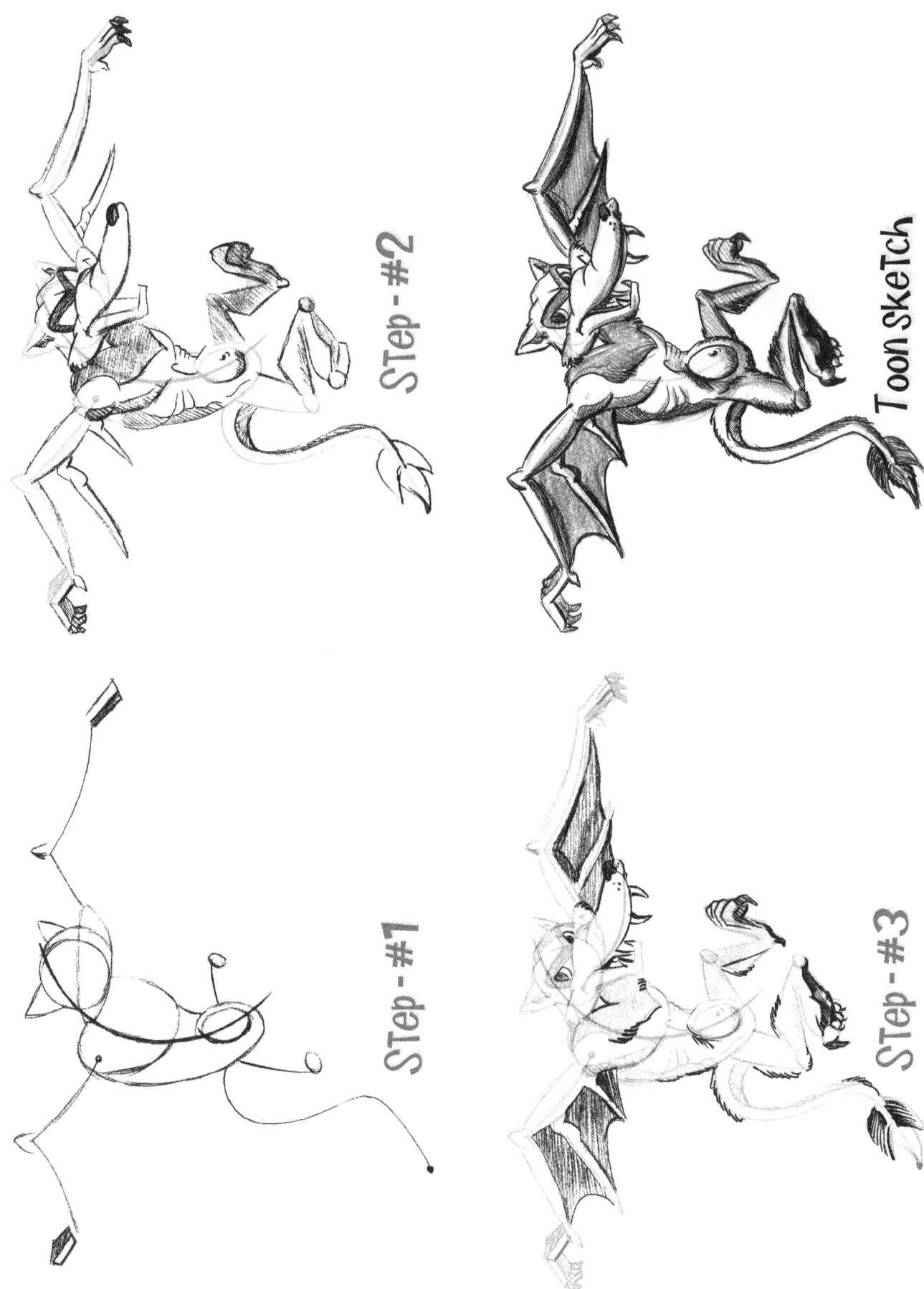

STep - #2

Toon SkeTch

STep - #1

STep - #3

75.

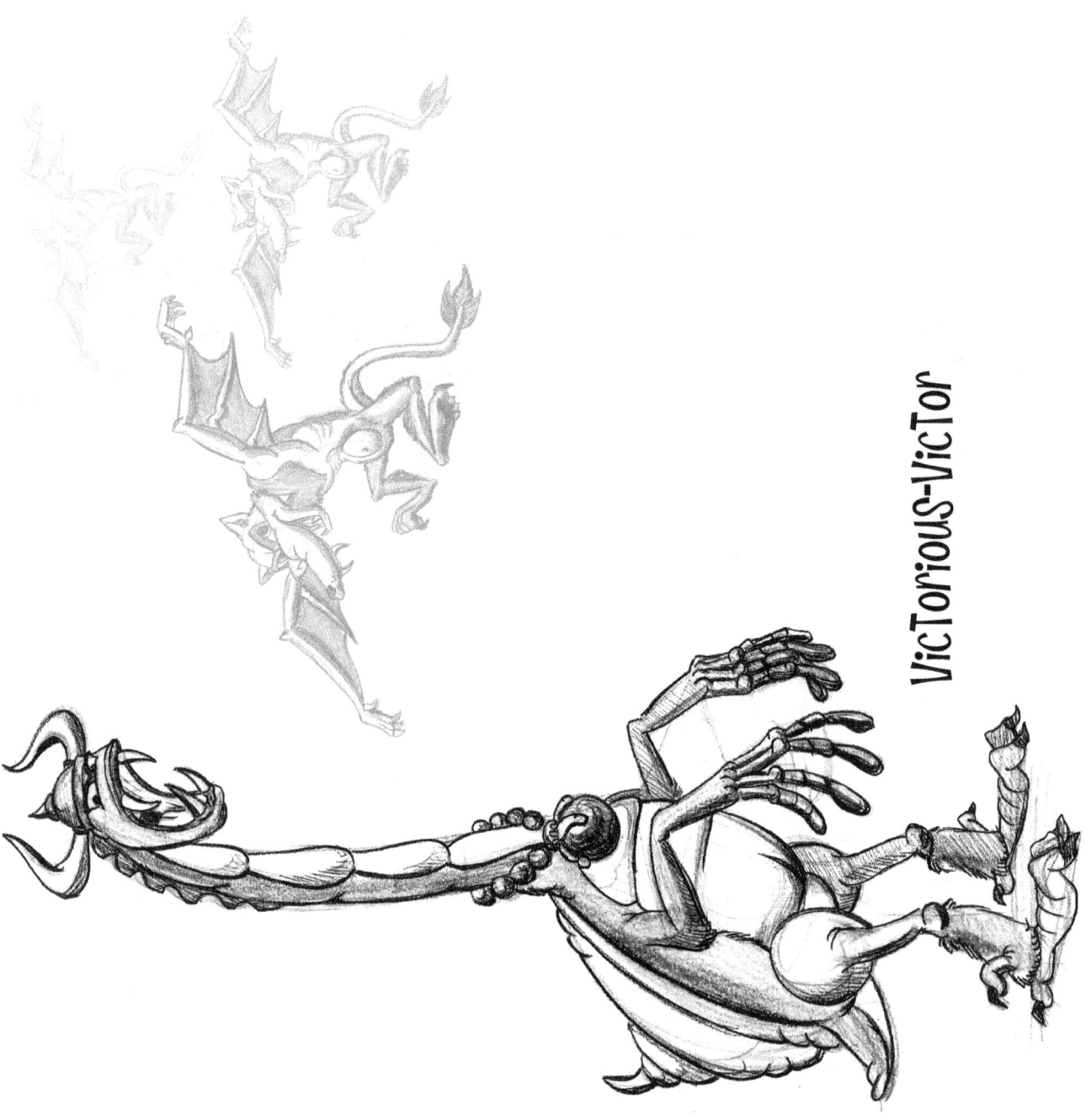

VicTorious-VicTor

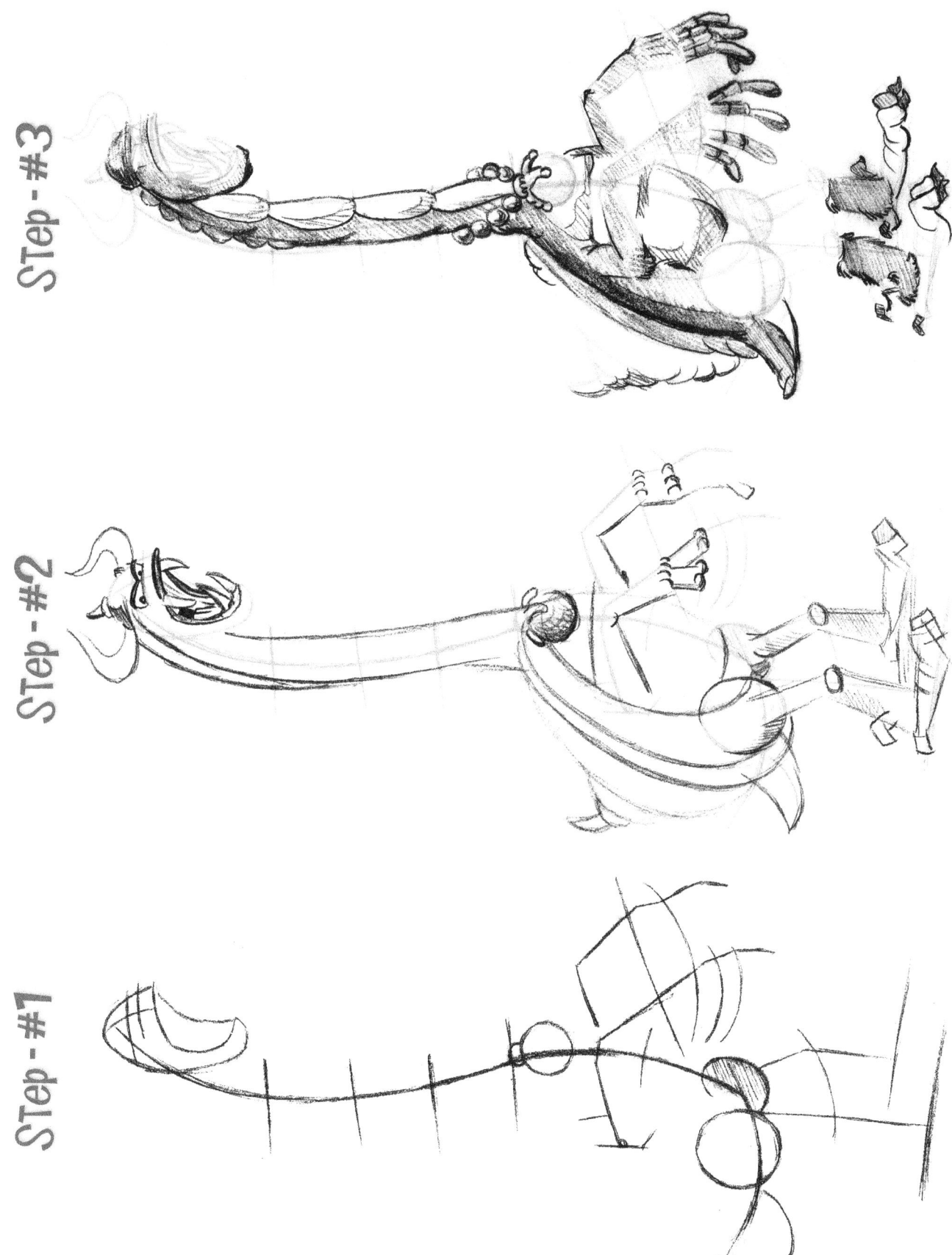

Step - #3

Step - #2

Step - #1

77.

# Drawing Space

# Ten monsters with Simple center axis

**Step 1.** The center line of the following characters will be simple and straight or slightly angled. Some center lines might also include limb lines for you to add arms and legs

**Step 2.** Once you have practiced creating toons form a basic center axis, you can explore with much more interesting curves and extreme lines. Try also adding horizontal lines for reference as you break down the different sections of the toons construction.

**Step 3.** As demonstrated in Chapter 1 Basic shape lessons, you will use the same methods in adding complete characters, body forms and significant masses. Use your line as the base construction of the toon and build your proportions over the center axis.

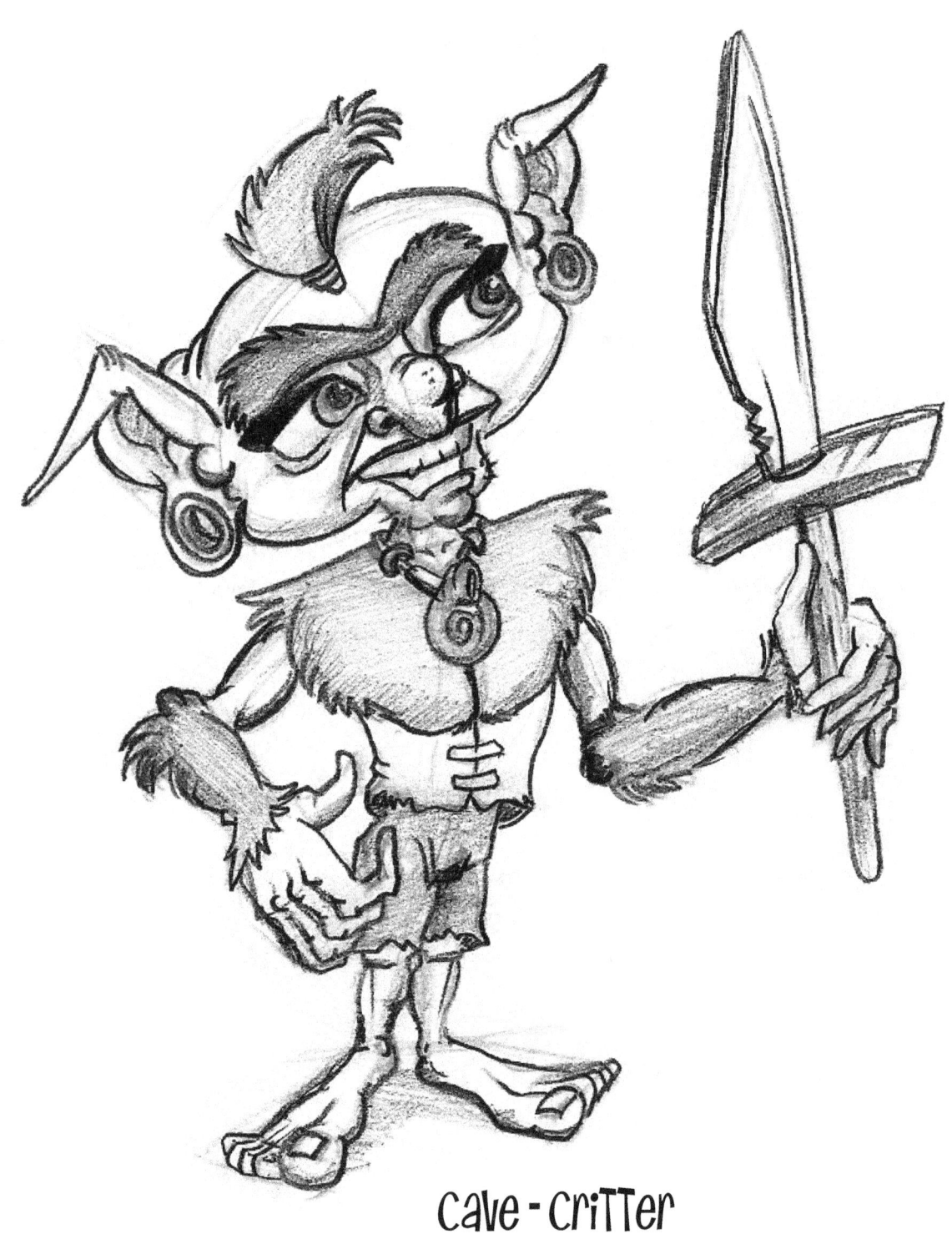

CAVE - CRITTER

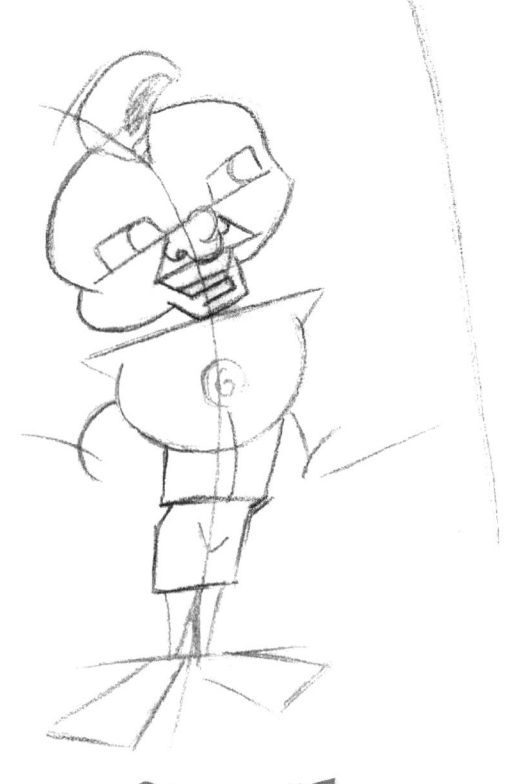

Step - #1

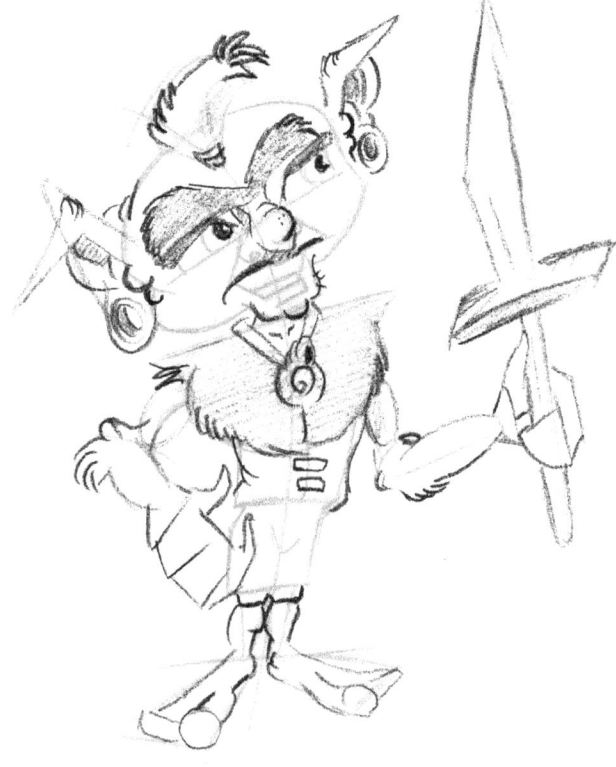

Step - #2

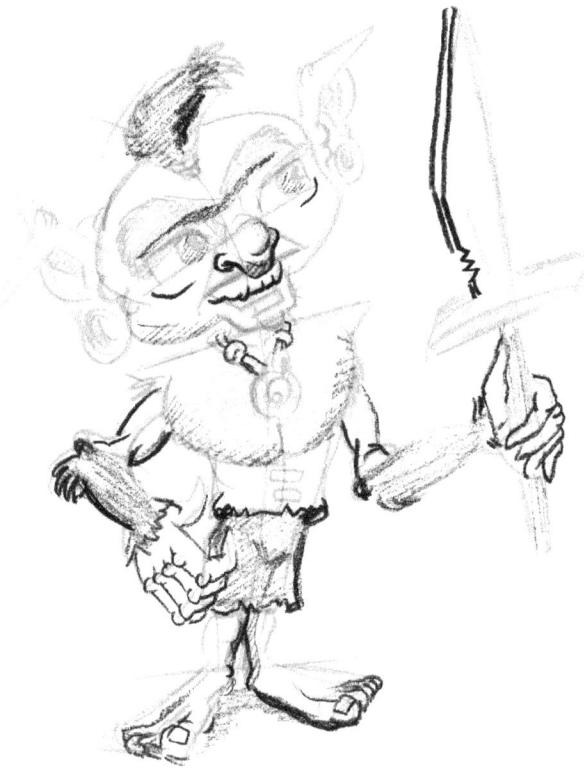

Step - #3

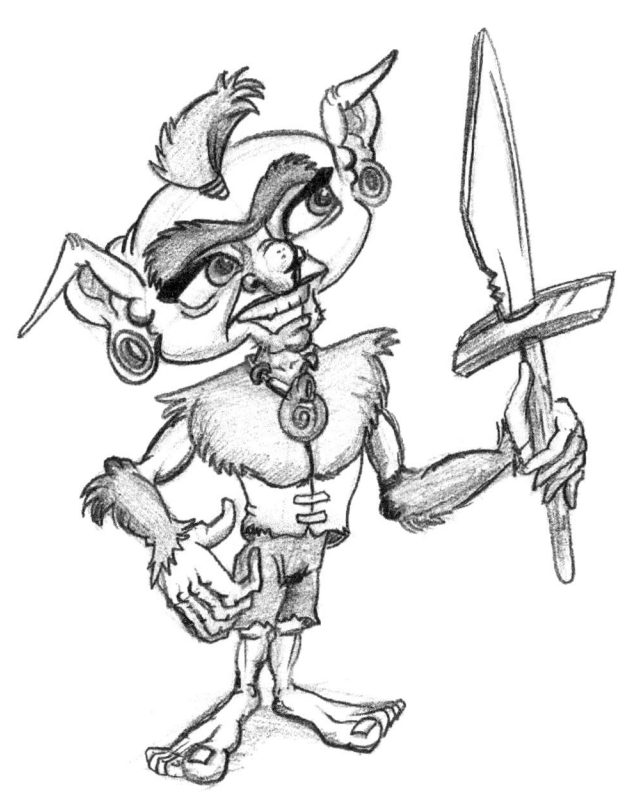

Toon sketch

81.

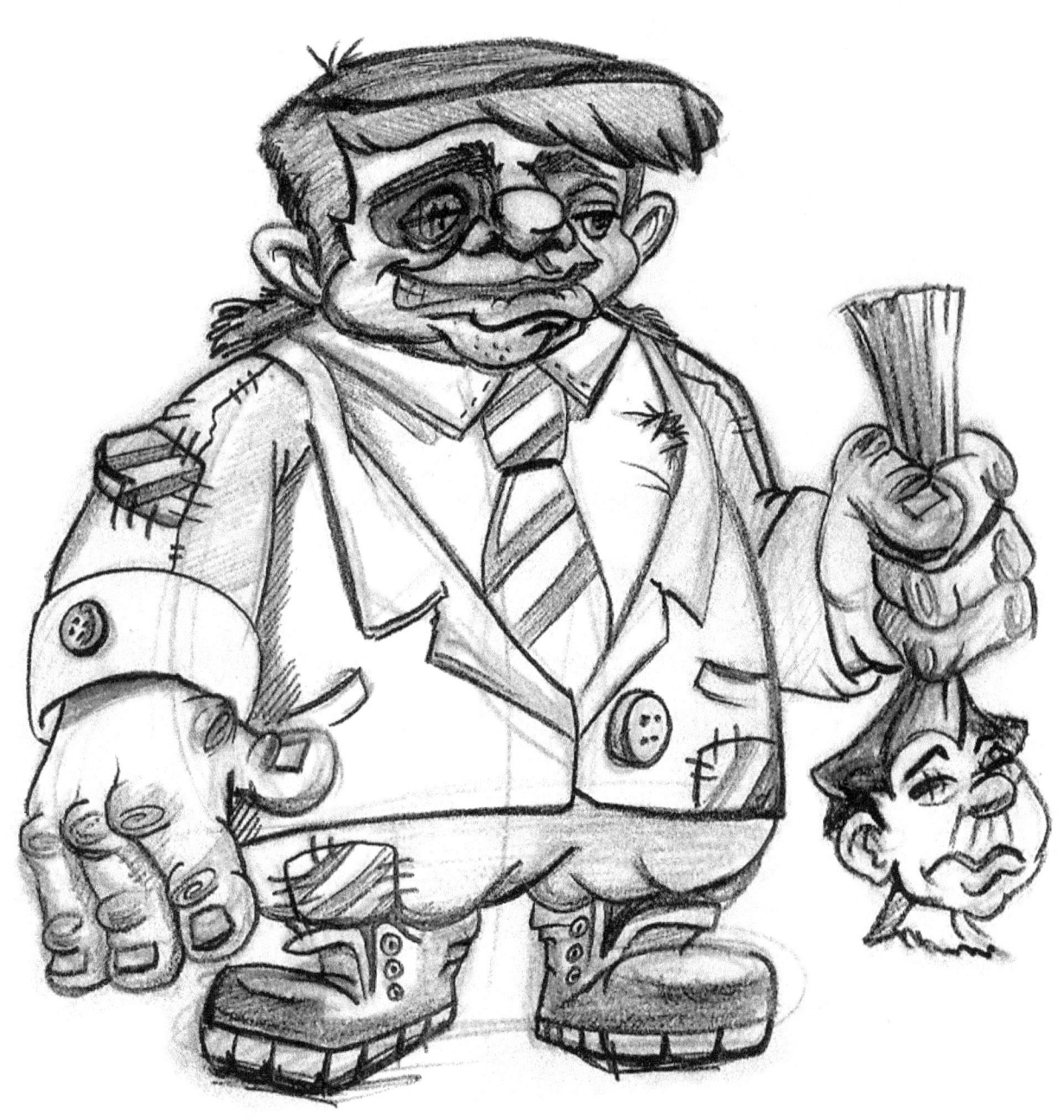

CLOTH-THE-SLOTH

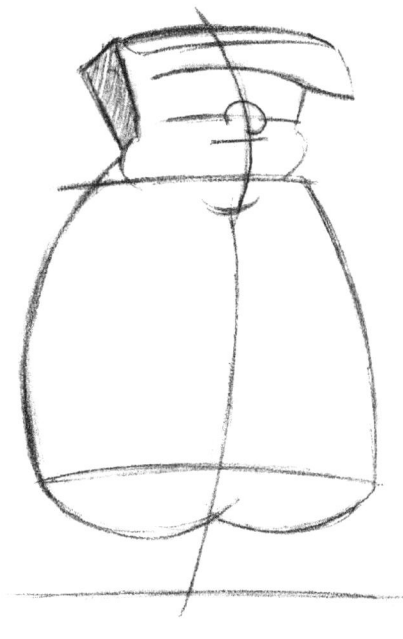

Step - #1

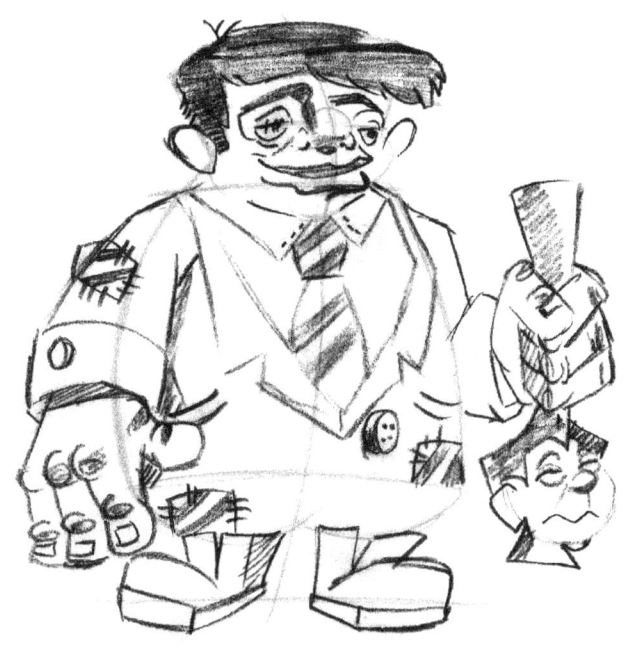

Step - #2

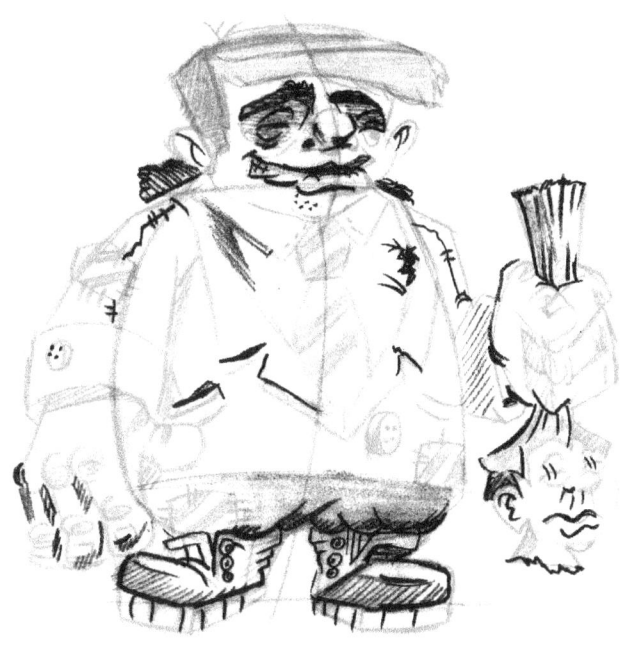

Step - #3

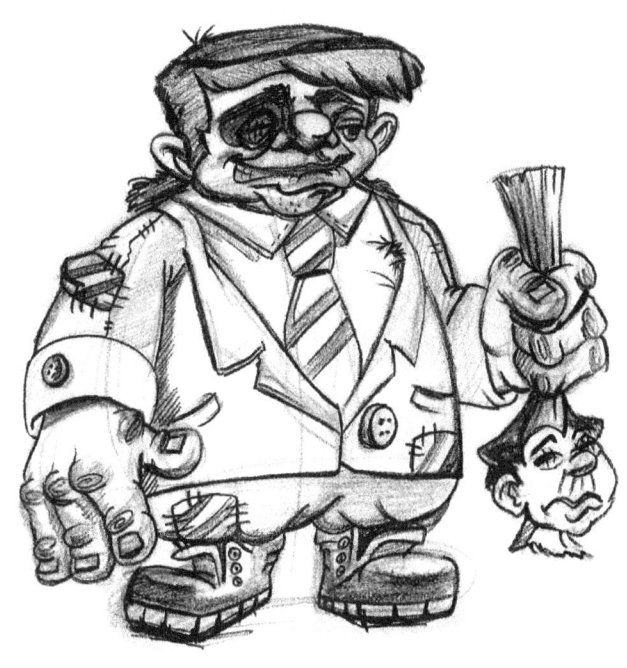

Toon sketch

83.

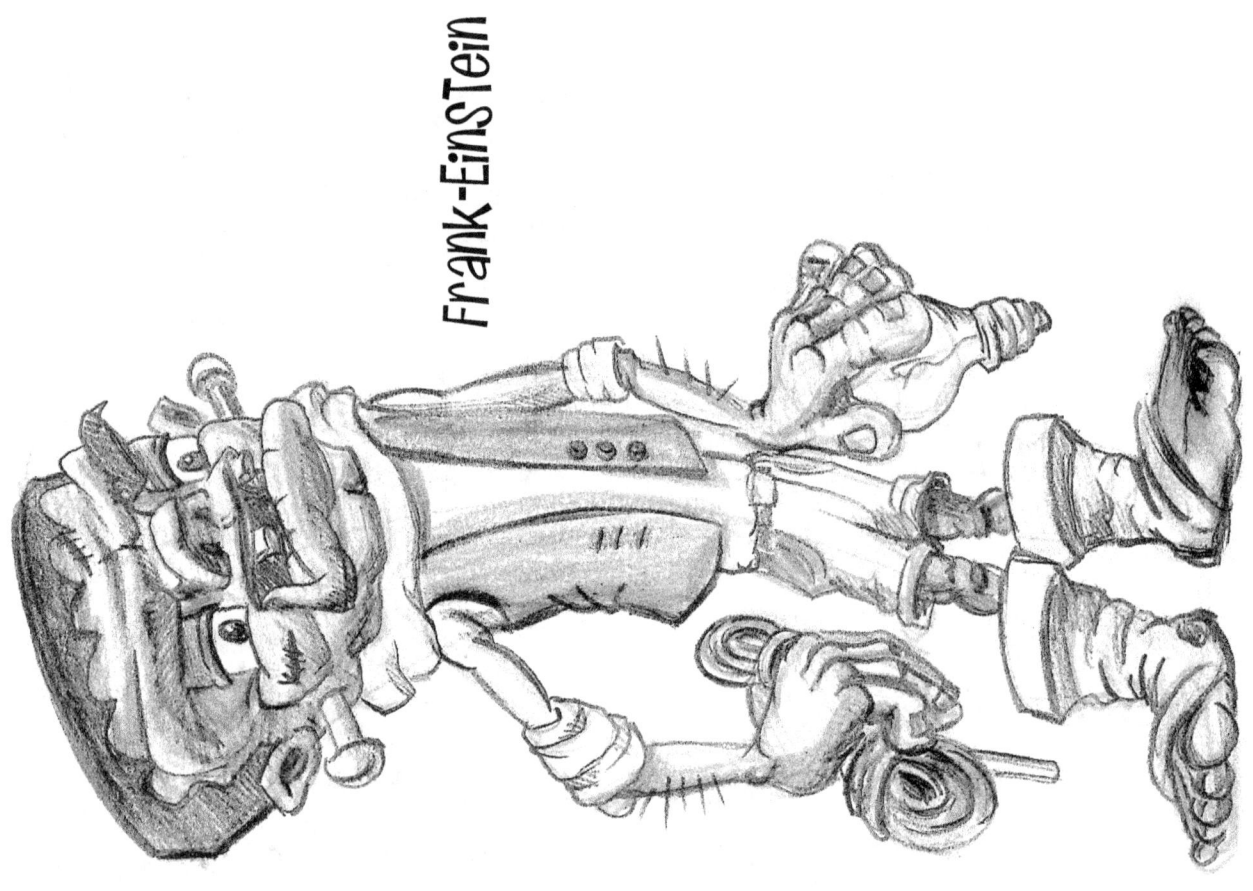

Frank-EinsTein

STep - #1

STep - #2

STep - #3

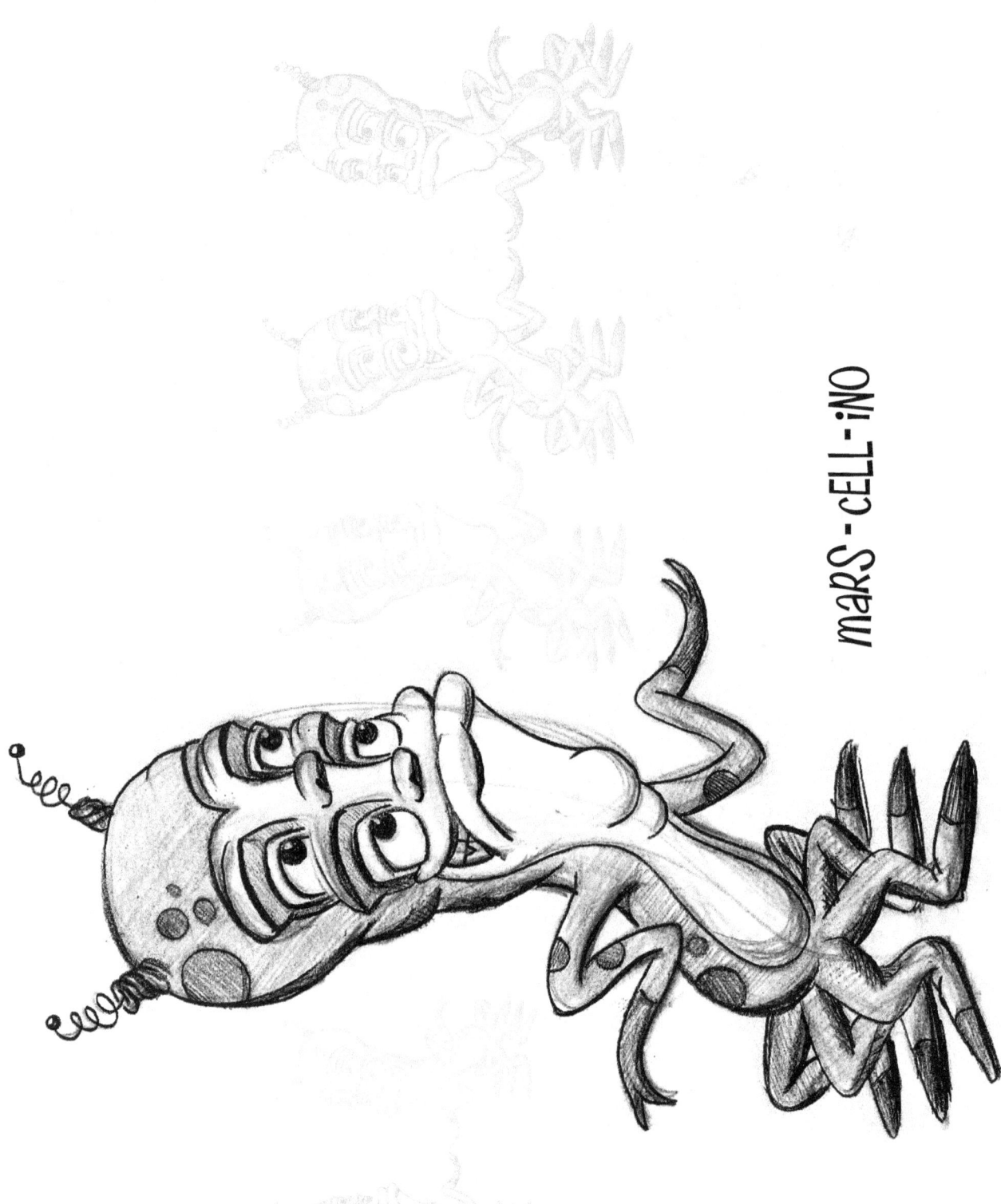

MaRS - cELL - iNO

STep - #3

STep - #2

STep - #1

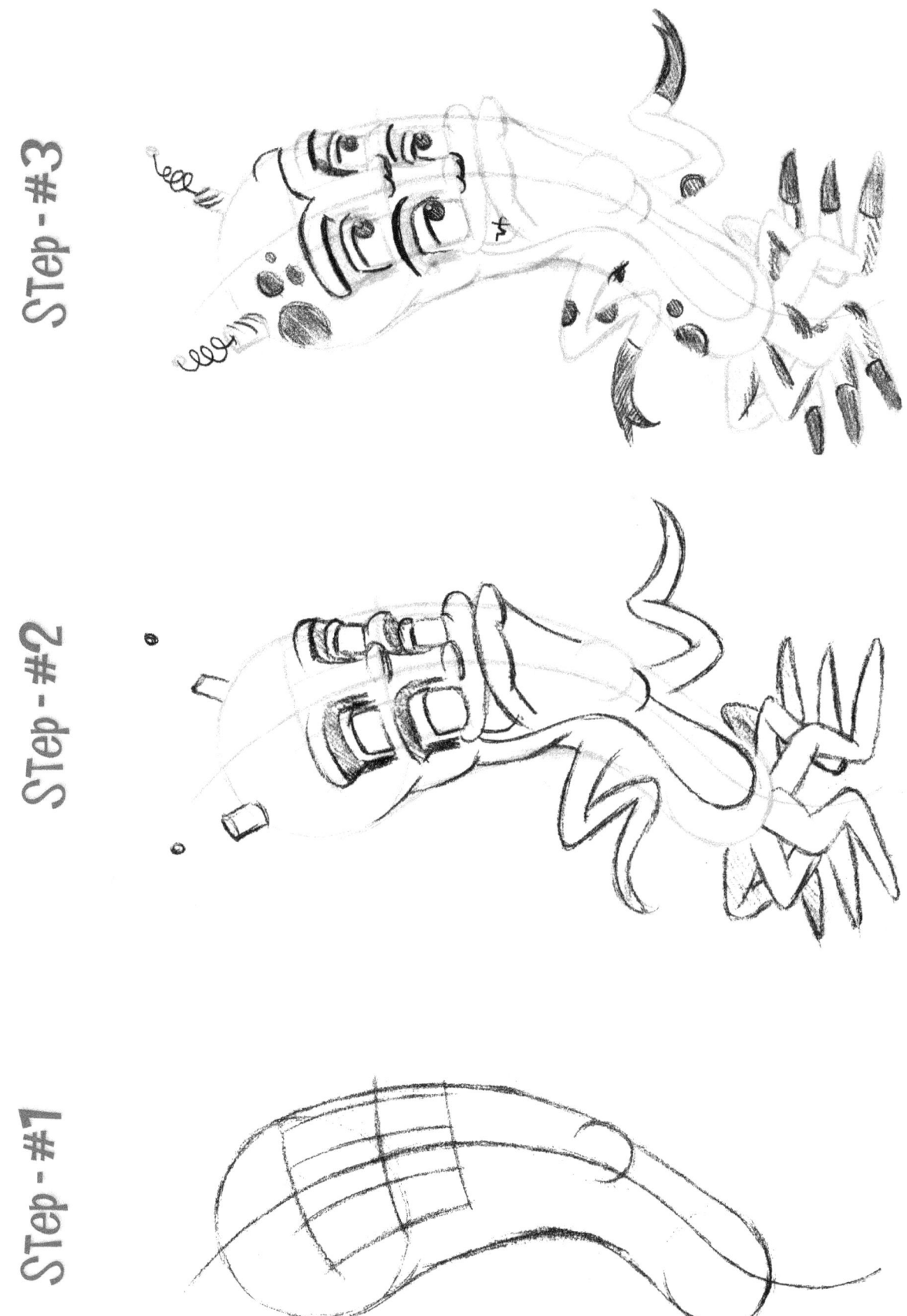

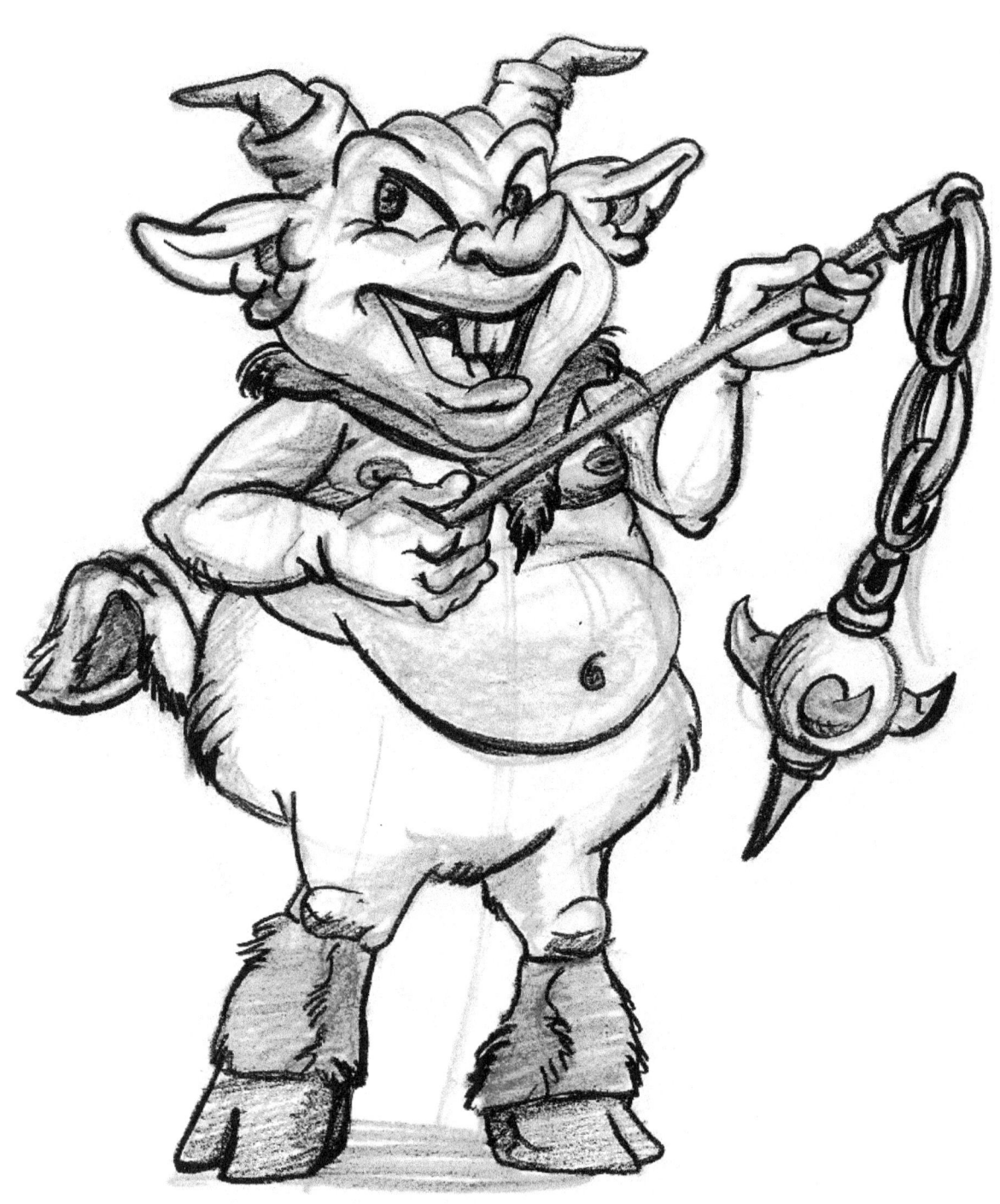

Horned-SLay-ErrH

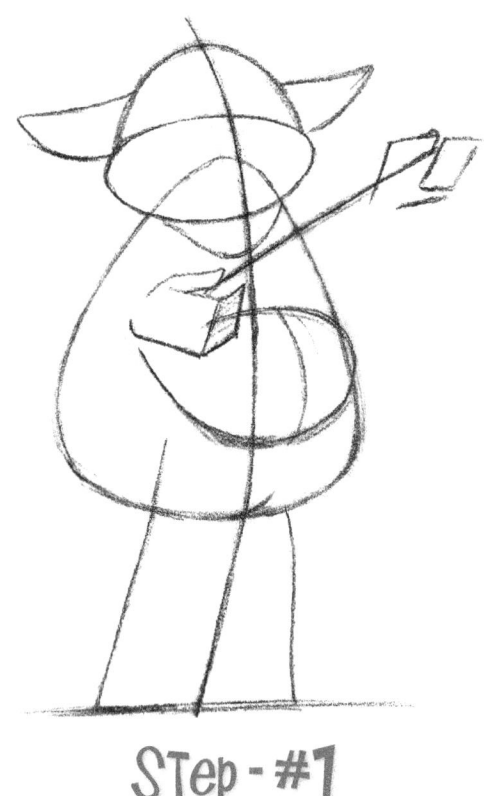

STep - #1

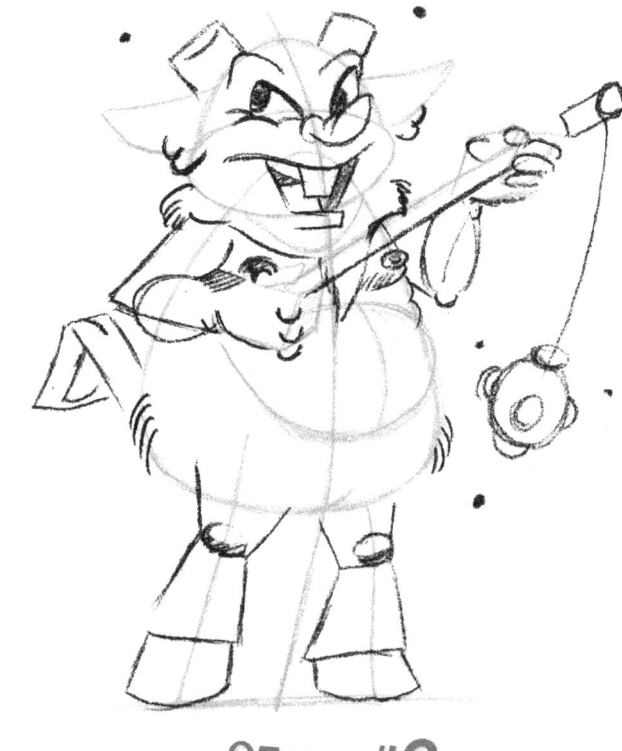

STep - #2

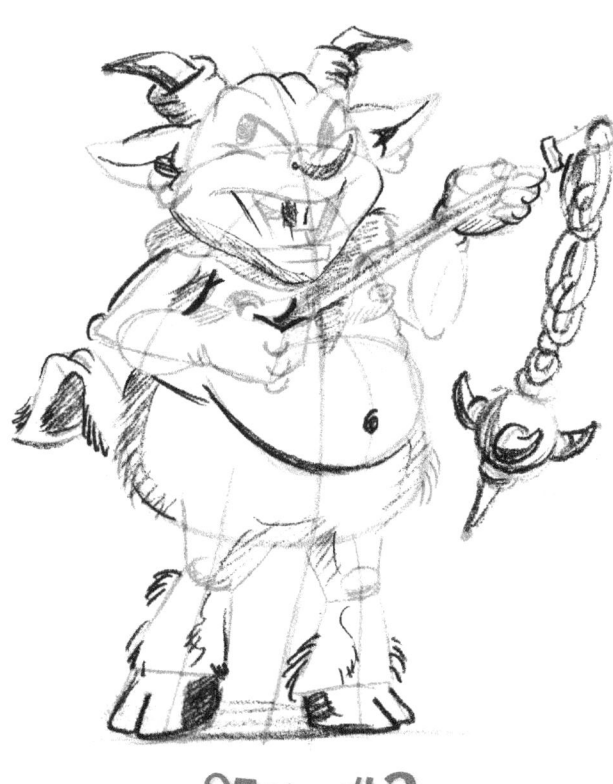

STep - #3

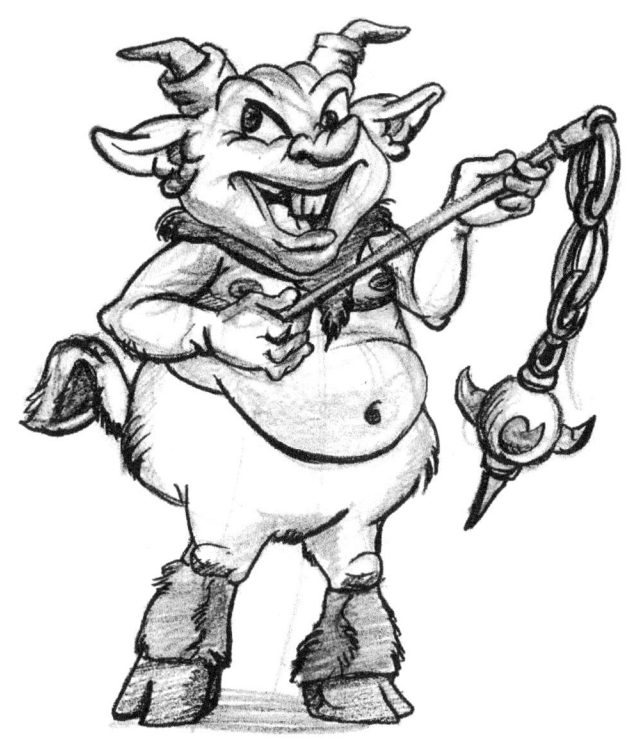

Toon sketch

89.

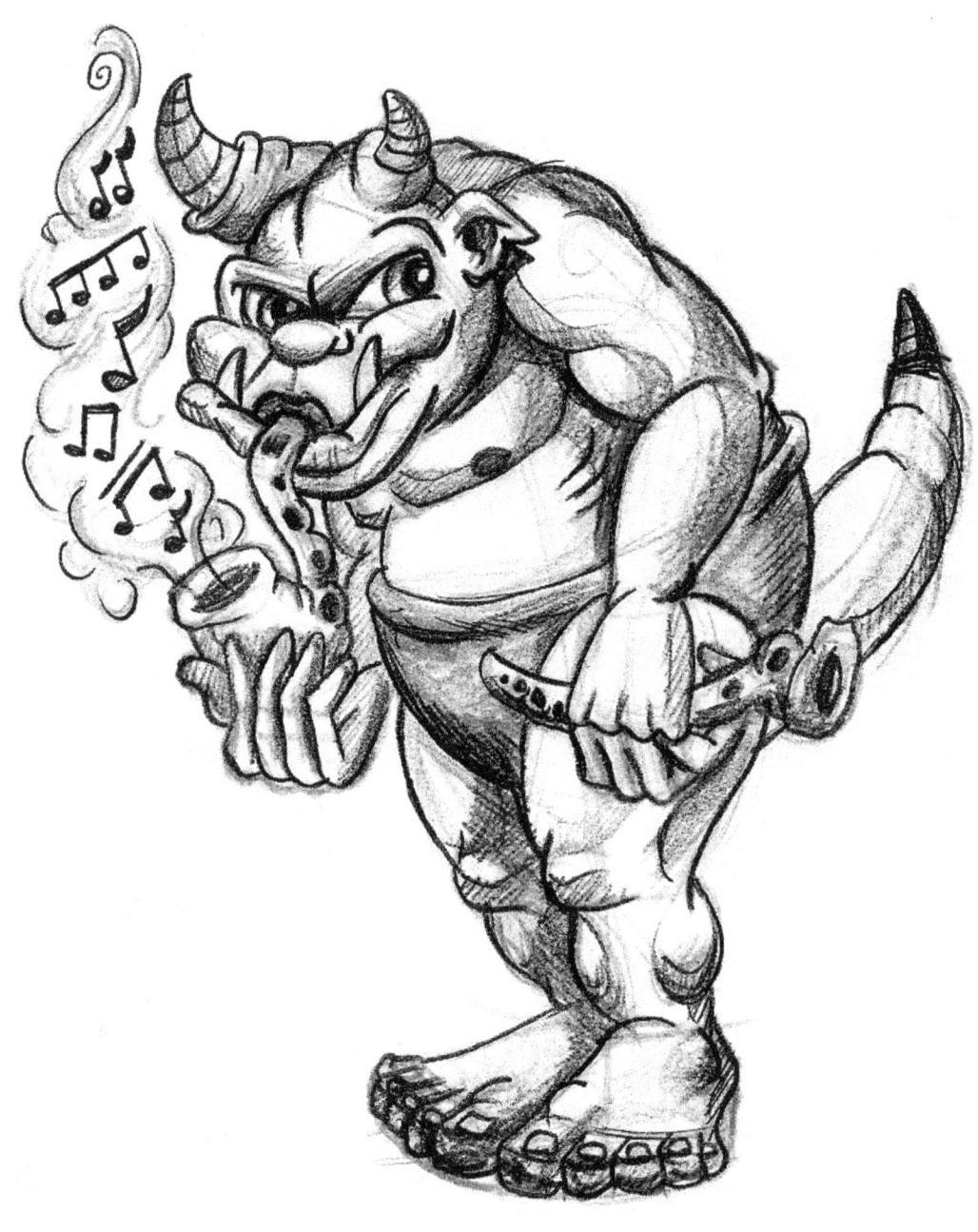

Horn-Z

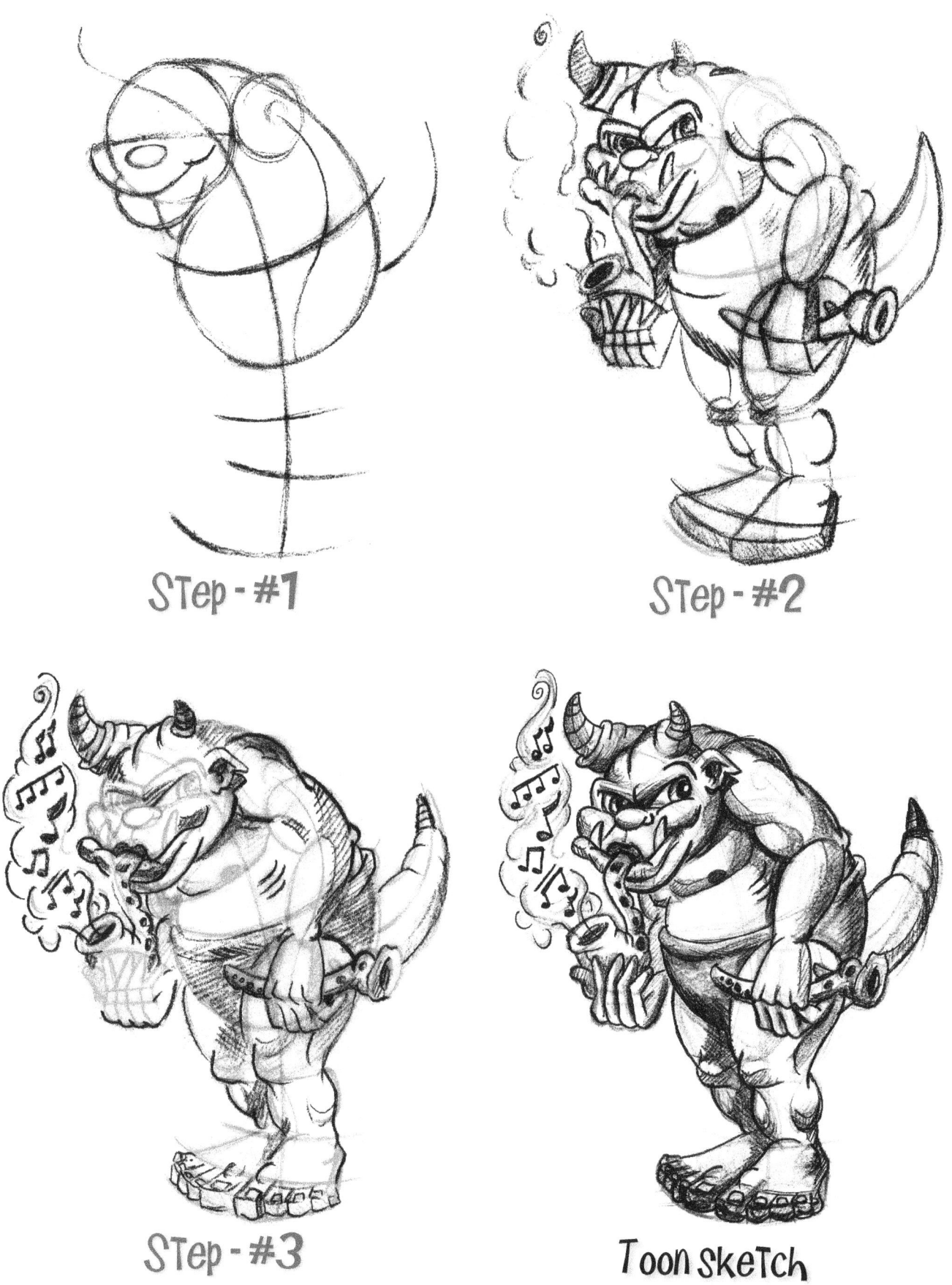

Step - #1

Step - #2

Step - #3

Toon Sketch

91.

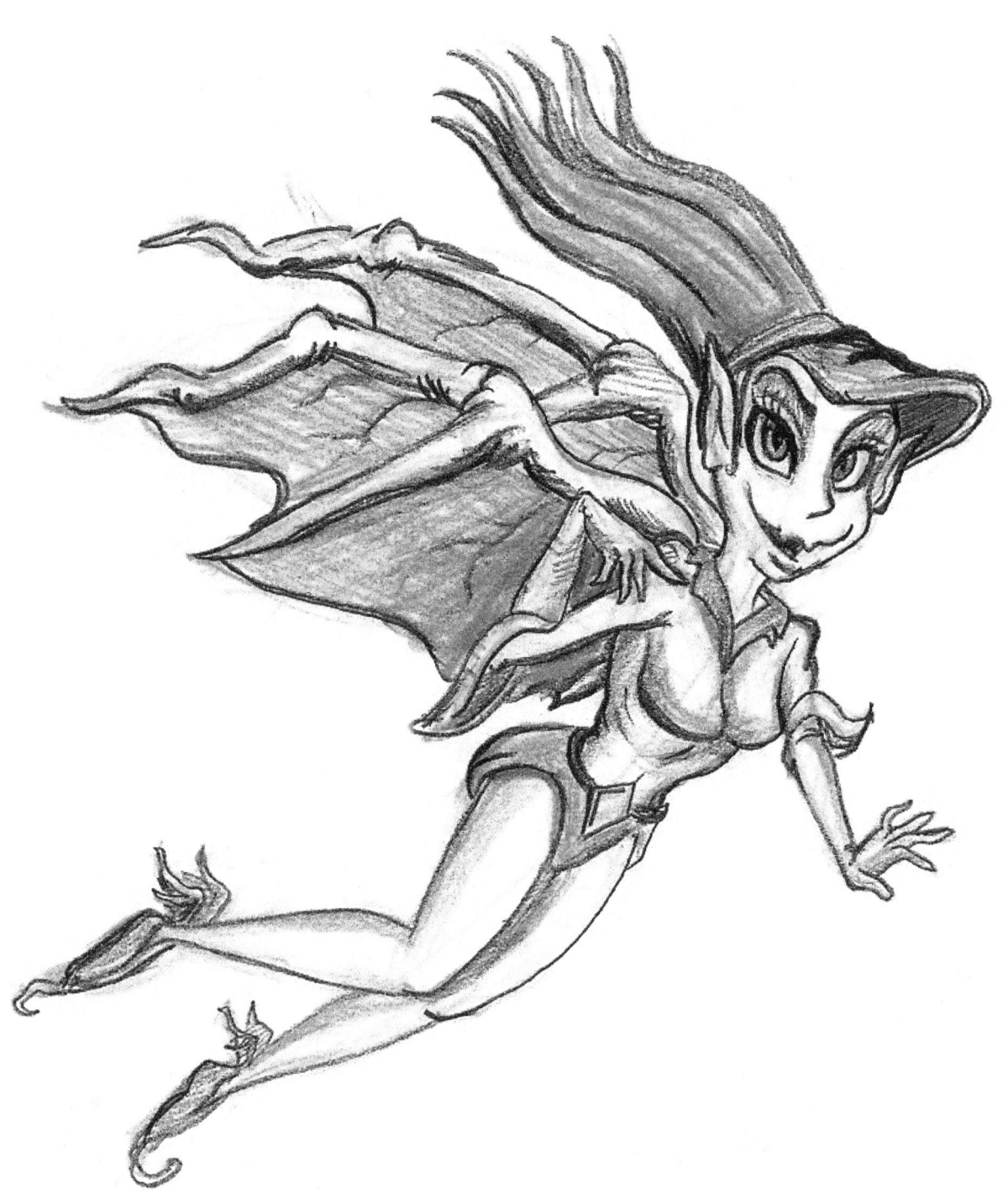

Gar - Goy - L - Gab - Bee

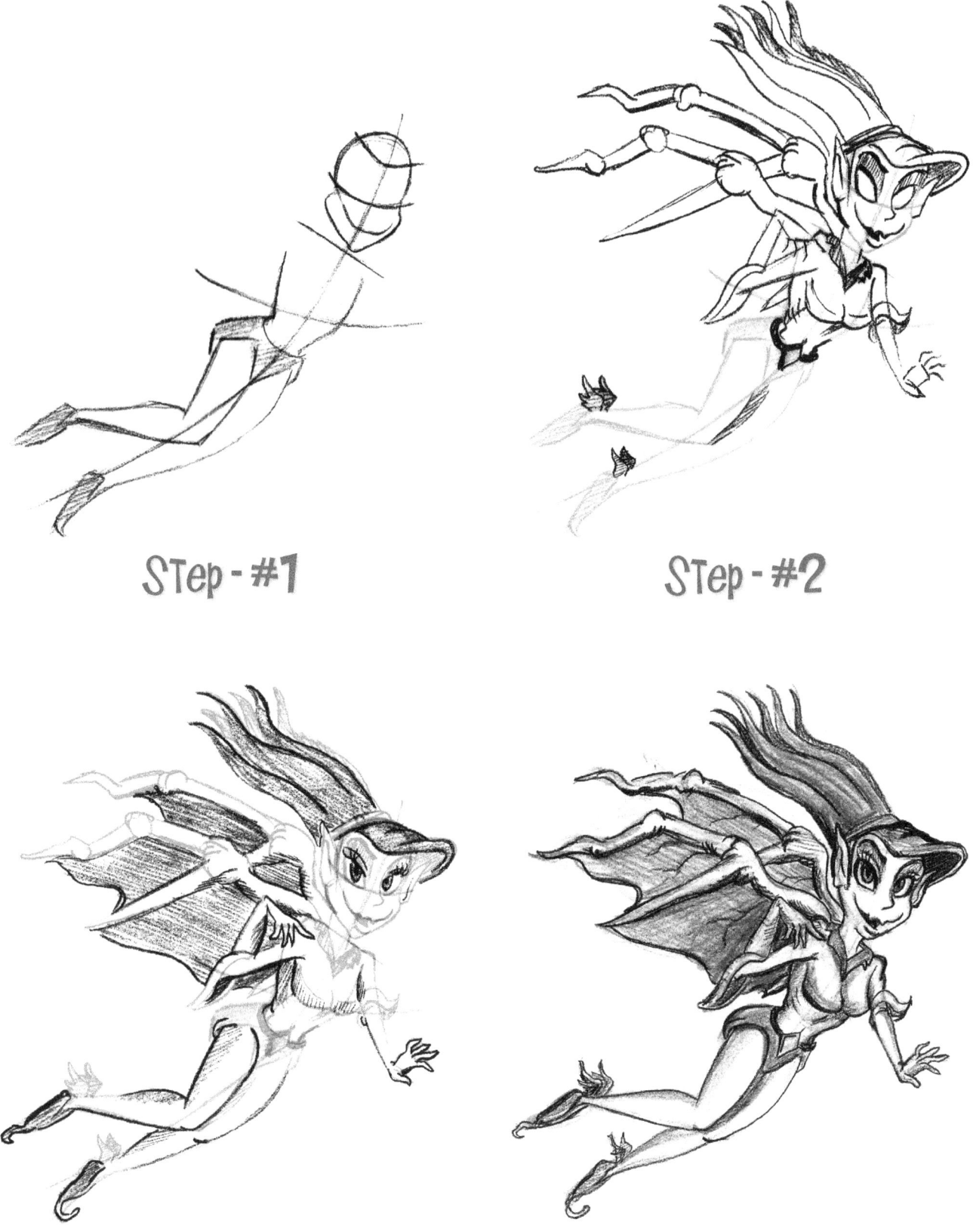

STep - #1

STep - #2

STep - #3

Toon sketch

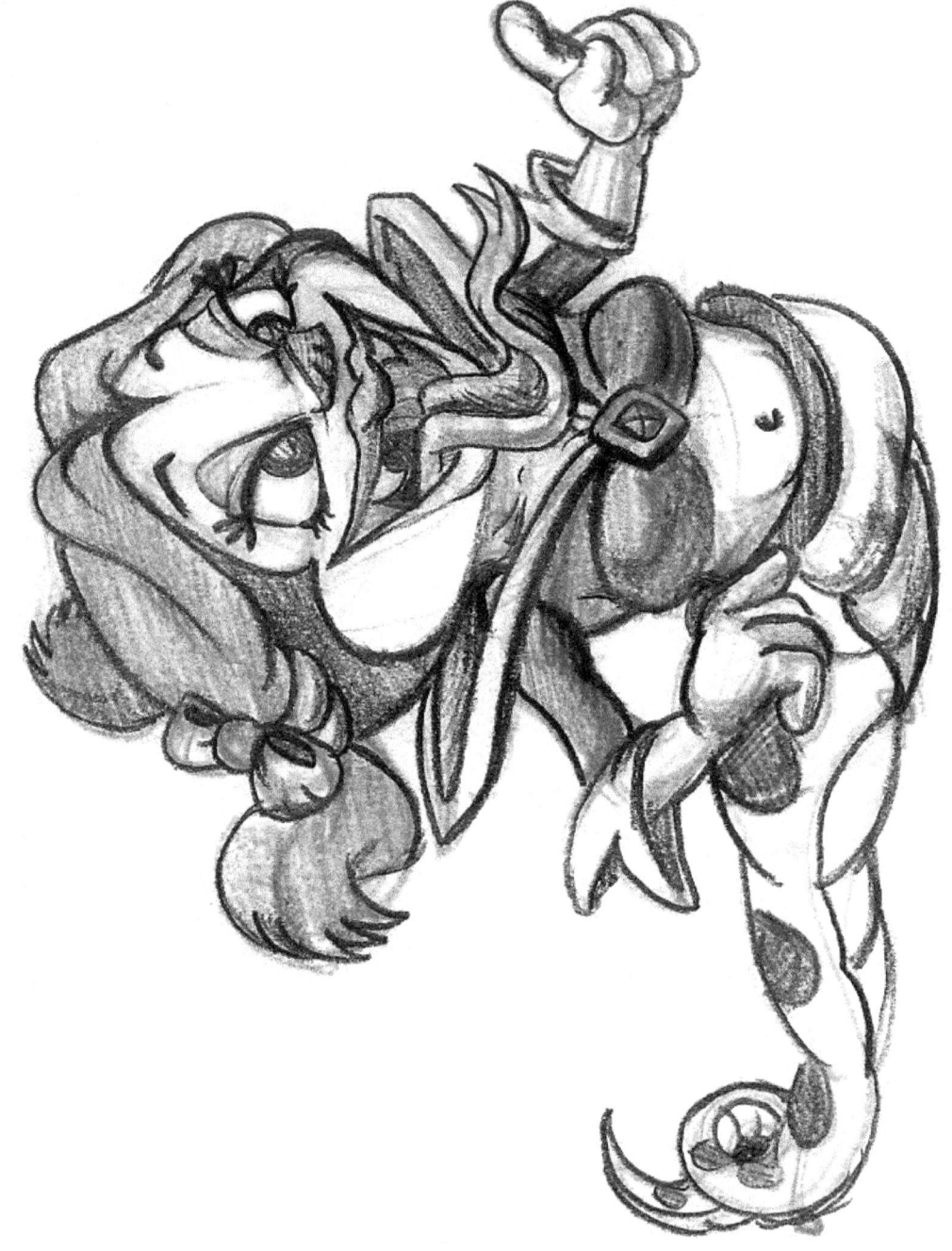

LeSLey-SLiThersz

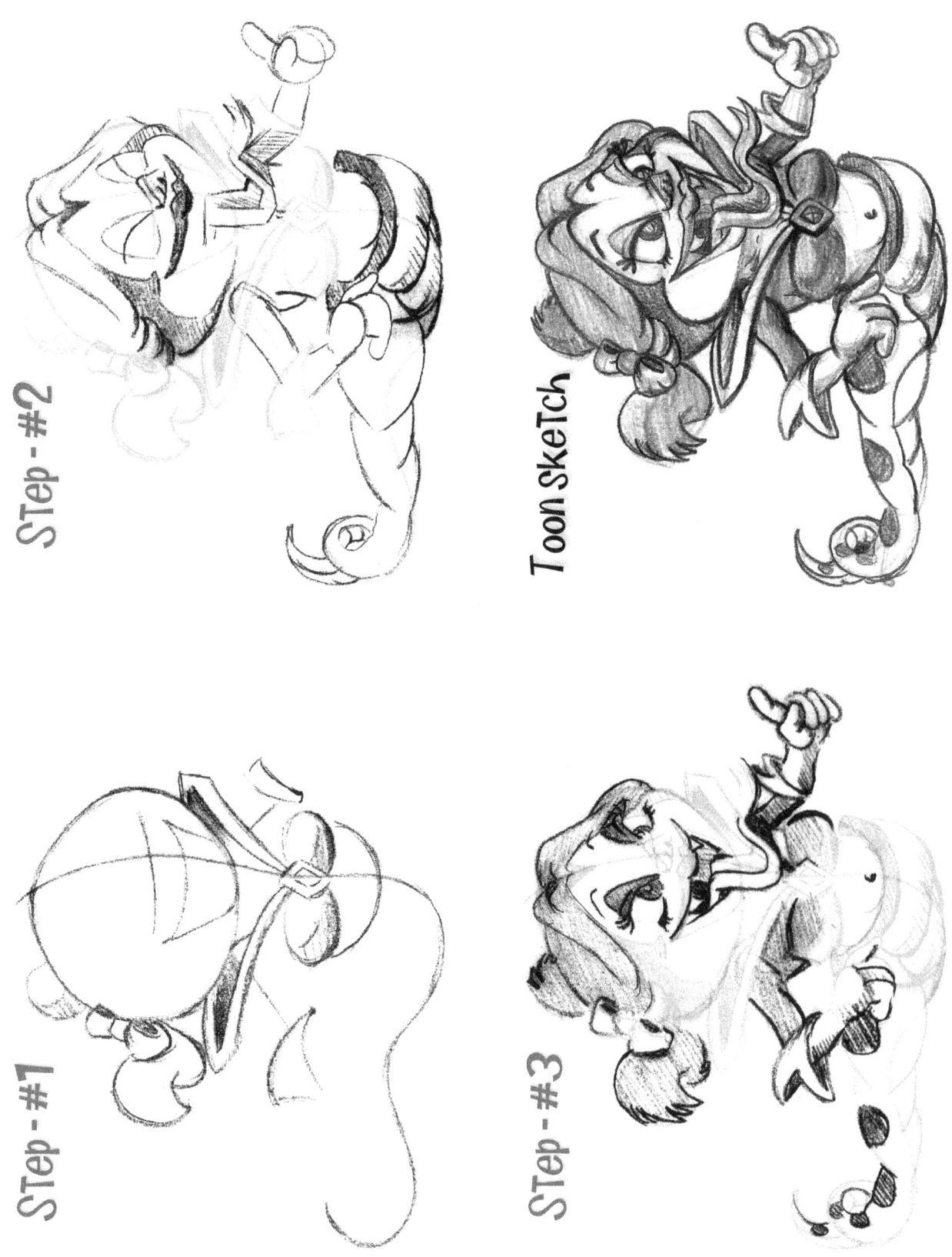

Step - #2

Toon Sketch

Step - #1

Step - #3

95.

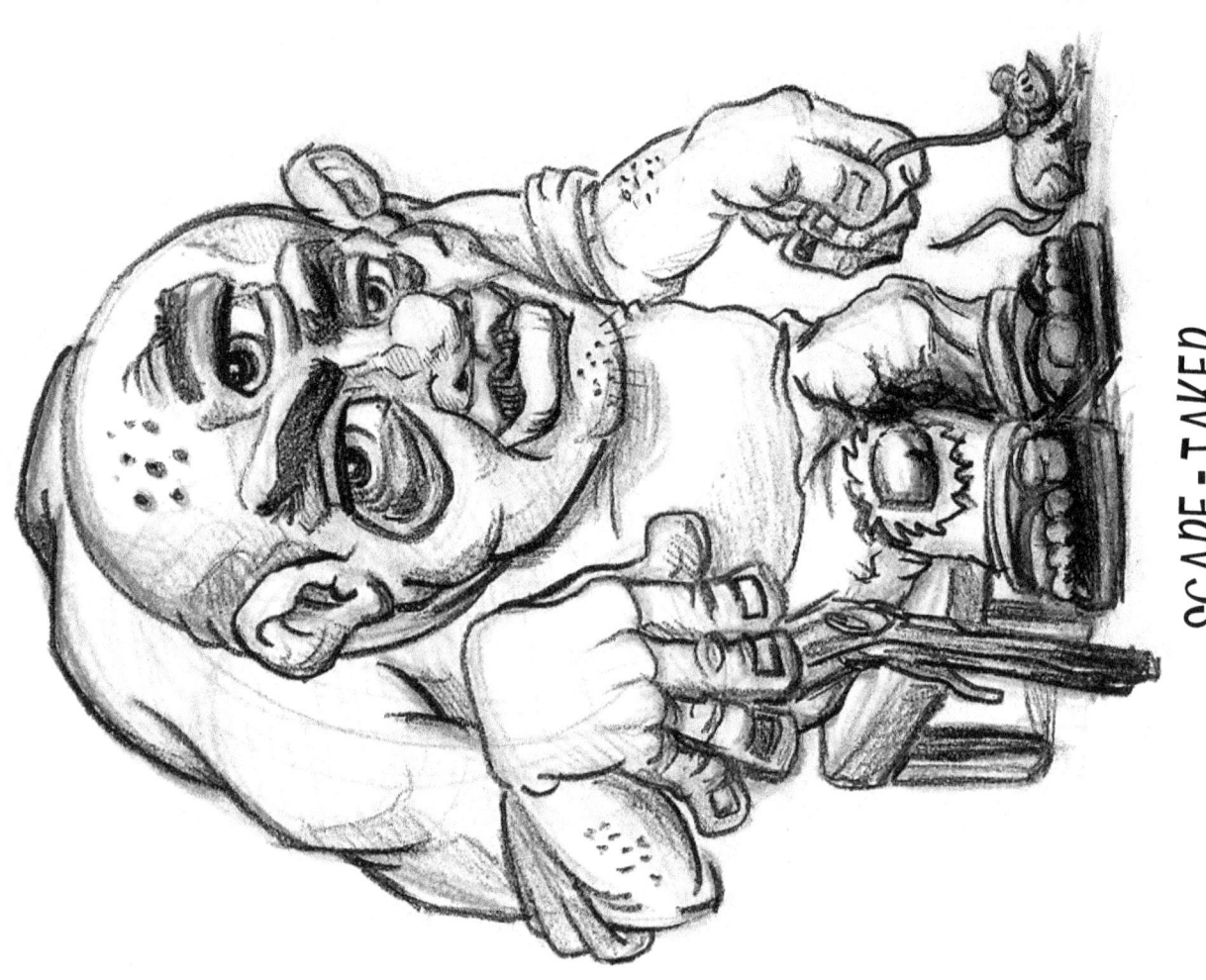

SCARE - TAKER

96.

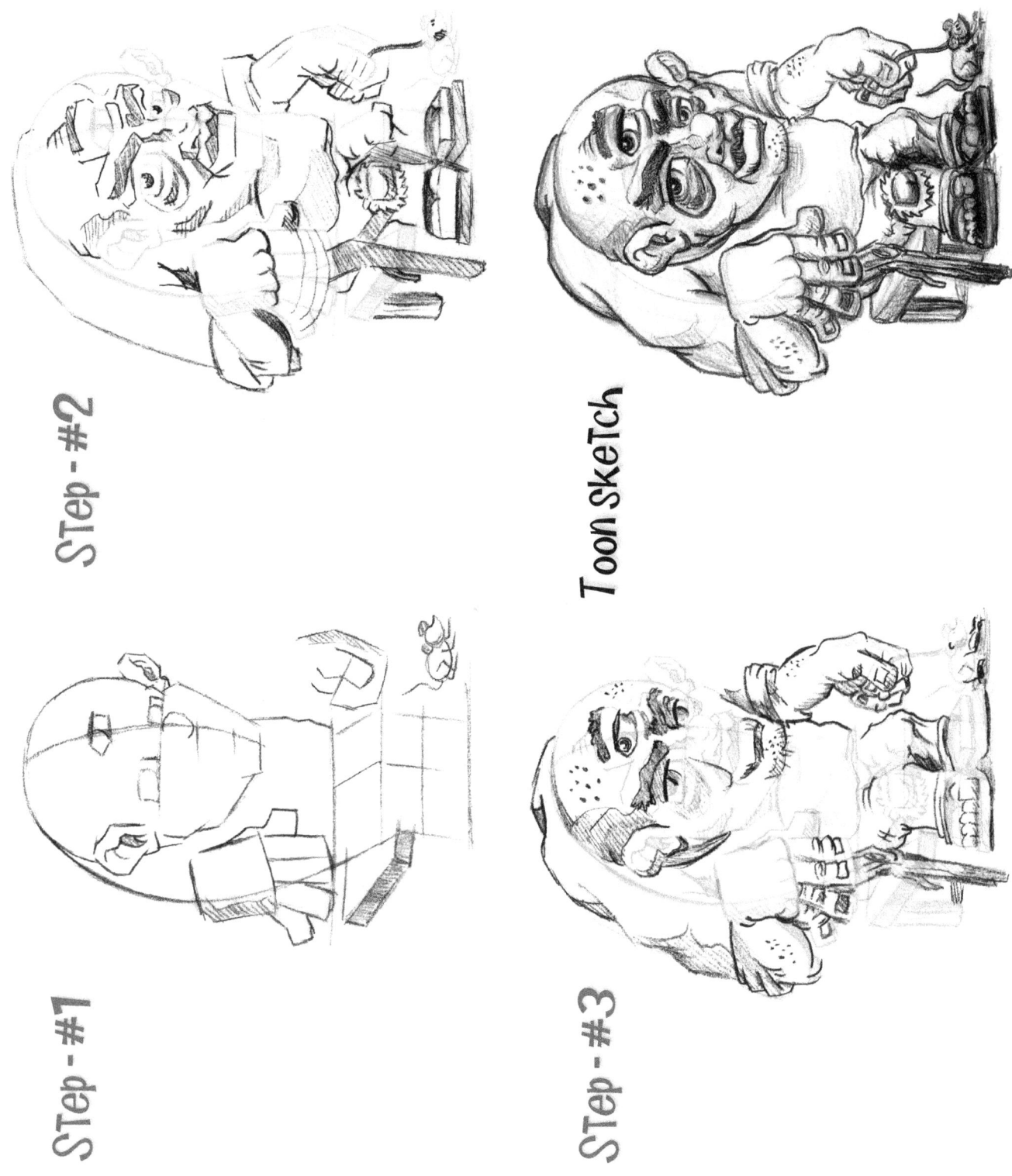

STep - #2

Toon SkeTch

STep - #1

STep - #3

Wolf - A - Saur - Ous

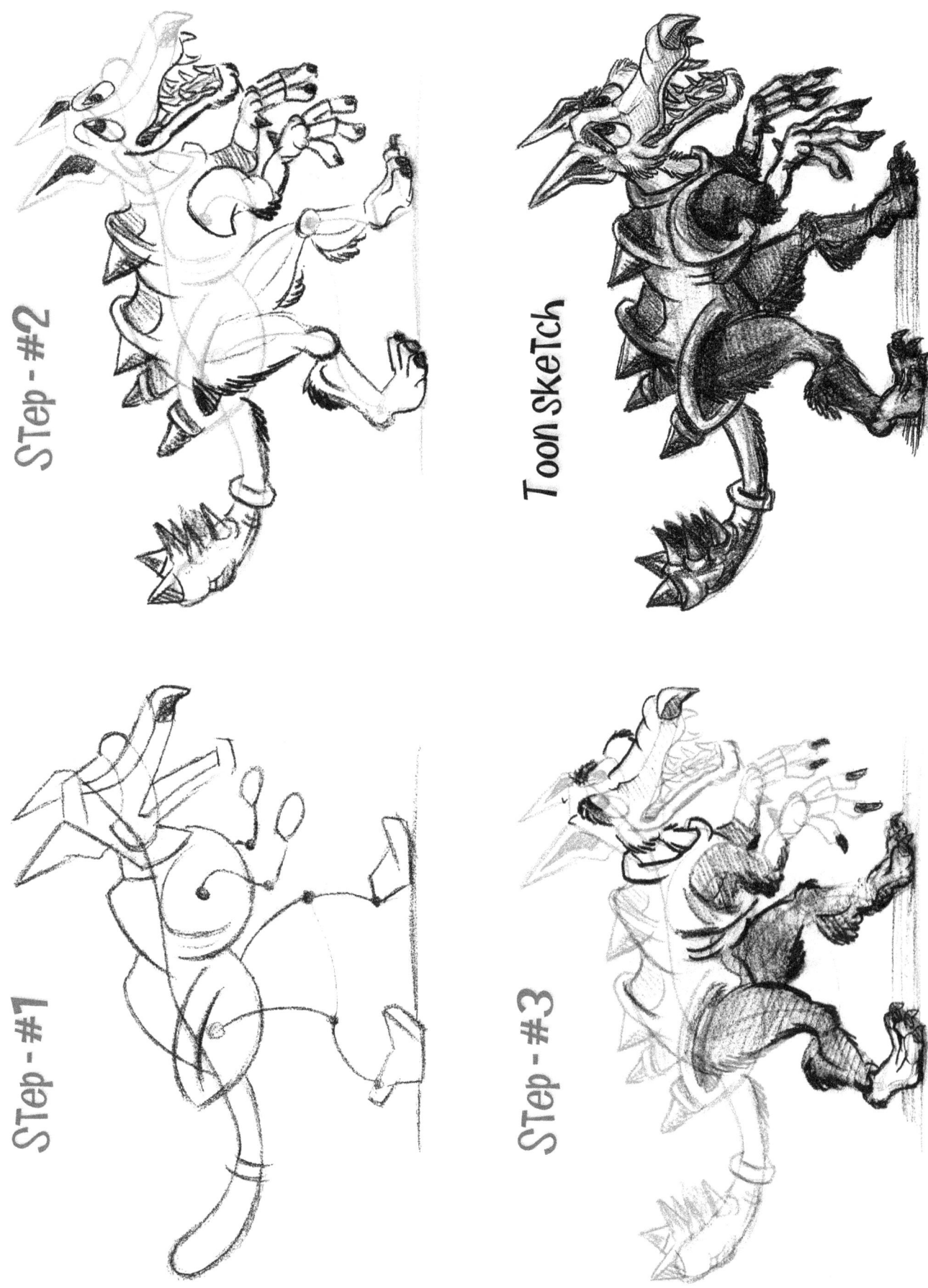

Step - #2

Toon Sketch

Step - #1

Step - #3

# Drawing Space

# Chapter 4 Drawing Cuddly Friends

## Five Cuddly creatures
## With Short Limbs

Step 1. The next five furry creatures are adorable.
You will enjoy Learning how to apply Short Limbs to your
cartoon characters. Short Limbs make toons Look so cute you
just want to hug them. You can also apply this
method when you develop baby toons.

Step 2. Try drawing a few circles and practice
making them furry, before you begin drawing
the fur on your cuddly creatures.

Step 3. Usually hair and fur is
drawn as simple lines. Experiment with vertical hatches
or small spikes that go in and out of areas that express fur.
Try also developing your own techniques for
creating fur on your soft and cuddly toons.

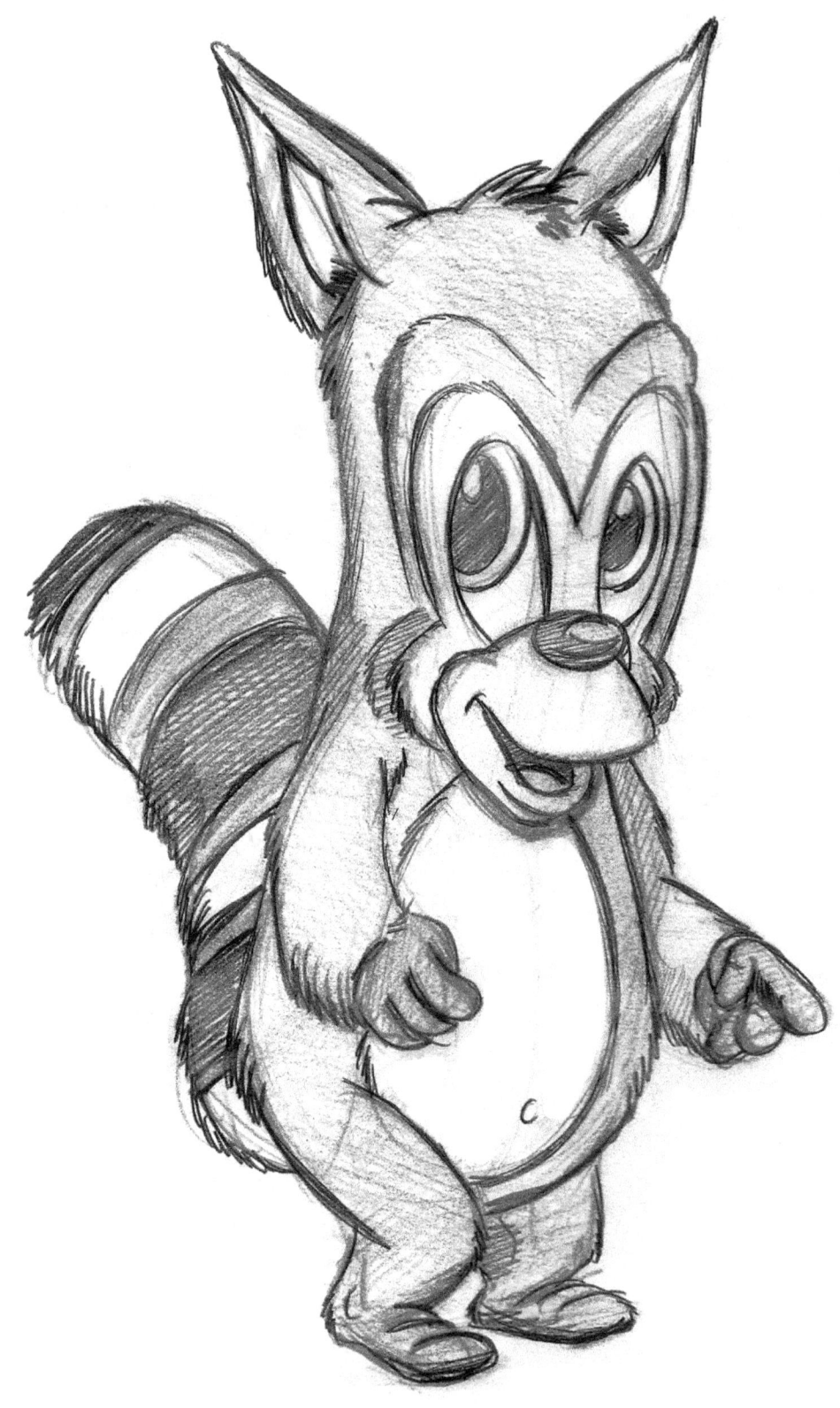

Funk - E - Fox - E

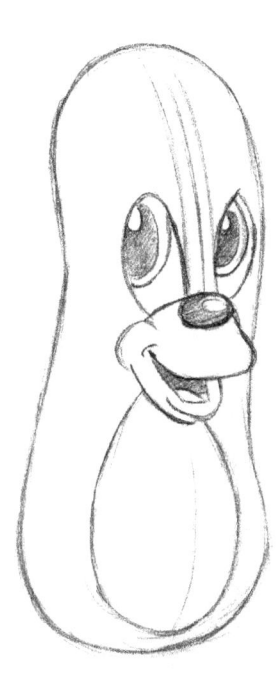

Step - #1

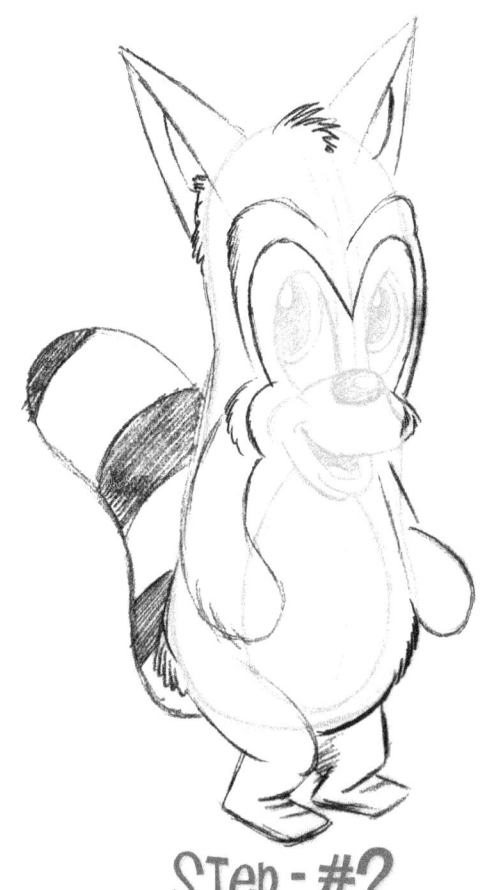

Step - #2

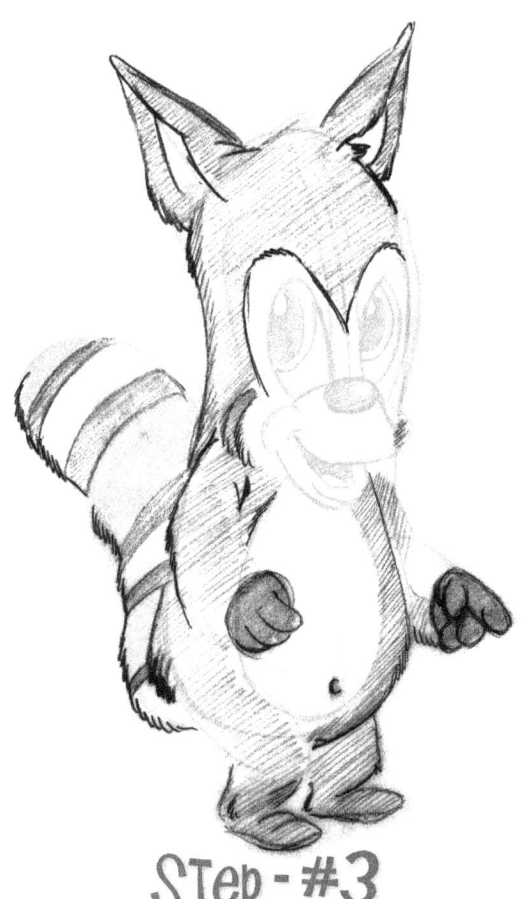

Step - #3

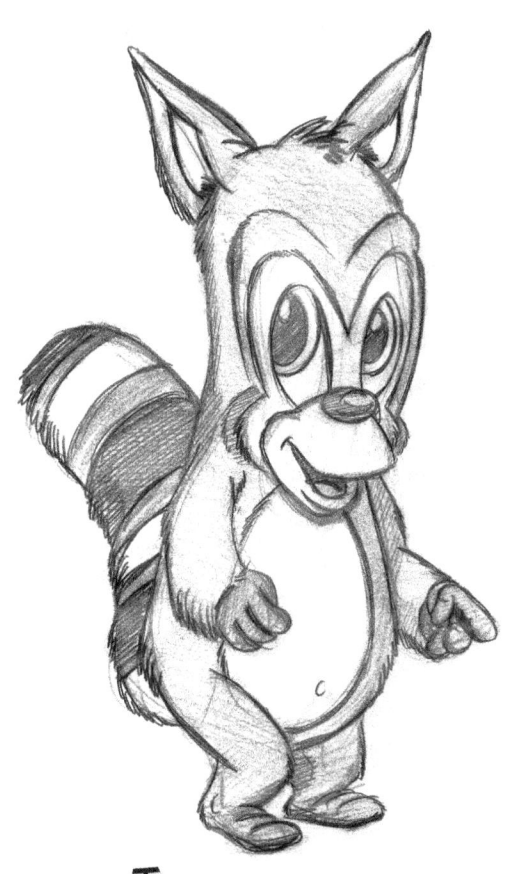

Toon sketch

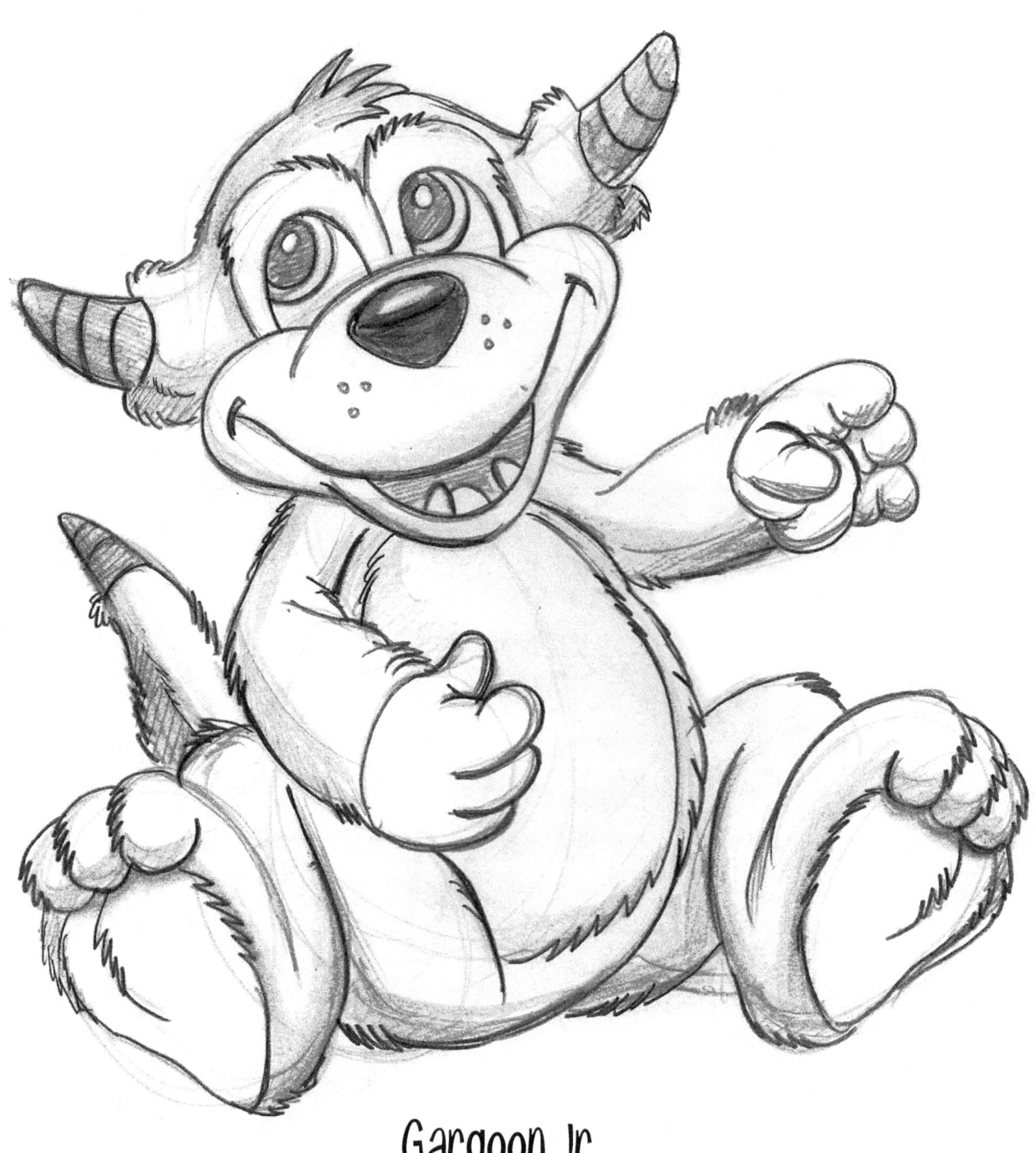

Gargoon Jr.

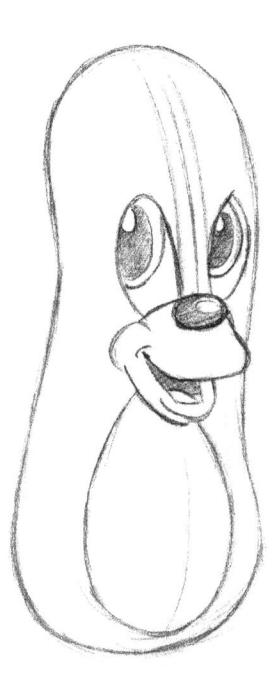

Step - #1

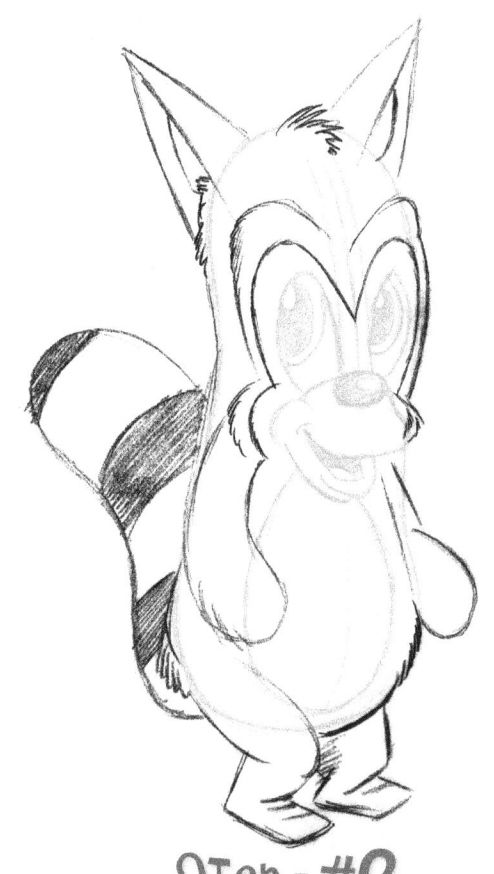

Step - #2

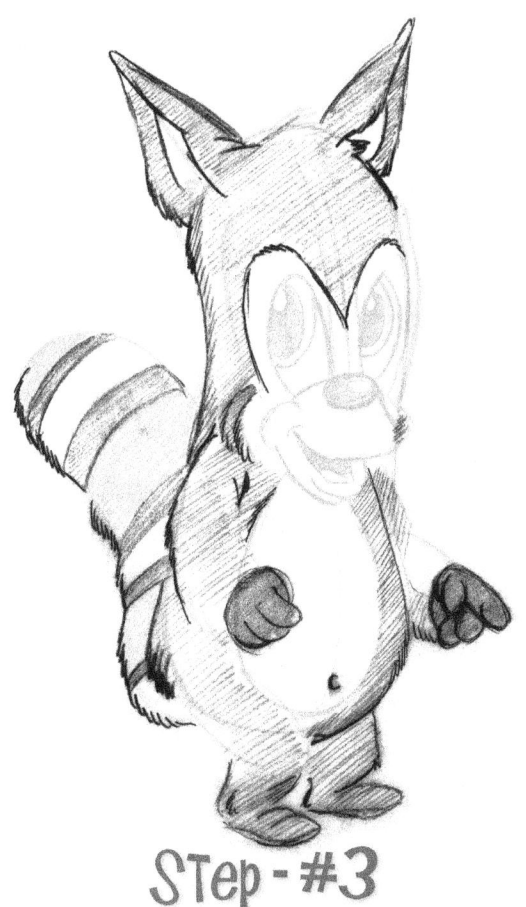

Step - #3

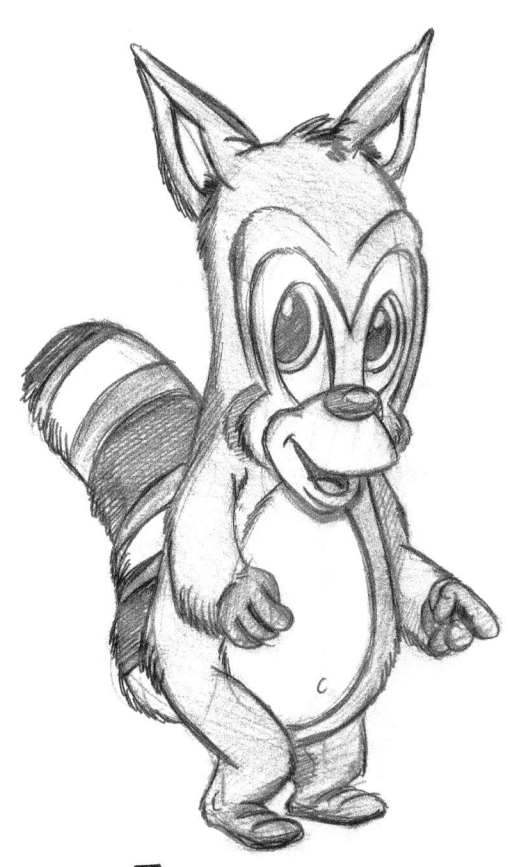

Toon sketch

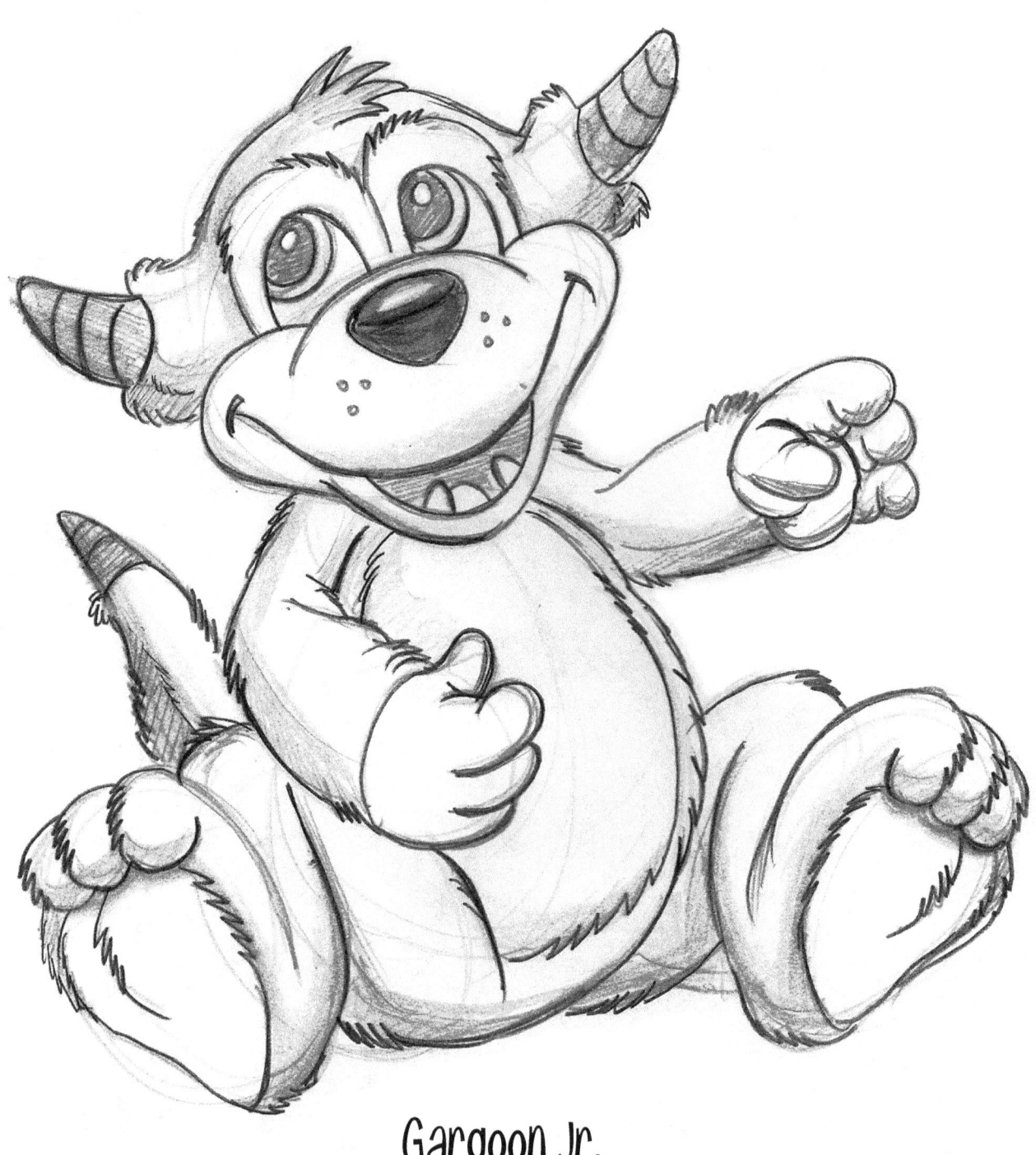

Gargoon Jr.

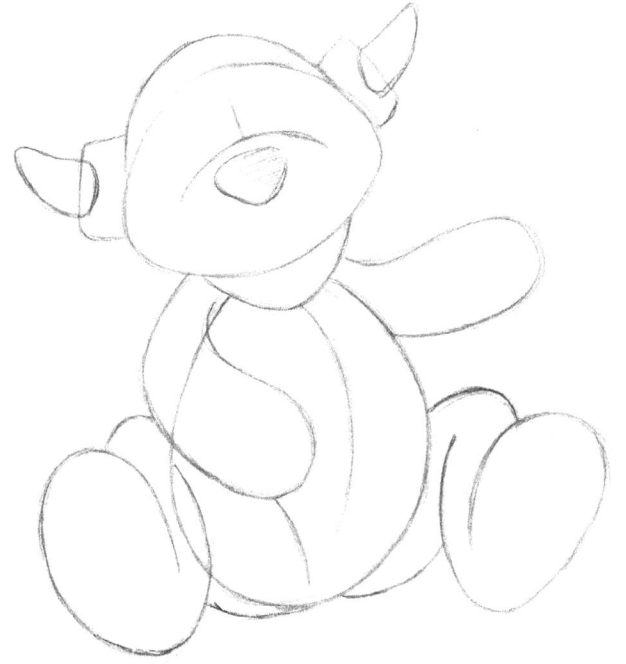

STep - #1

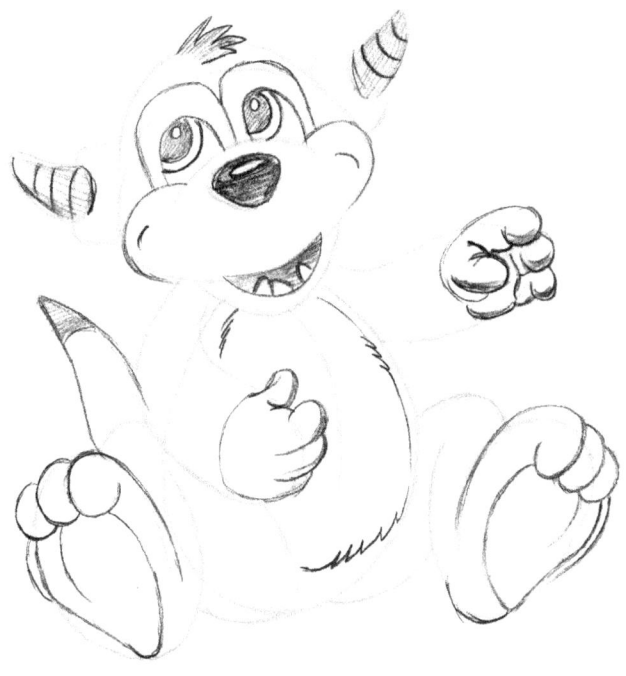

STep - #2

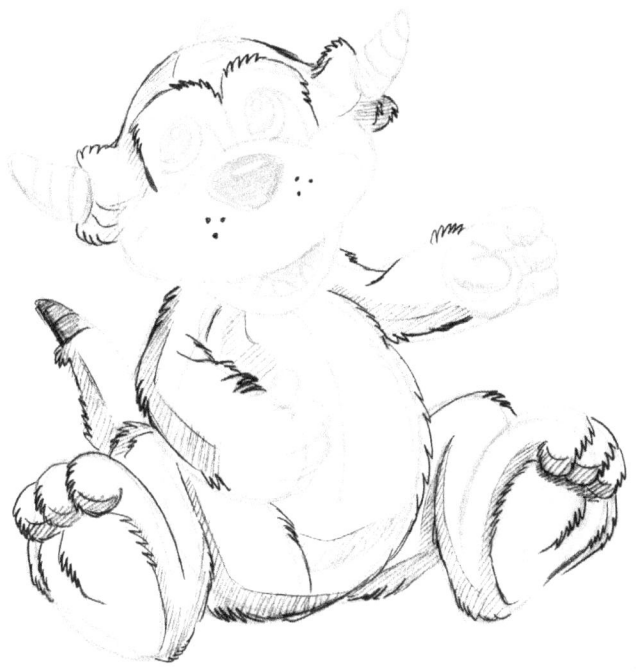

STep - #3

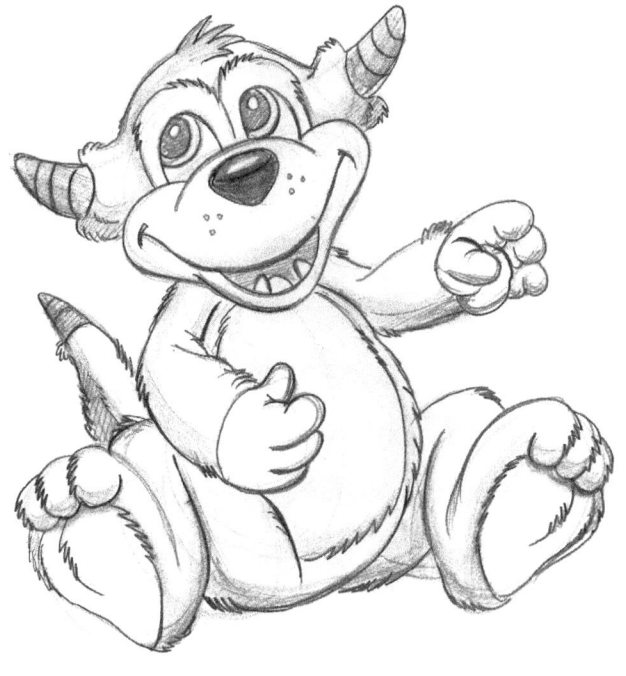

Toon sketch

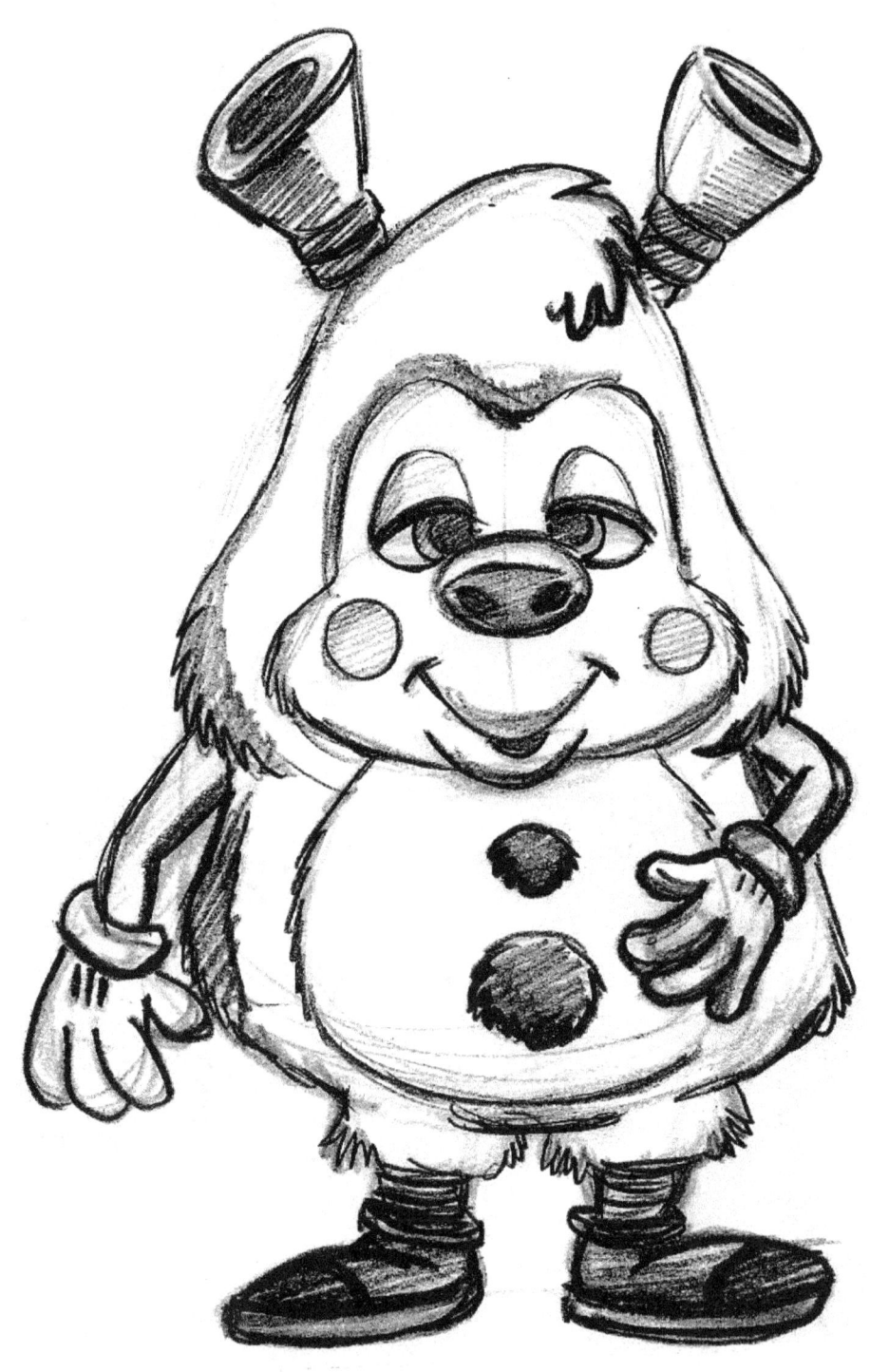

Polly - Pom-Pom - Belly

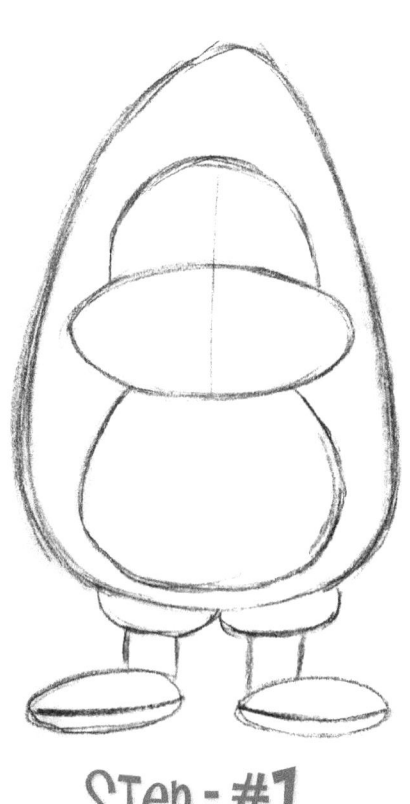

STep - #1

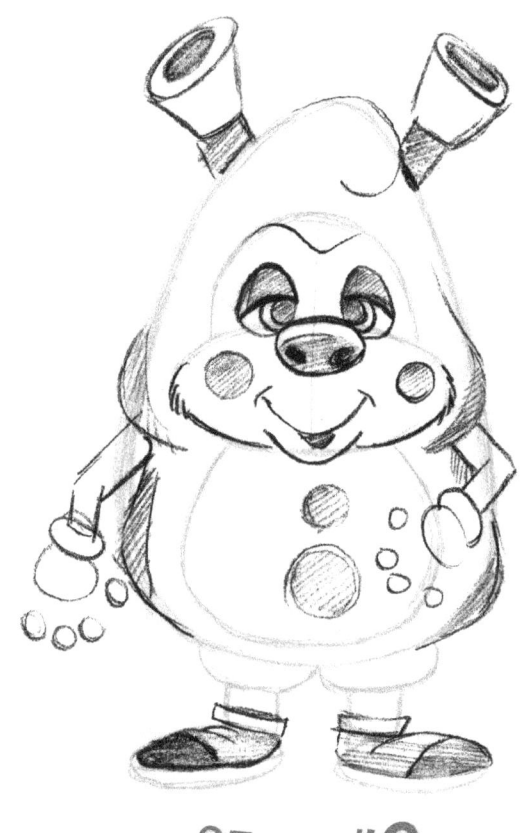

STep - #2

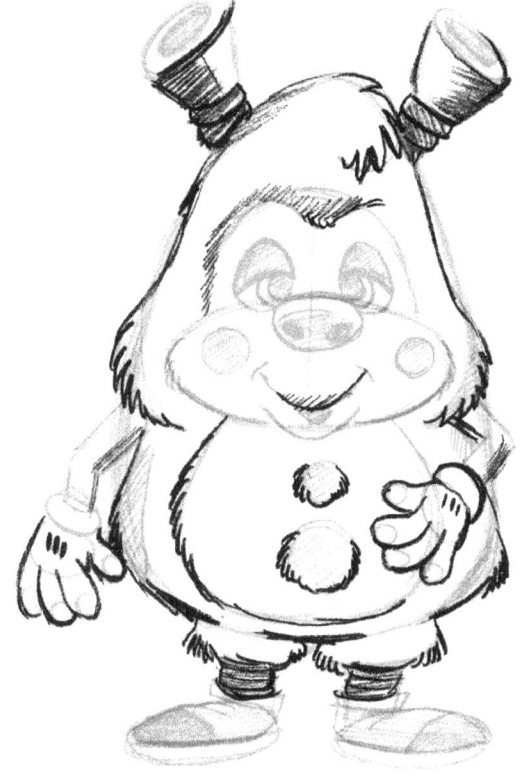

STep - #3

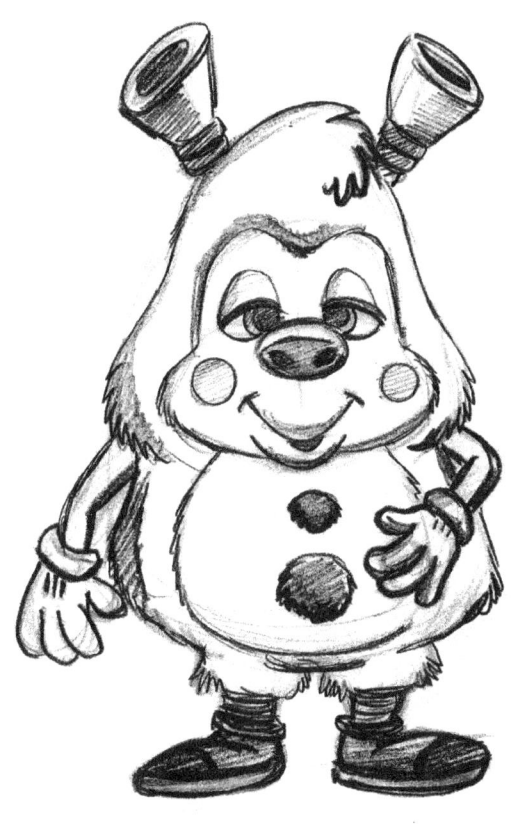

Toon sketch

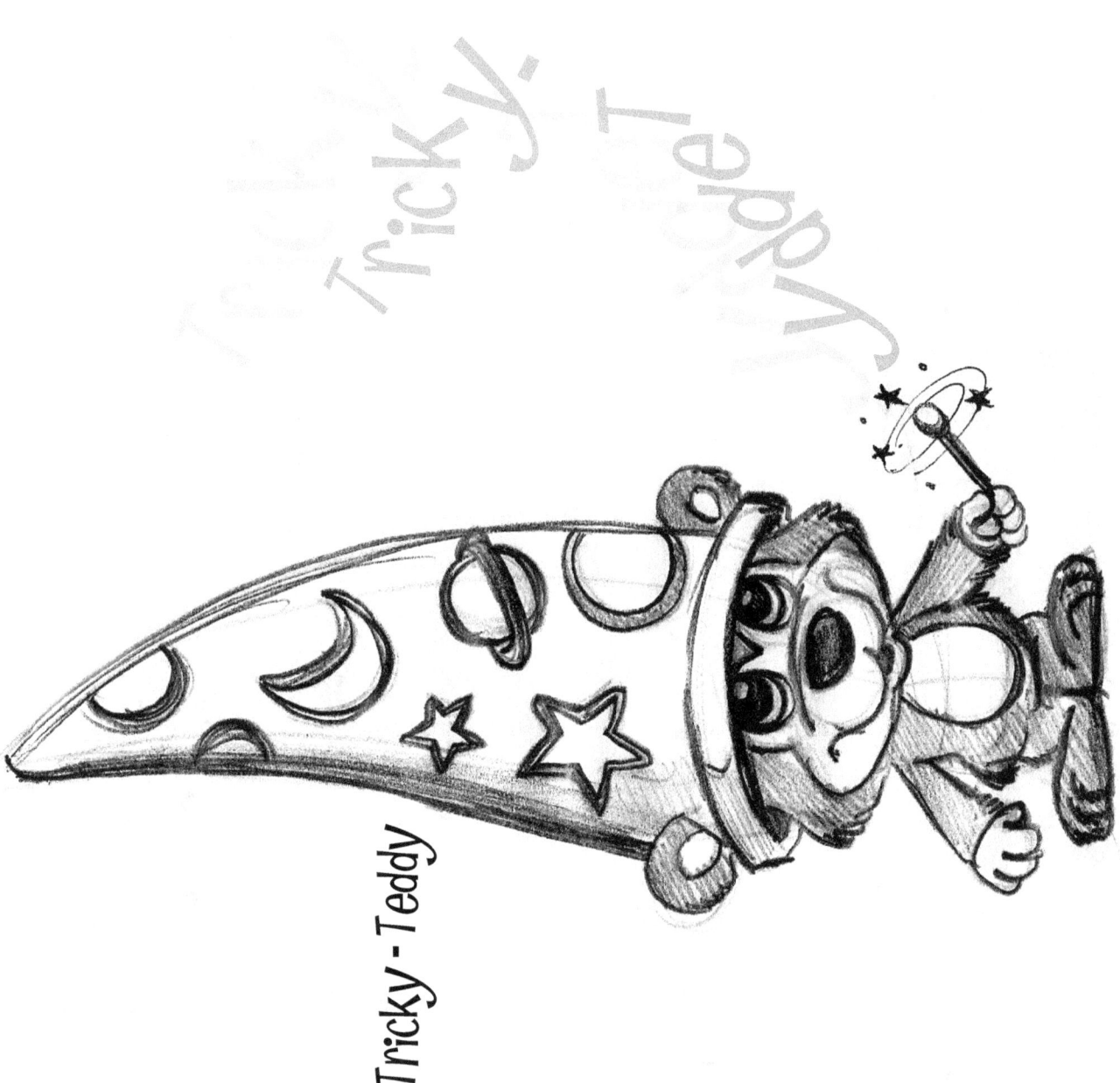

Tricky - Teddy

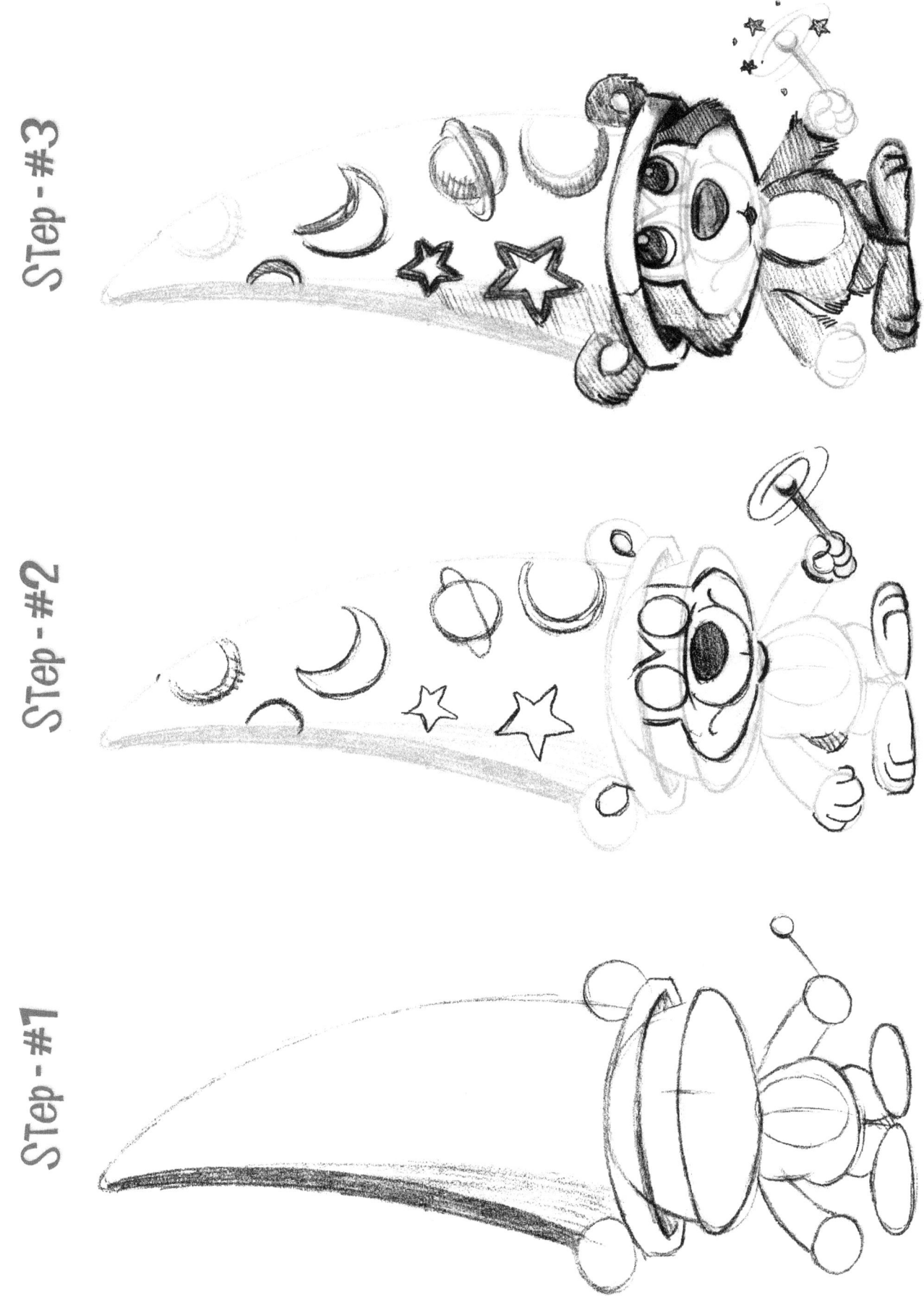

STep-#1

STep-#2

STep-#3

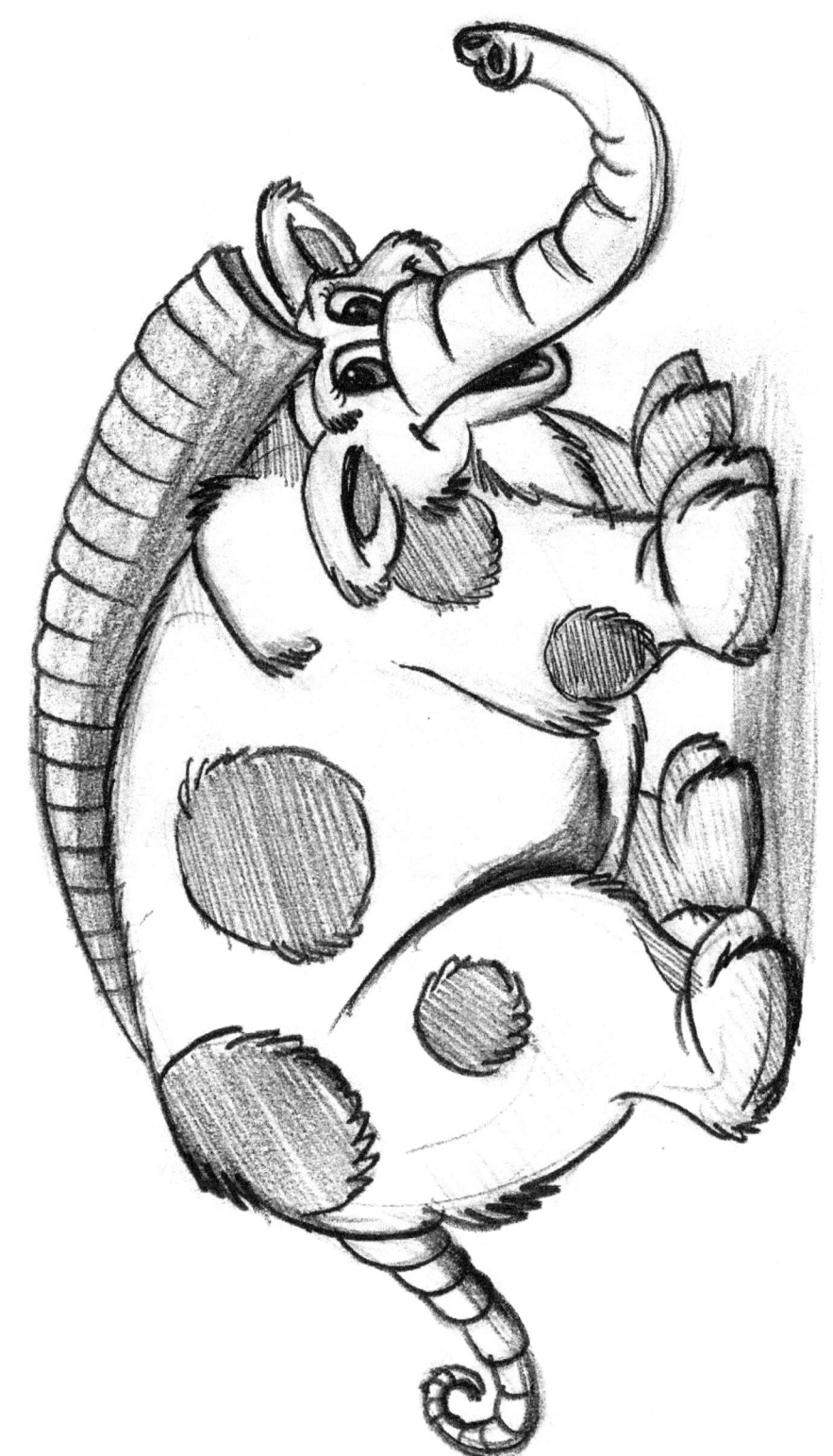

Trunky - Tree - nah

STep - #2

Toon SkeTch

STep - #1

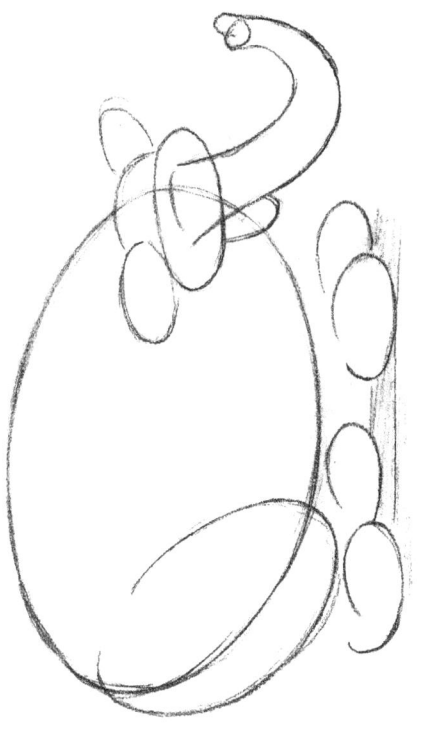

STep - #3

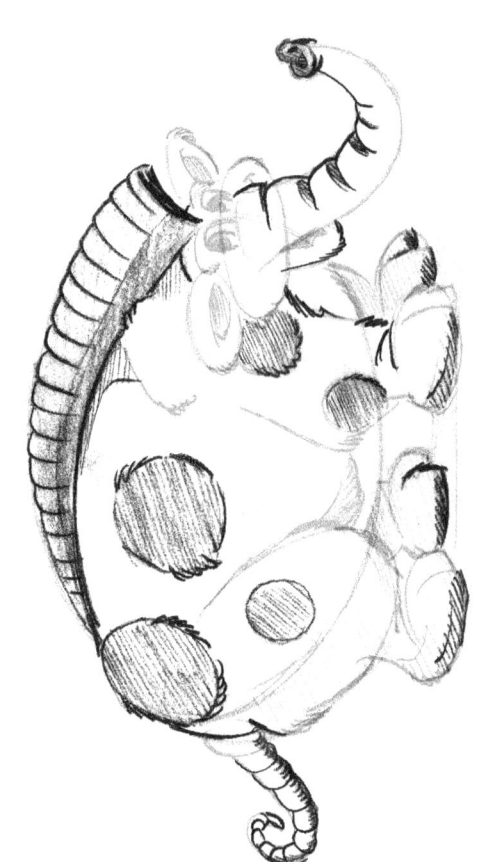

# Drawing Space

# Ten cuddly creatures with Long Limbs

Step 1. The characters you are about to meet are furry and rather cuddly friends. In this Lesson you can explore how to add Long Limbs and Fur to a cartoon character.

Step 2. After your Toon is drawn and ready for fur, visit the Helpful Hints chapter 7 for Lessons and ideas for applying the fur. Try also inventing new ways to texture your furry friends.

Step 3. Once you have finished drawing all your cuddly creatures, you are now a professional Toon hair Designer. Always practice applying fur to your new characters, especially if you want them to be cute and cuddly.

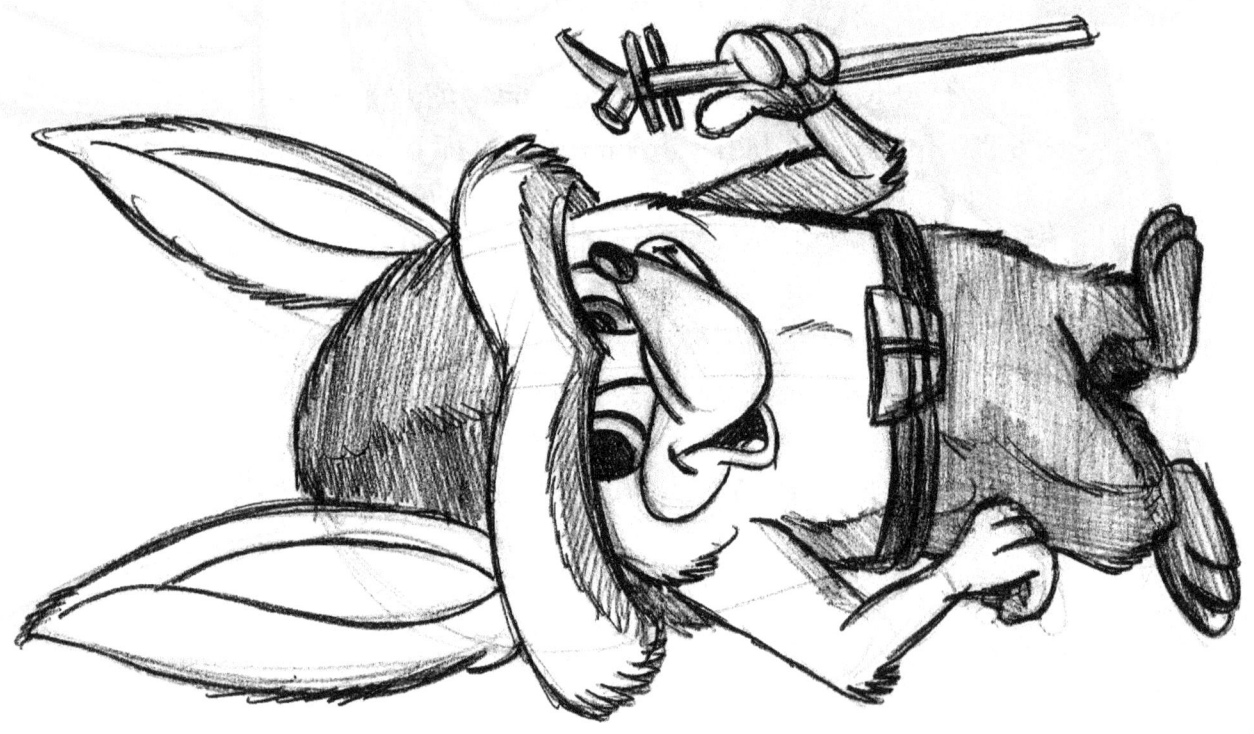

Bum-Zee

Step - #1

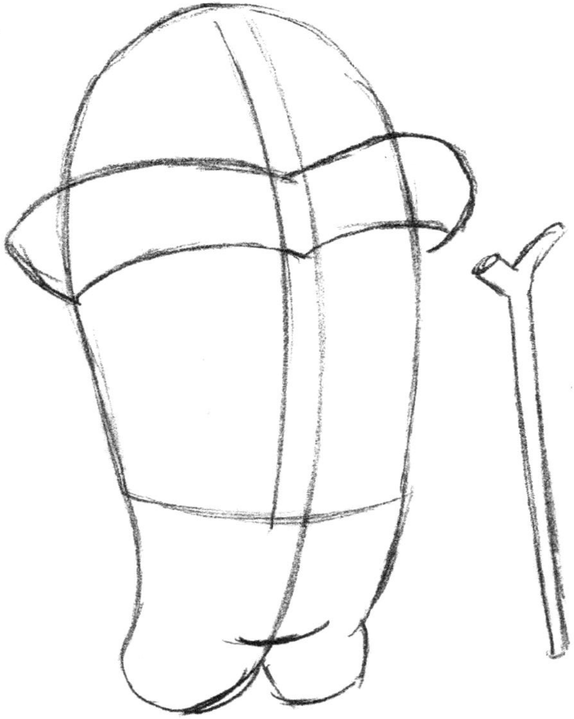

Step - #2

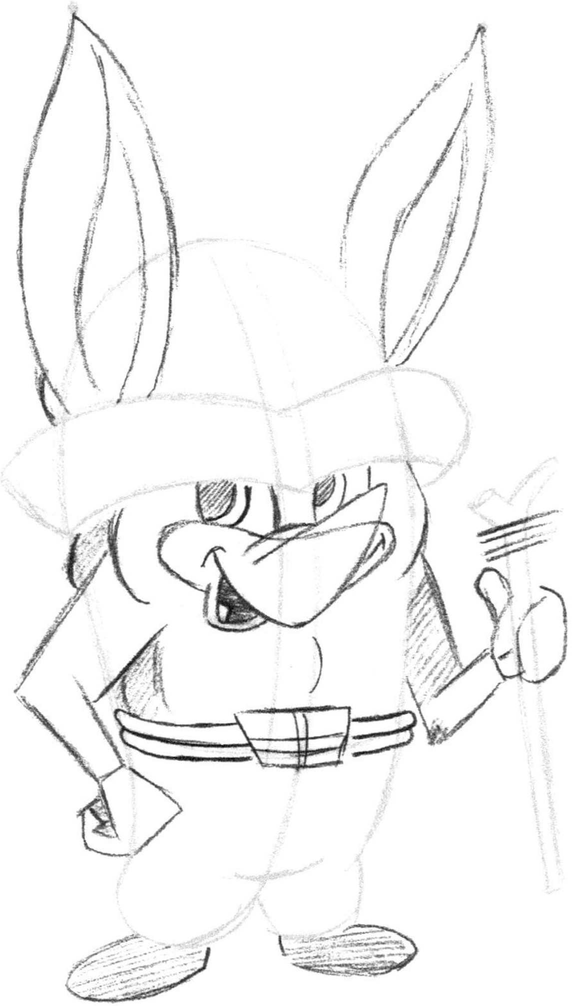

Step - #3

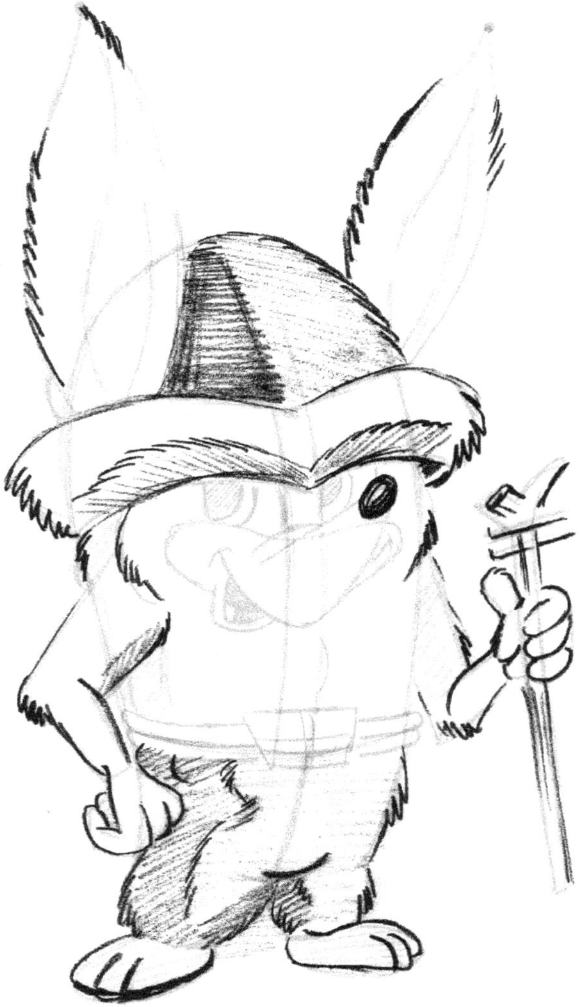

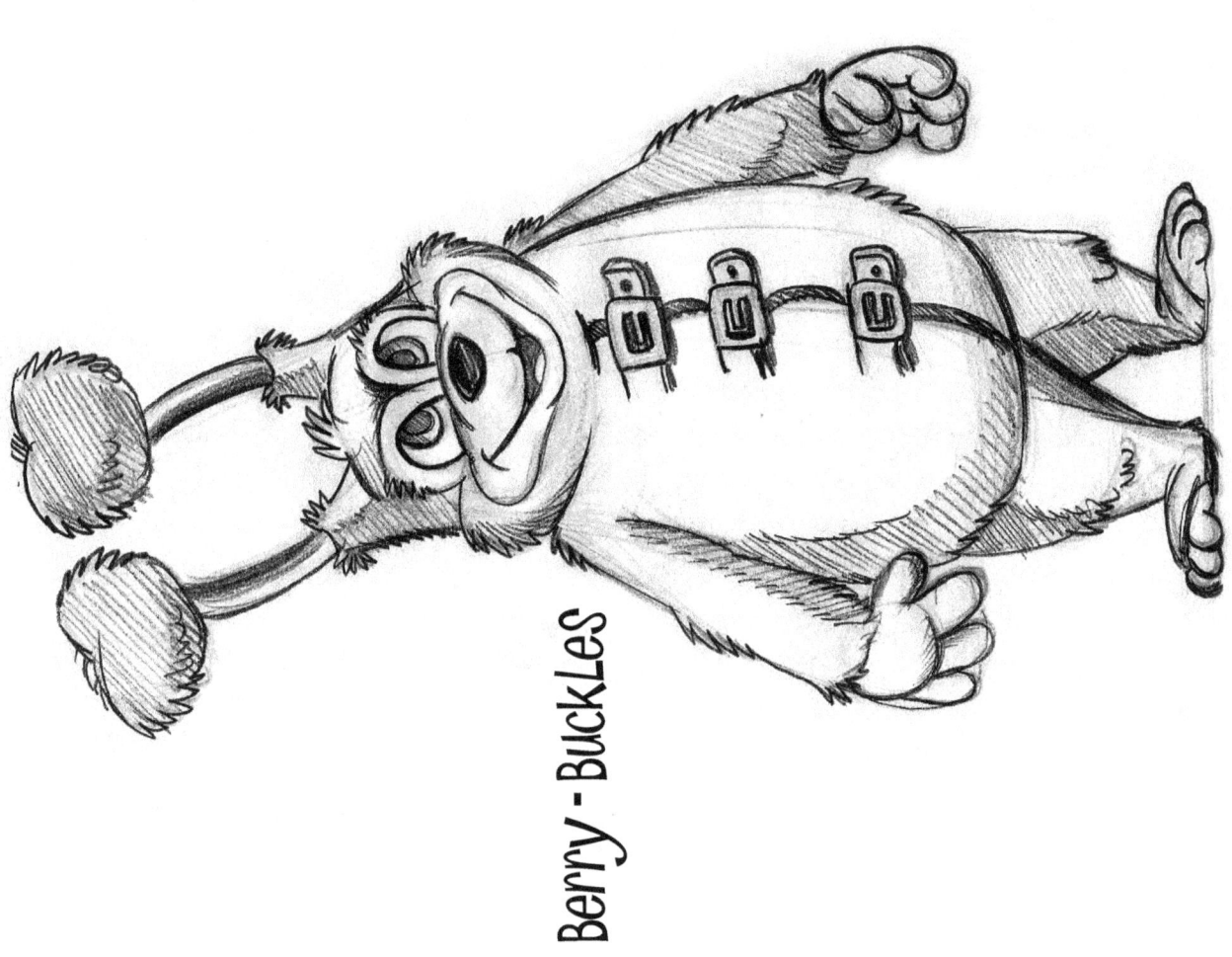

Berry - BuckLeS

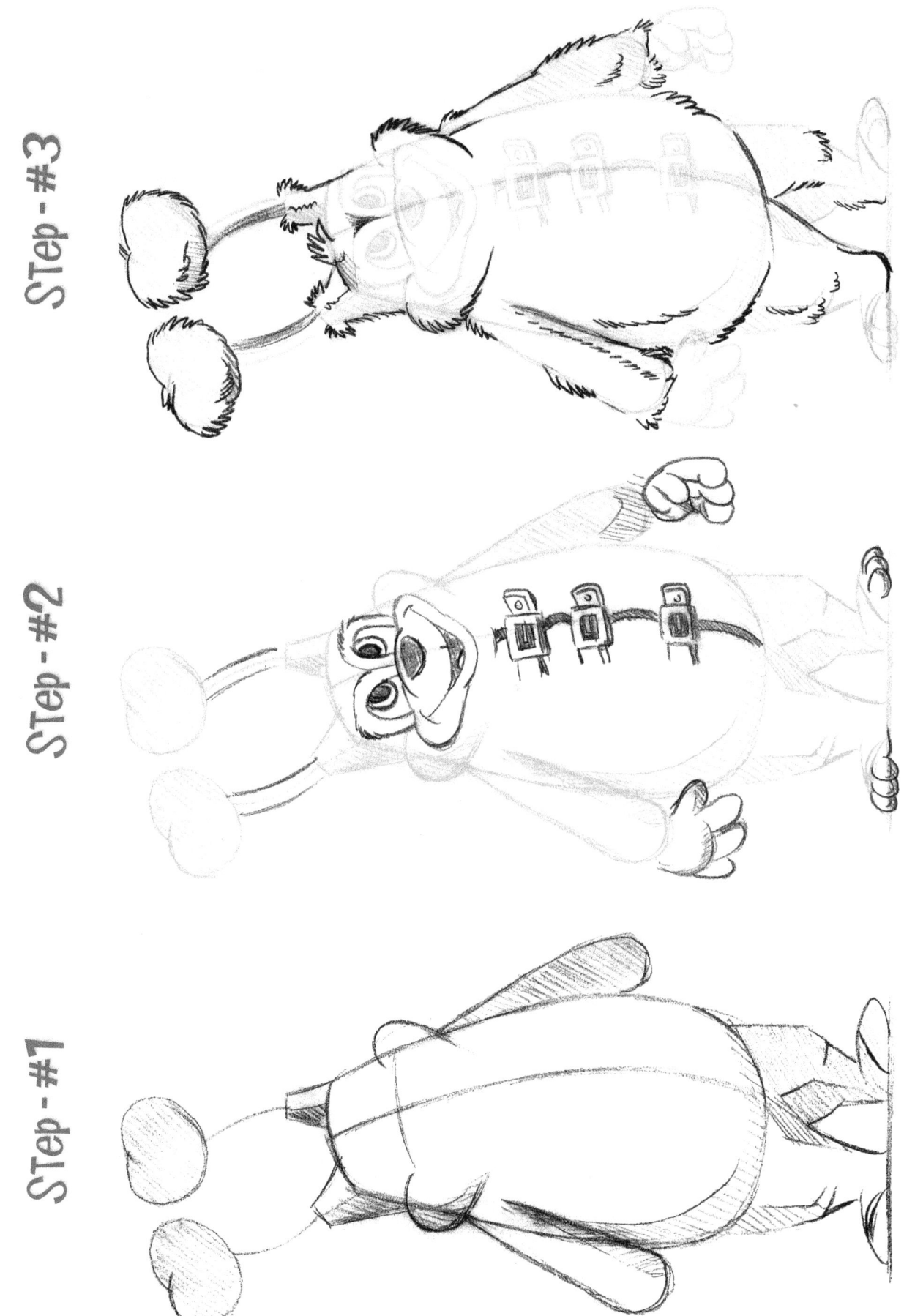

STep-#1

STep-#2

STep-#3

117

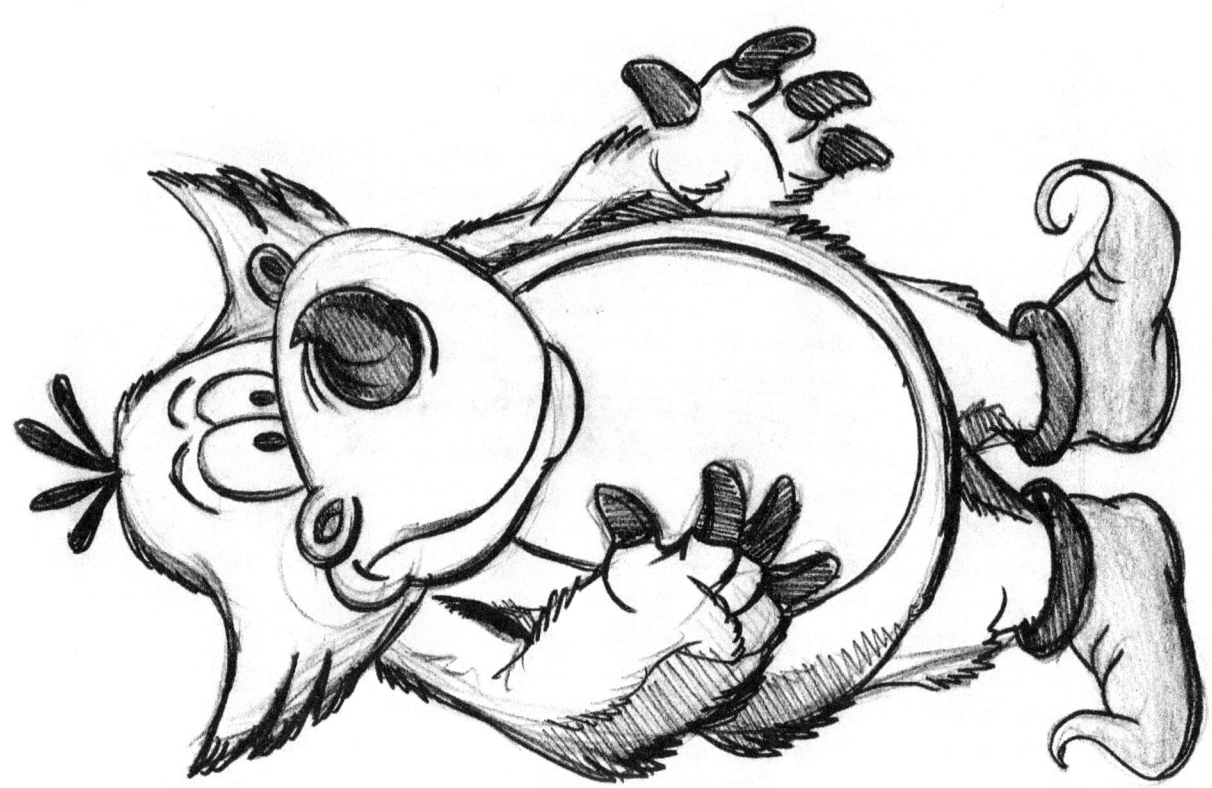

CorneLiousse

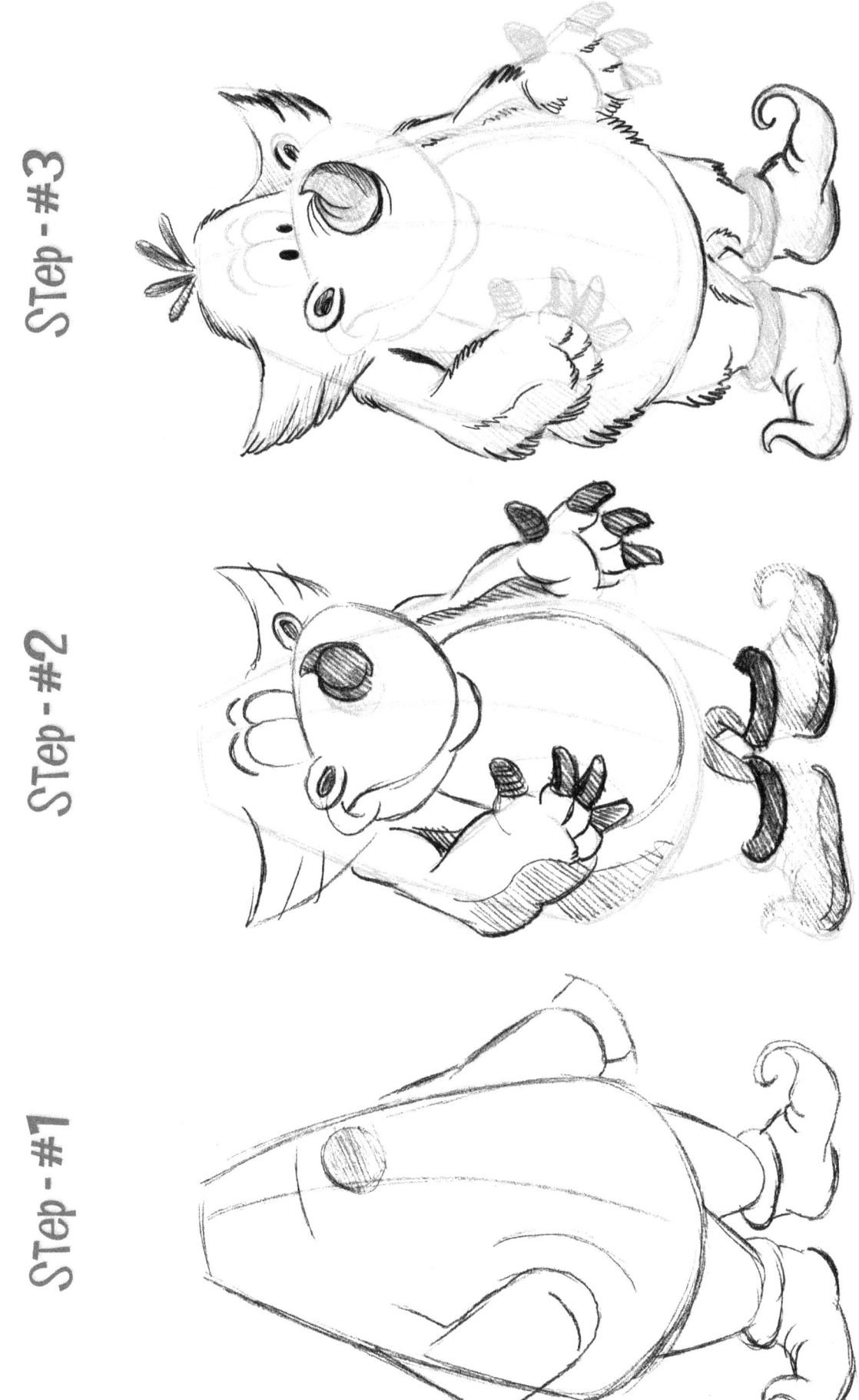

FeLina

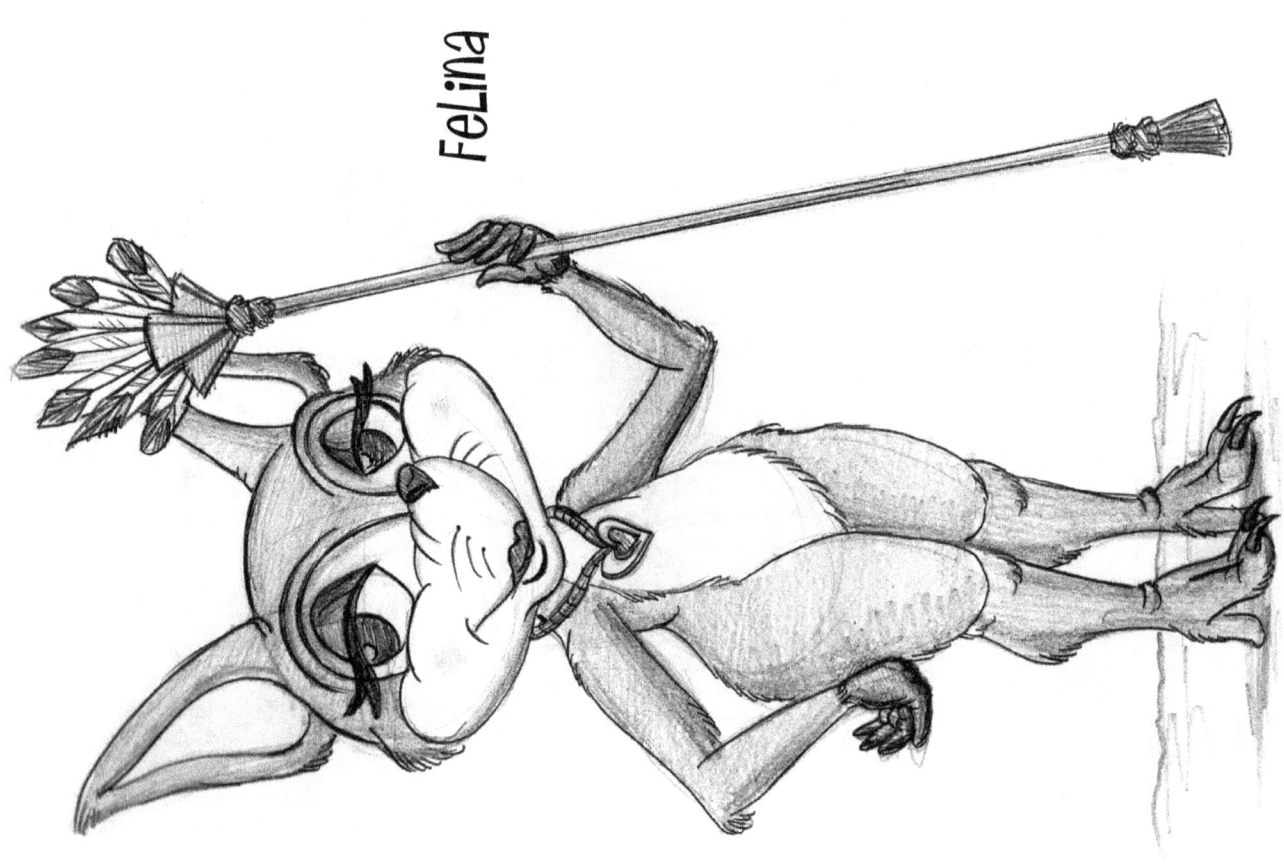

STep - #1

STep - #2

STep - #3

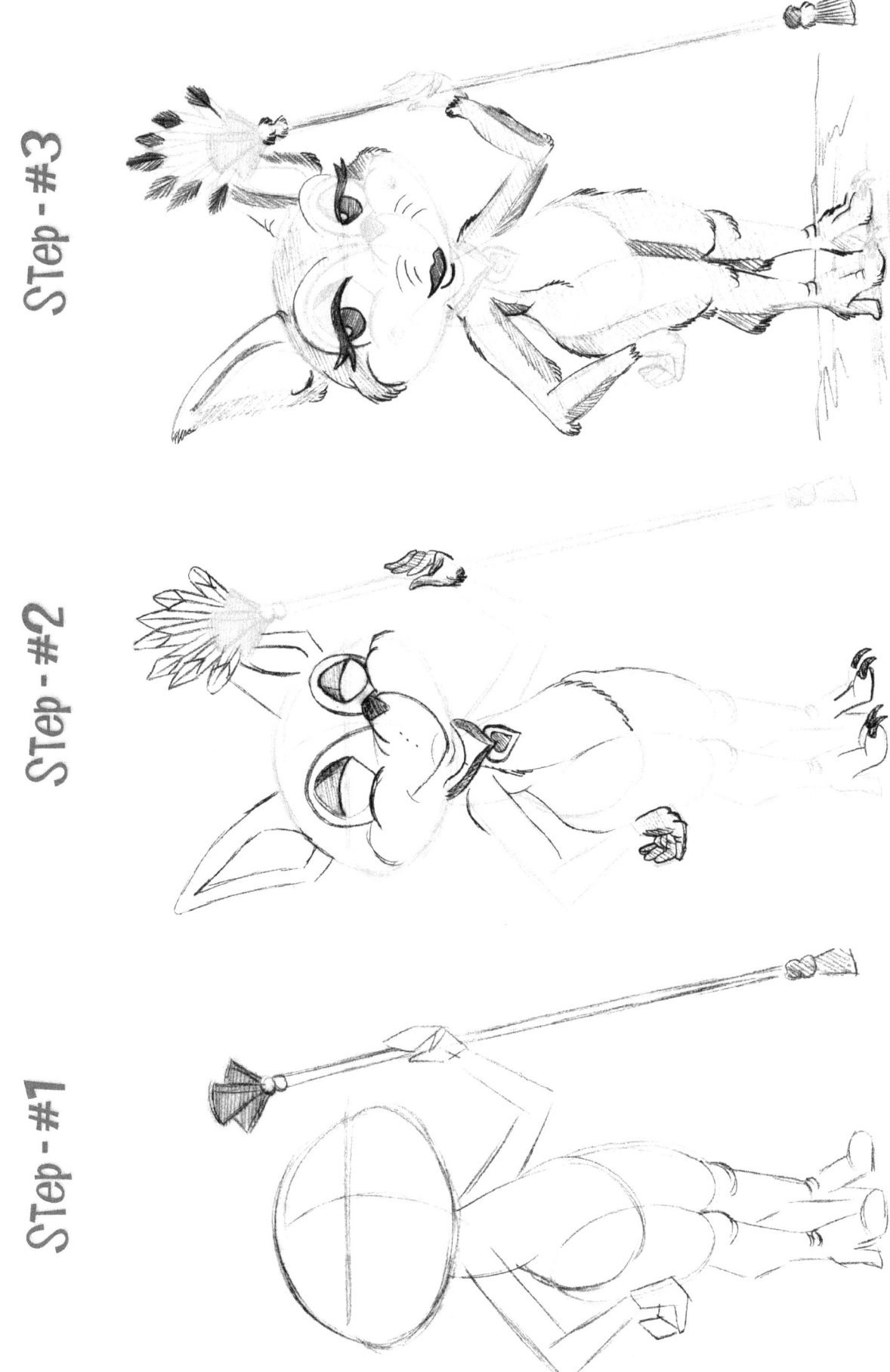

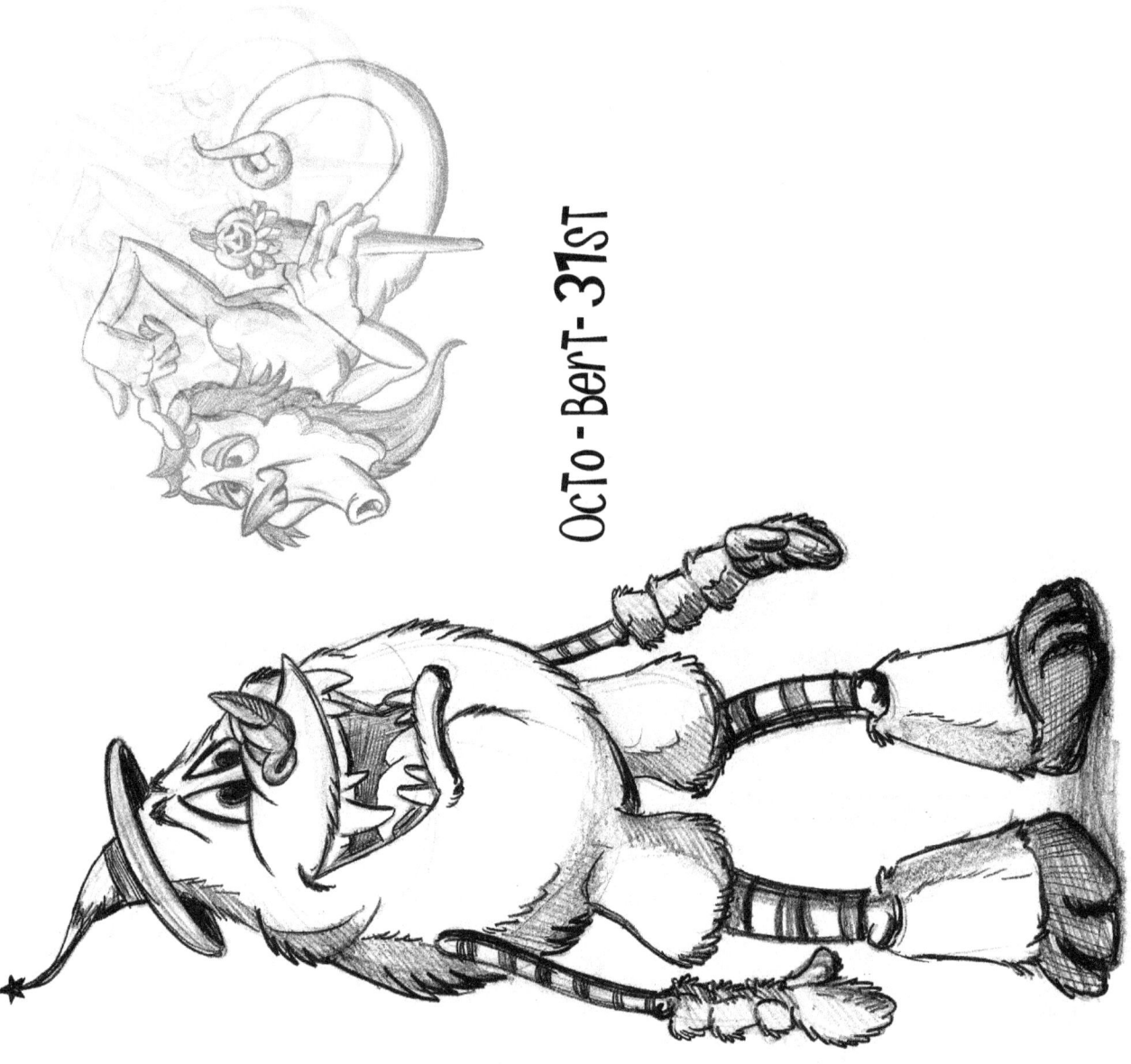

OcTo - BerT - 31st

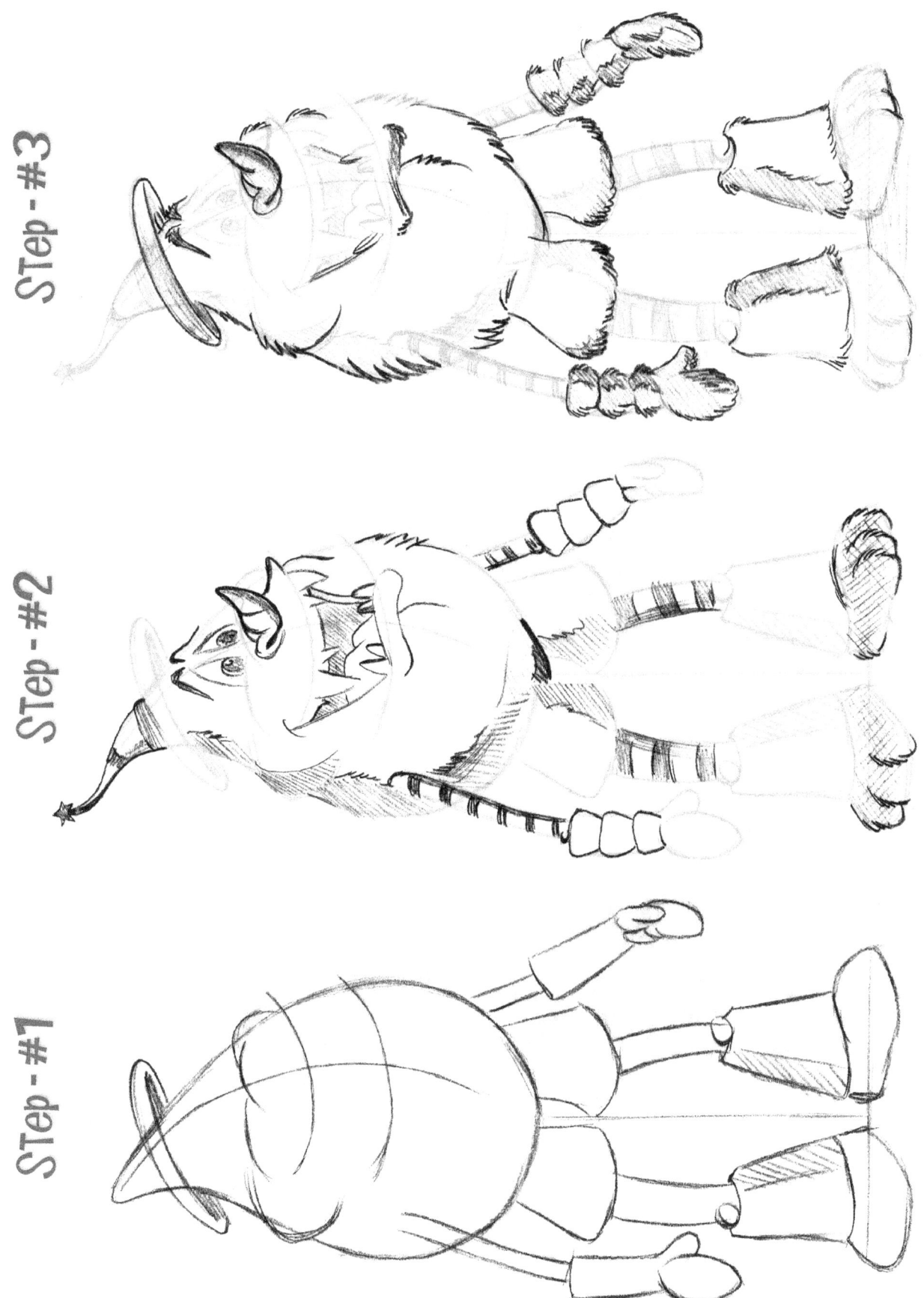

STep - #1

STep - #2

STep - #3

123.

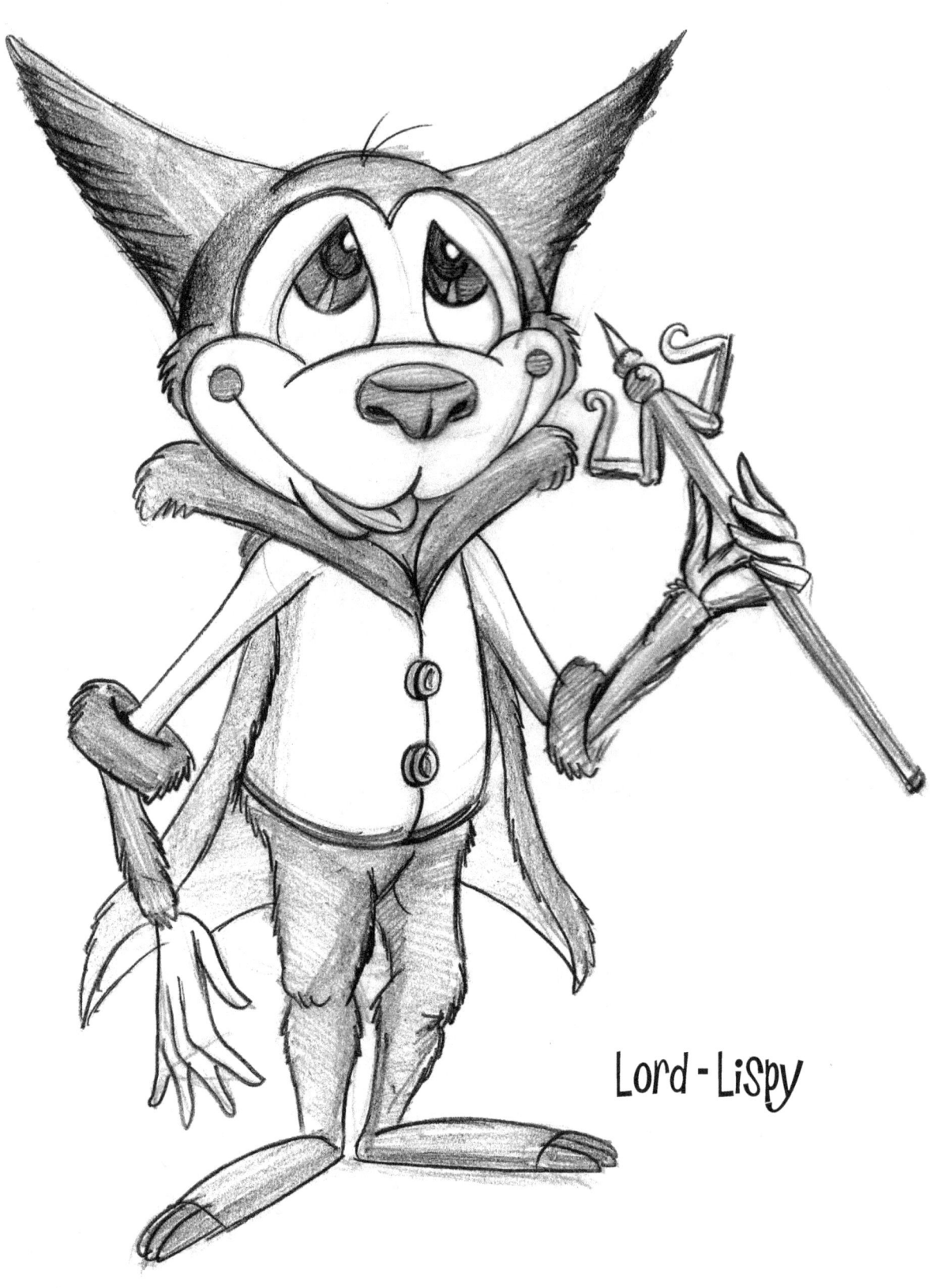

Lord - Lispy

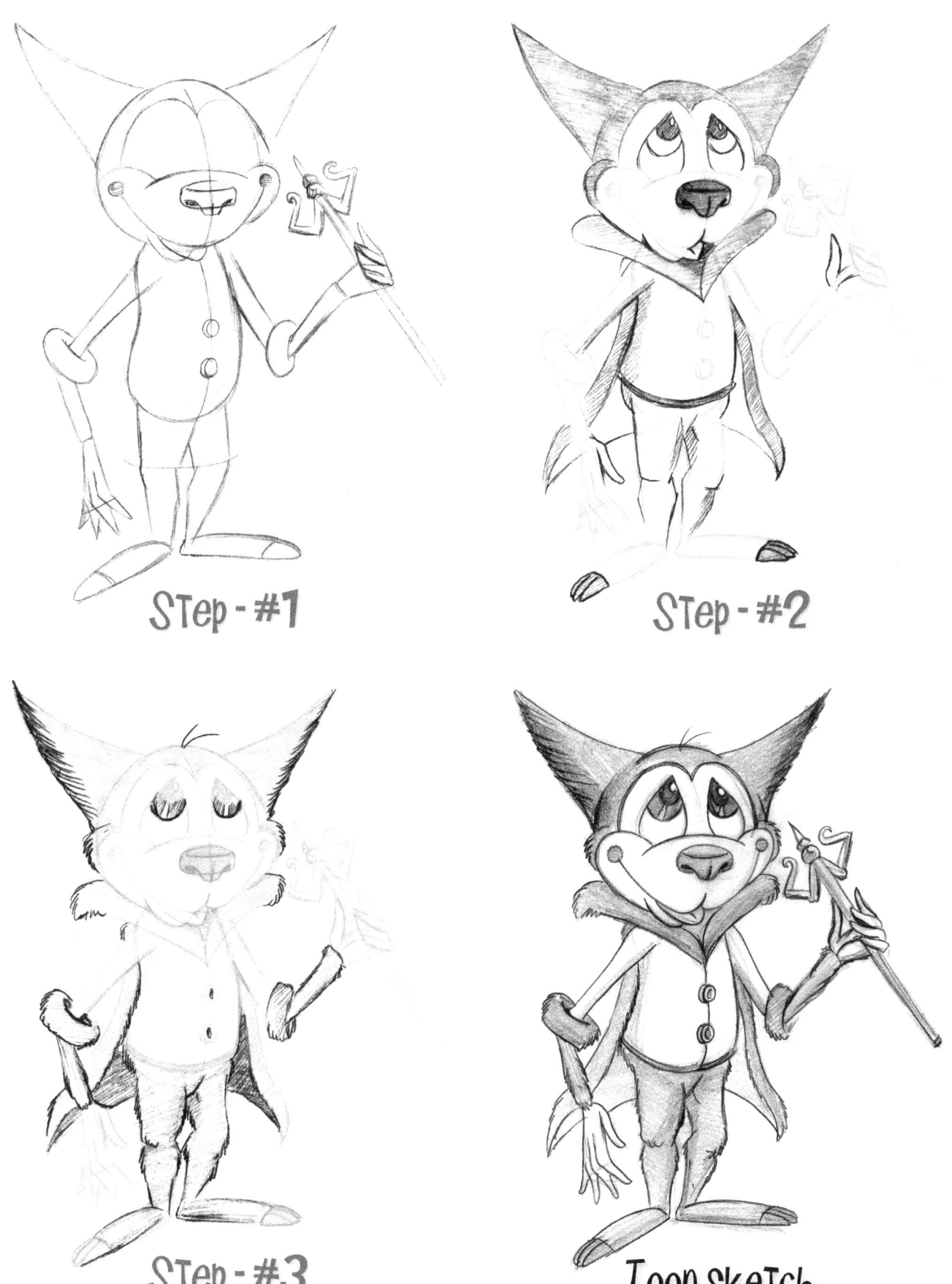

Step - #1

Step - #2

Step - #3

Toon sketch

125.

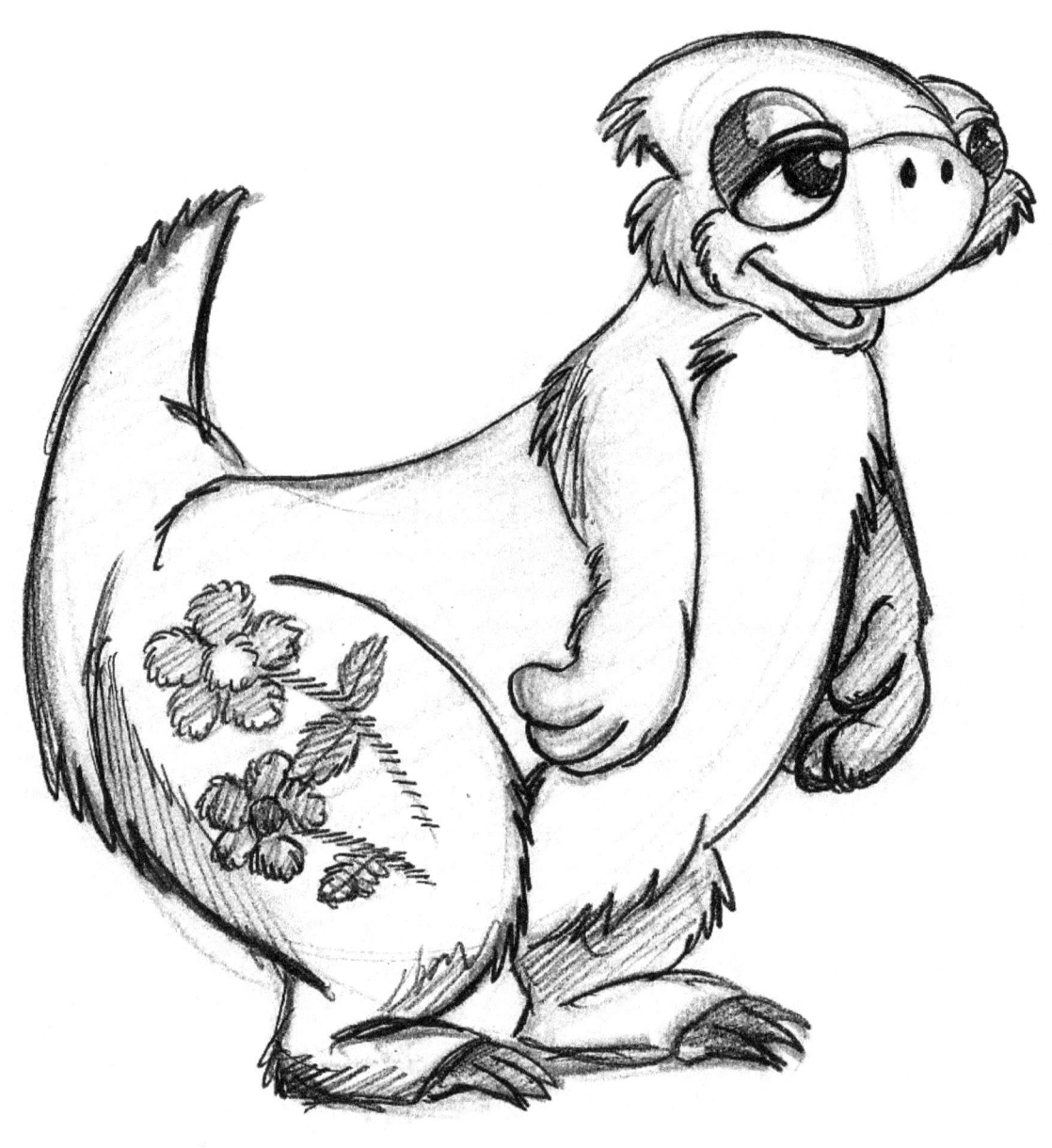

Mrs. Goo-Goo

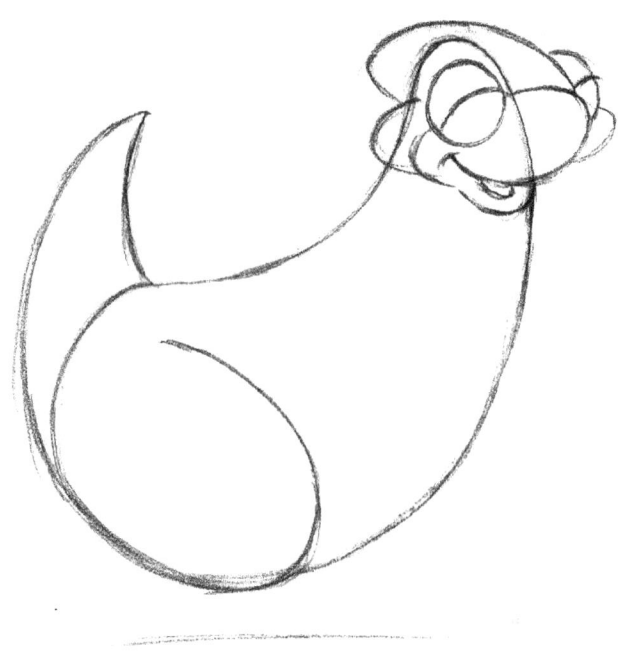

Step - #1

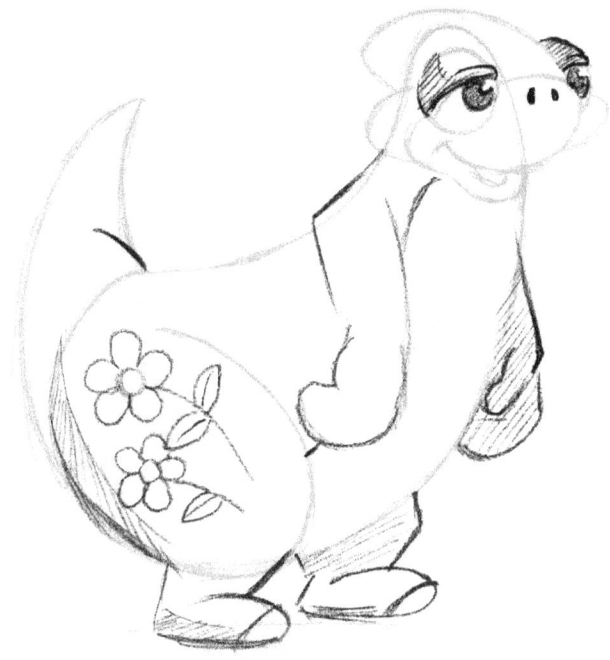

Step - #2

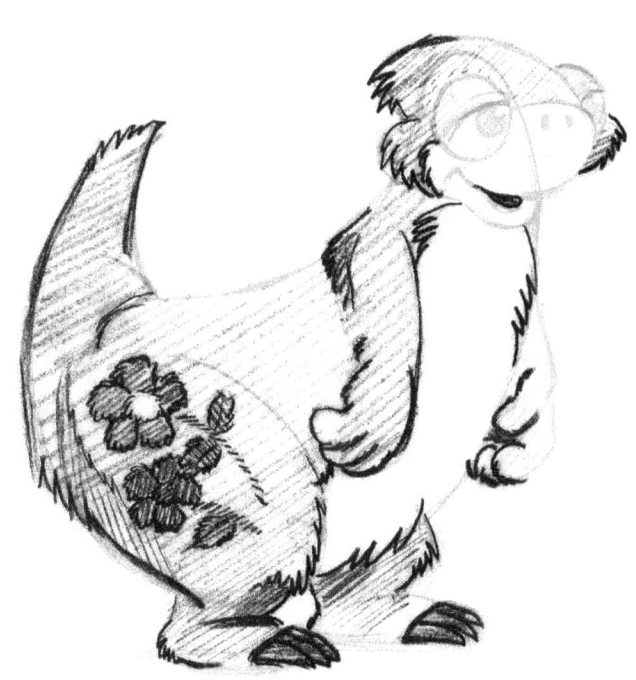

Step - #3

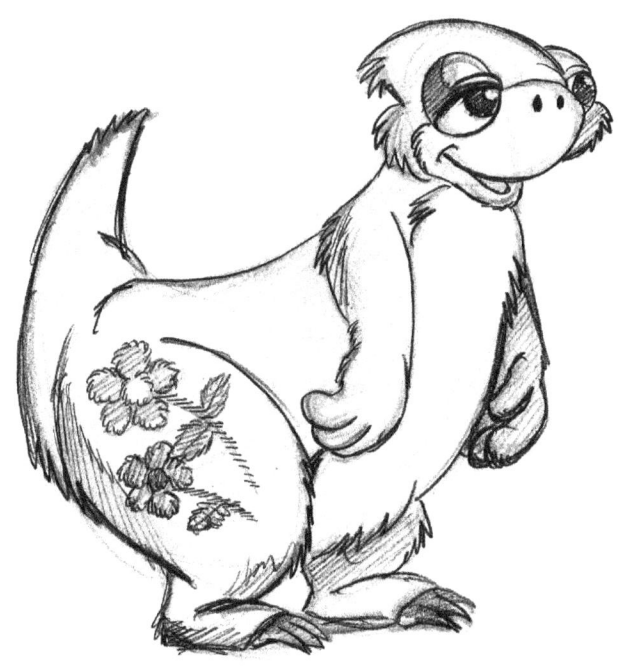

Toon sketch

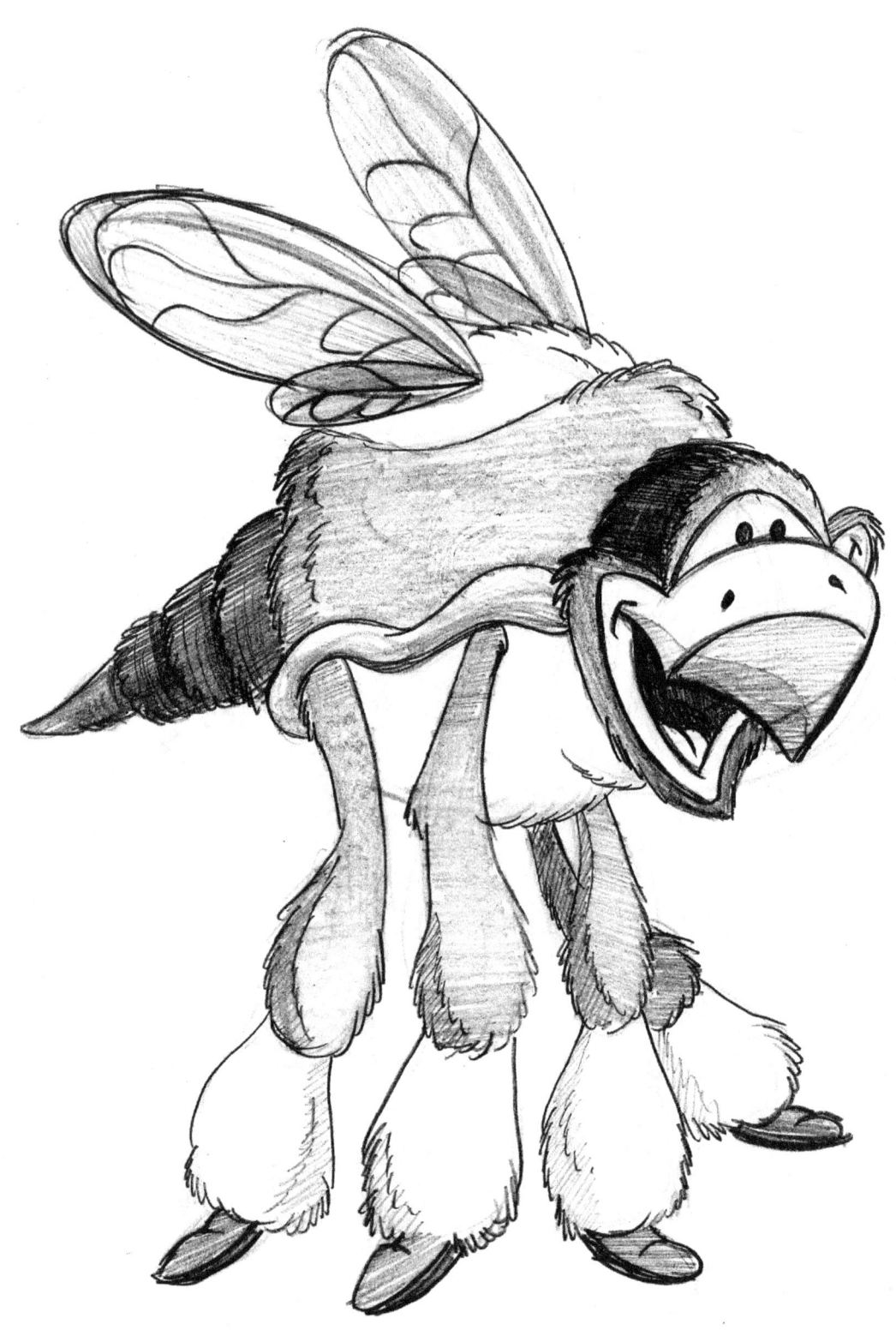

FuZZ-ie BuZZ-ie

# STep - #1

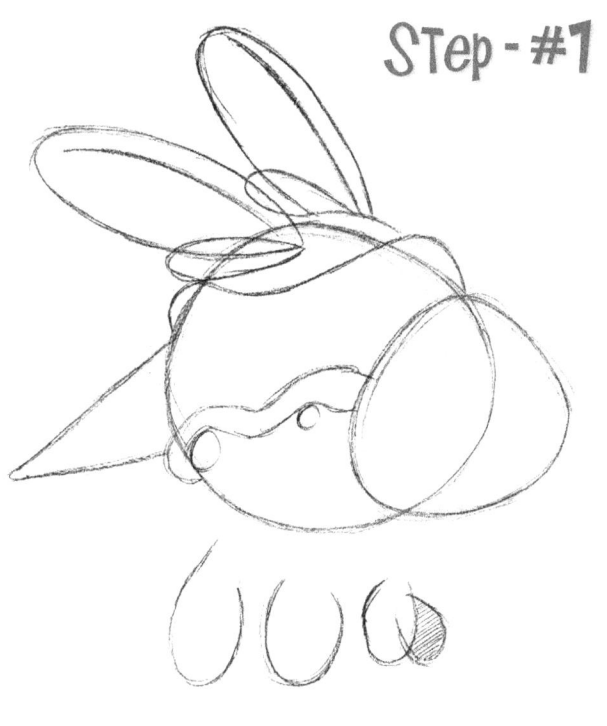

# STep - #2

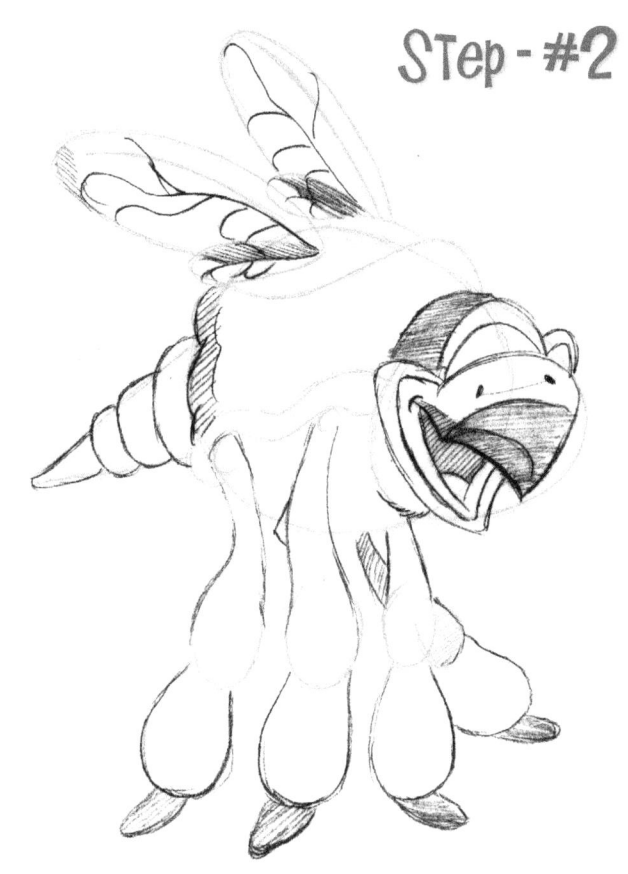

# STep - #3

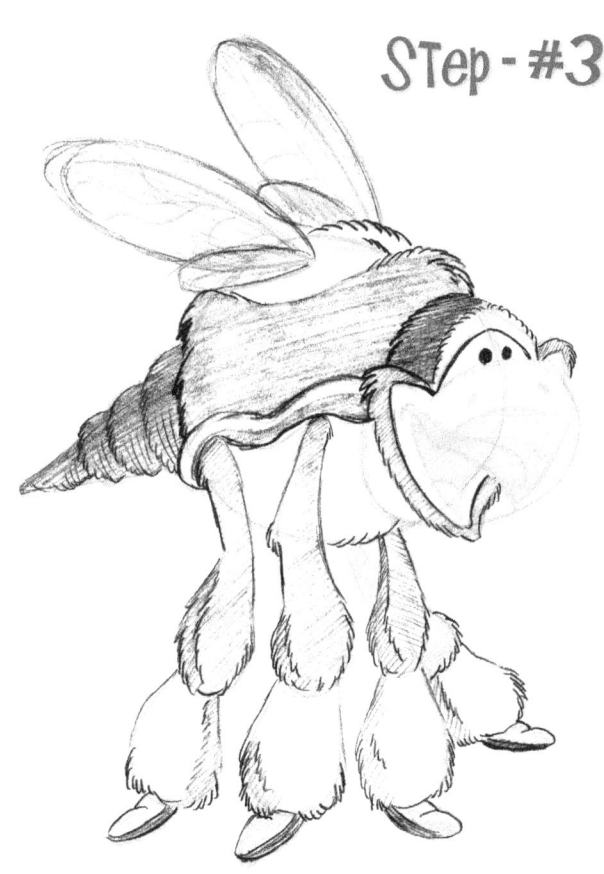

# Toon sketch

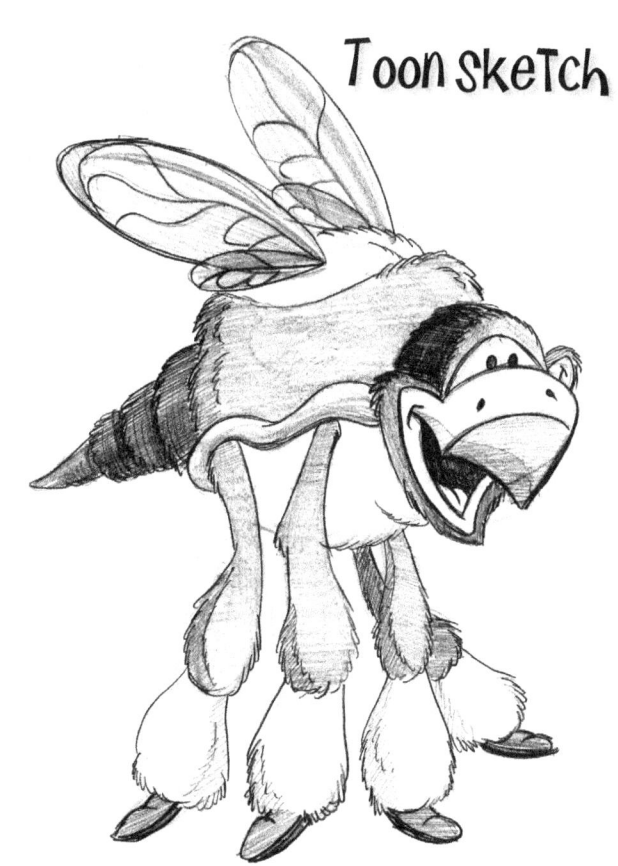

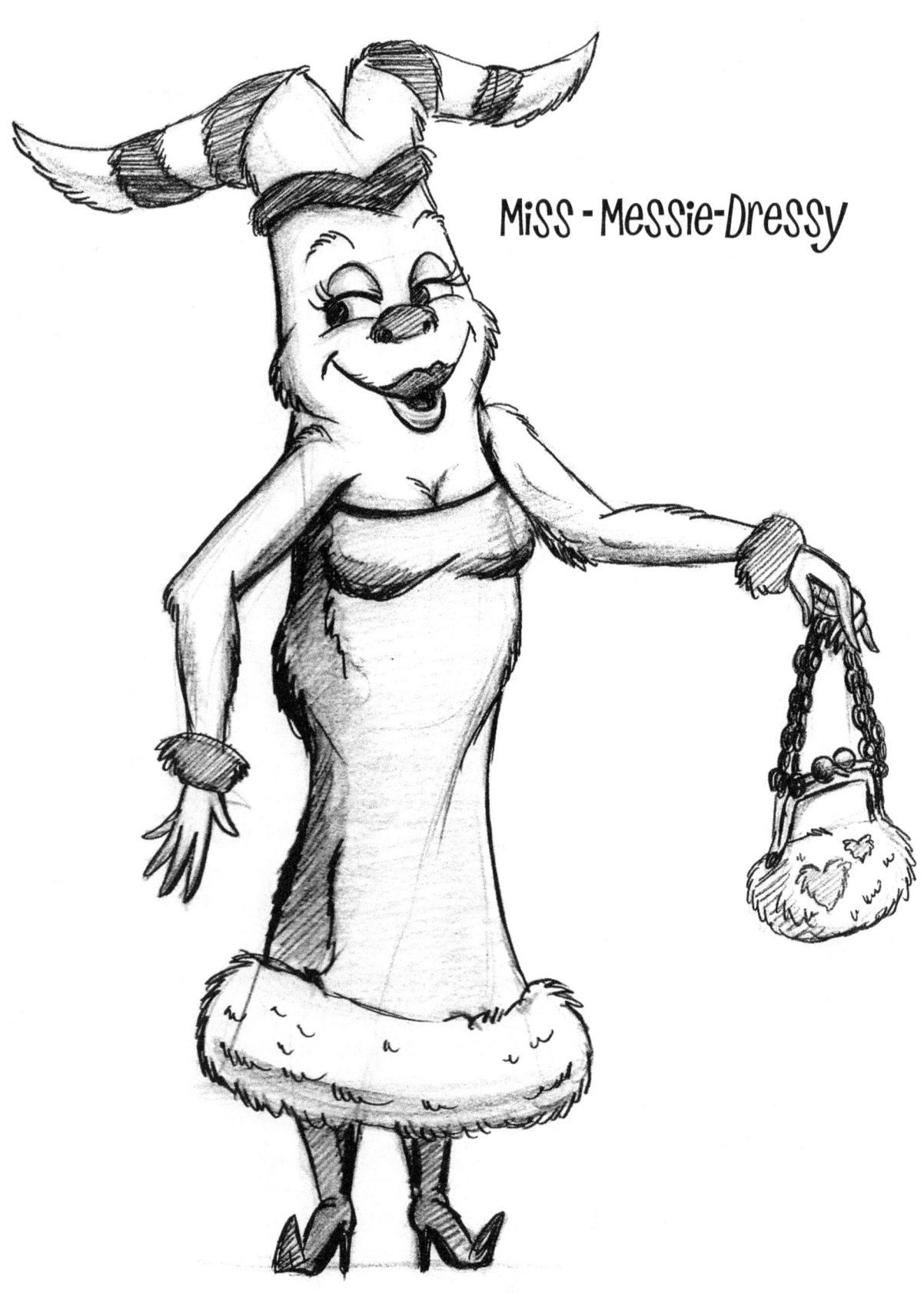

Miss - Messie-Dressy

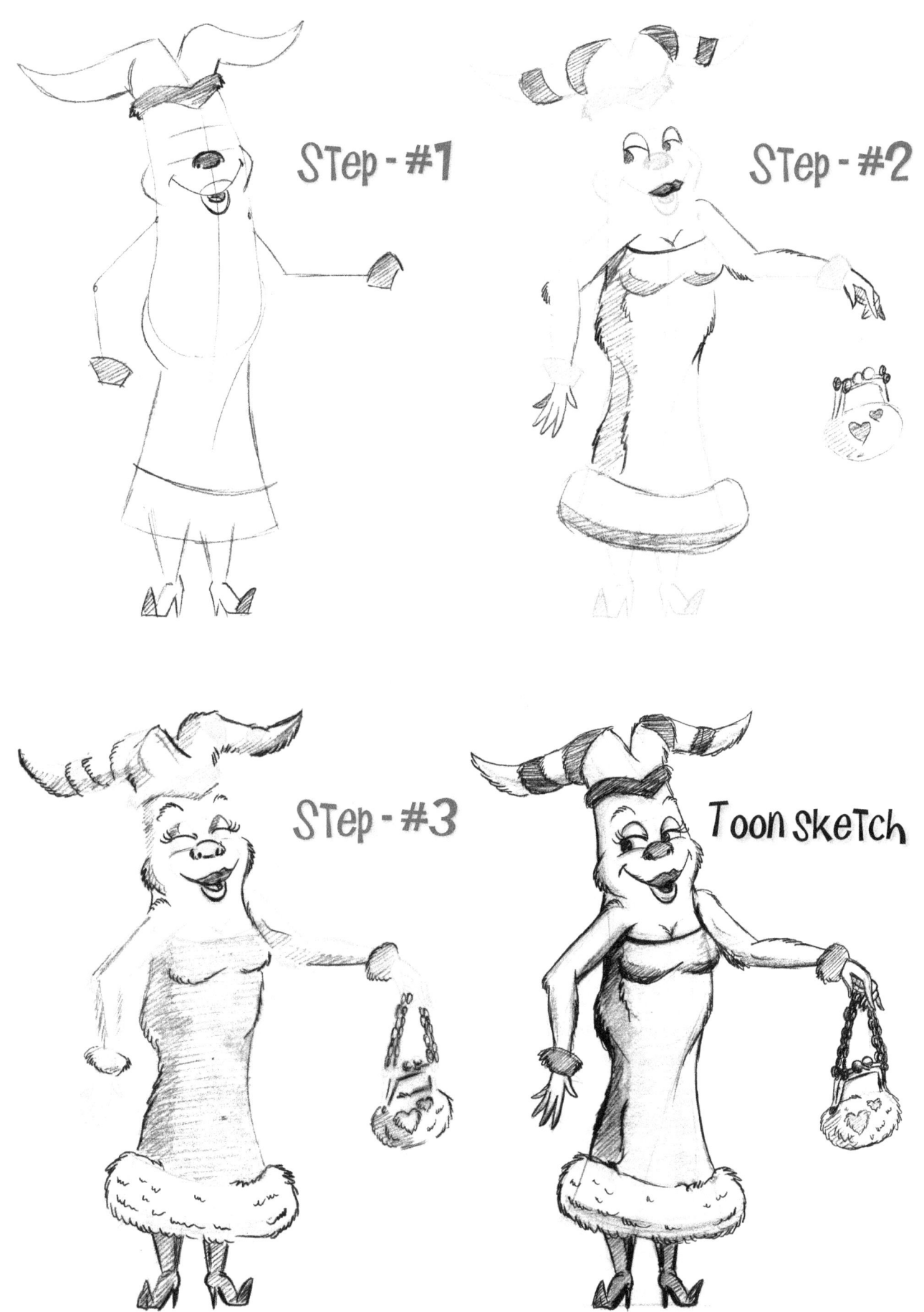

STeP - #1

STeP - #2

STeP - #3

Toon sketch

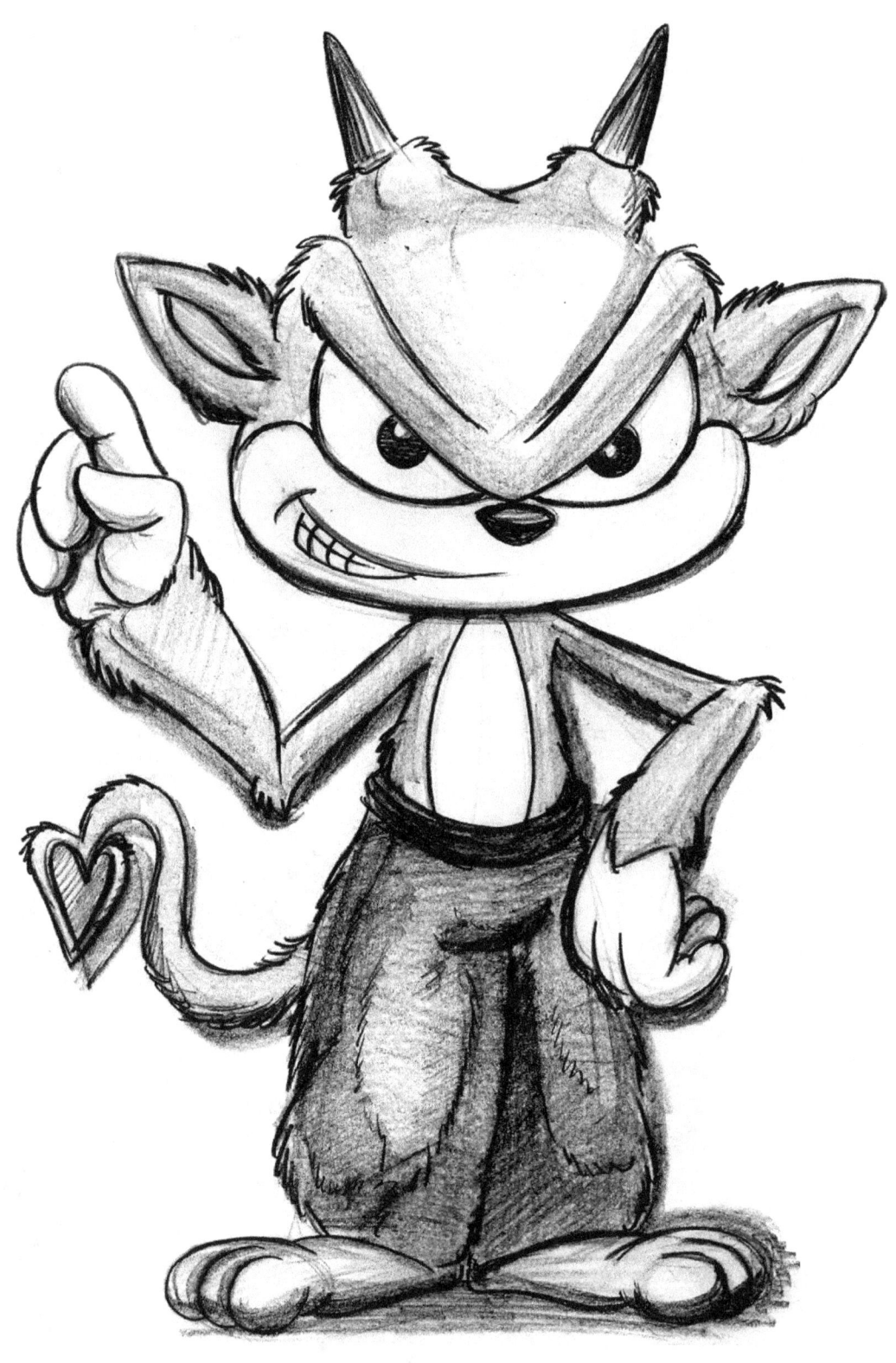

Slick-Vick

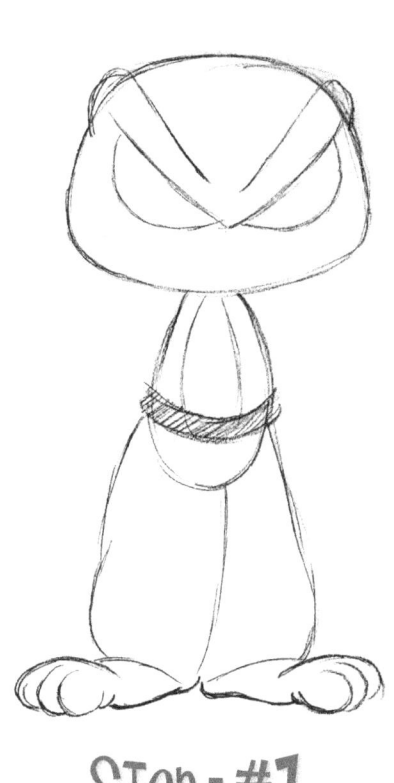

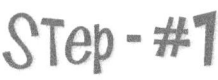

STep - #1

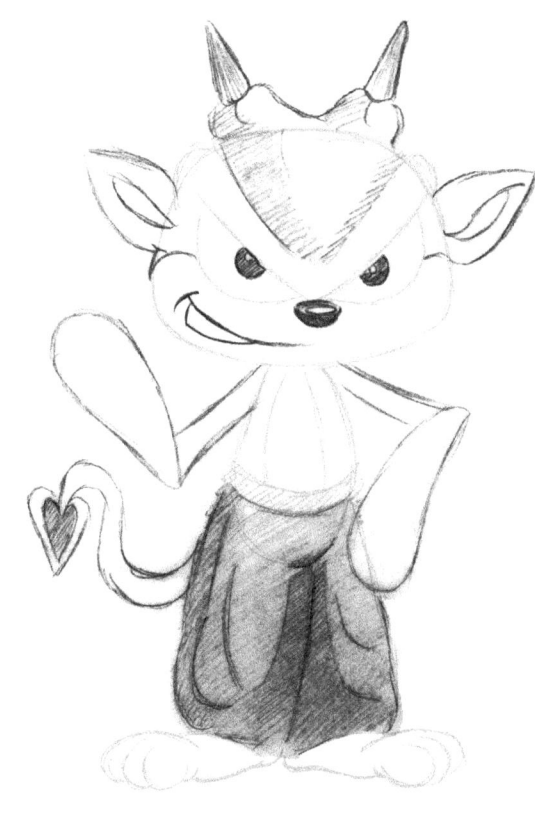

STep - #2

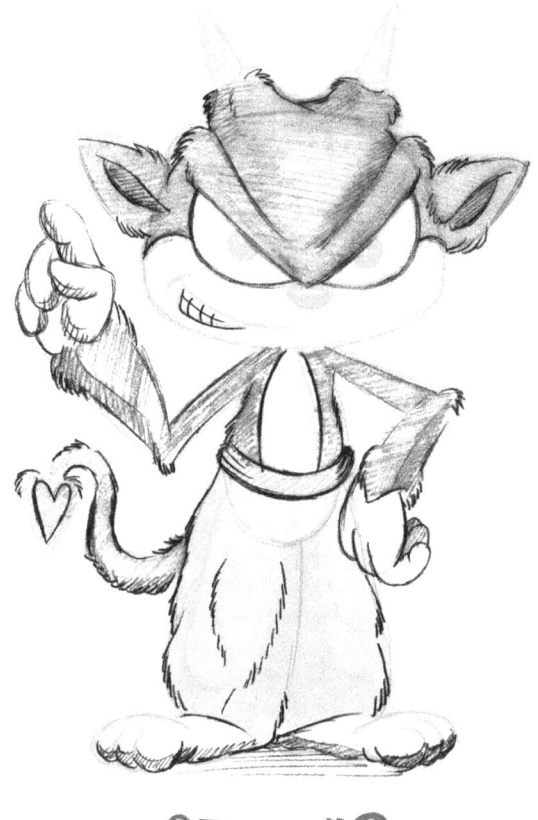

STep - #3

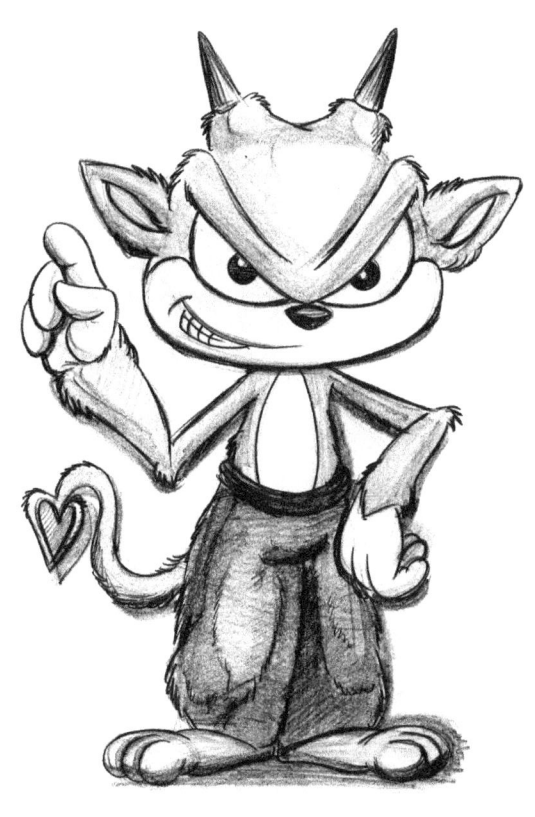

Toon skeTch

133.

# Drawing Space

# Chapter 5 Mirroring a Character

## Using Half a character and Mirror effect To make a Toon

Step 1. Using Tracing paper, make a vertical Line on your drawing space. Then create only the right side of a cartoon character. This will be the character Template.

Step 2. Next with a clean sheet of Tracing paper, Trace the Line and the right side of your Toon.

Step 3. Flip the Template over and align with the vertical Line. Now Trace the Left side. Try Exploring with other Artistic creations and designing your own Toon designs.

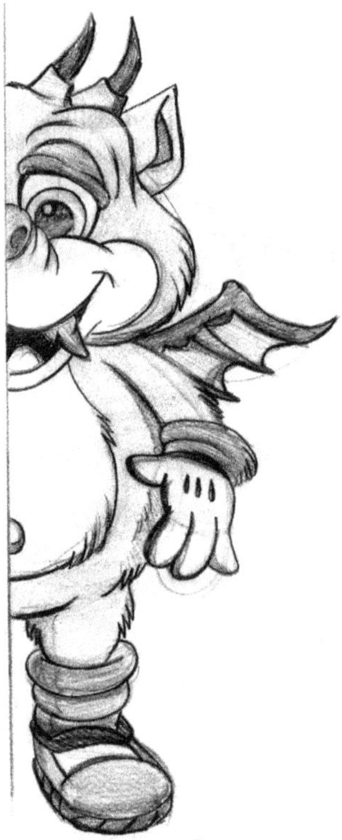

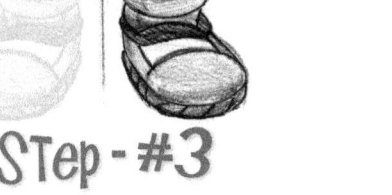

Step - #1

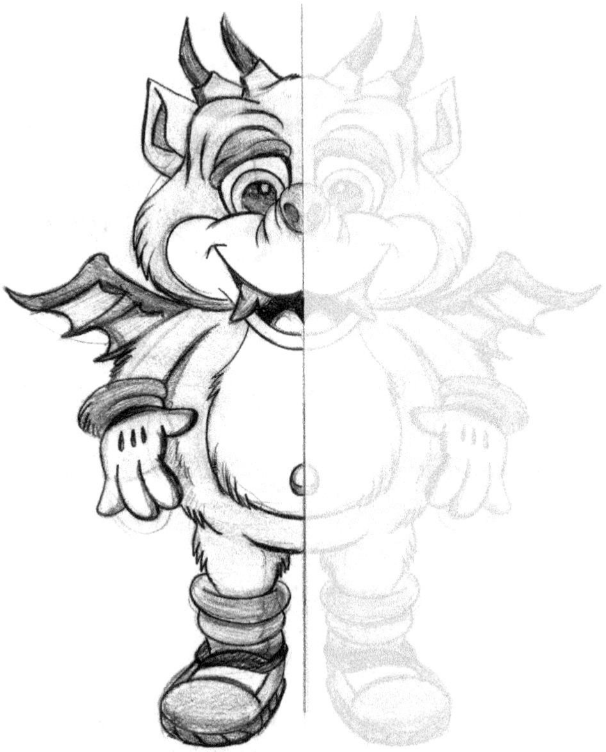

Step - #2

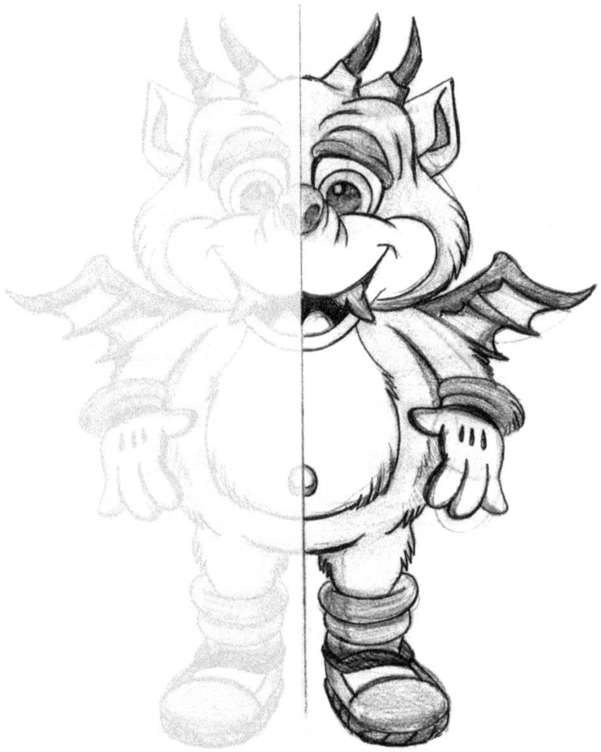

Step - #3

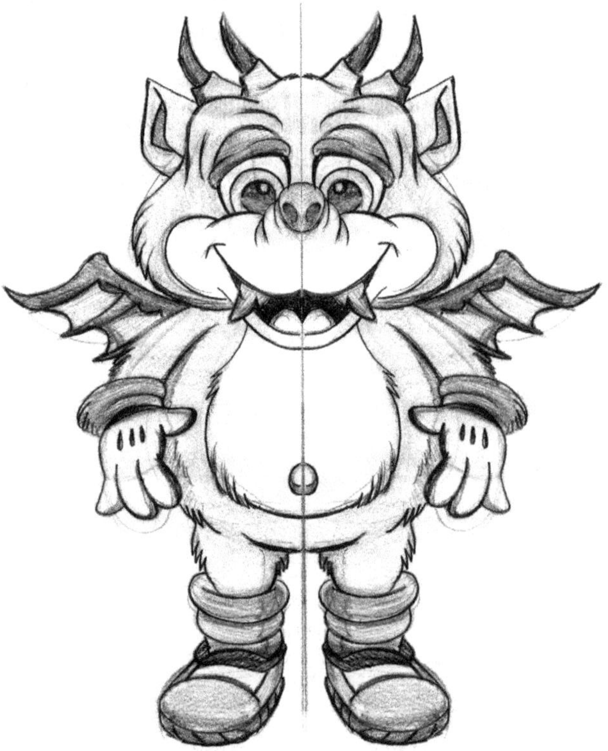

Toon sketch

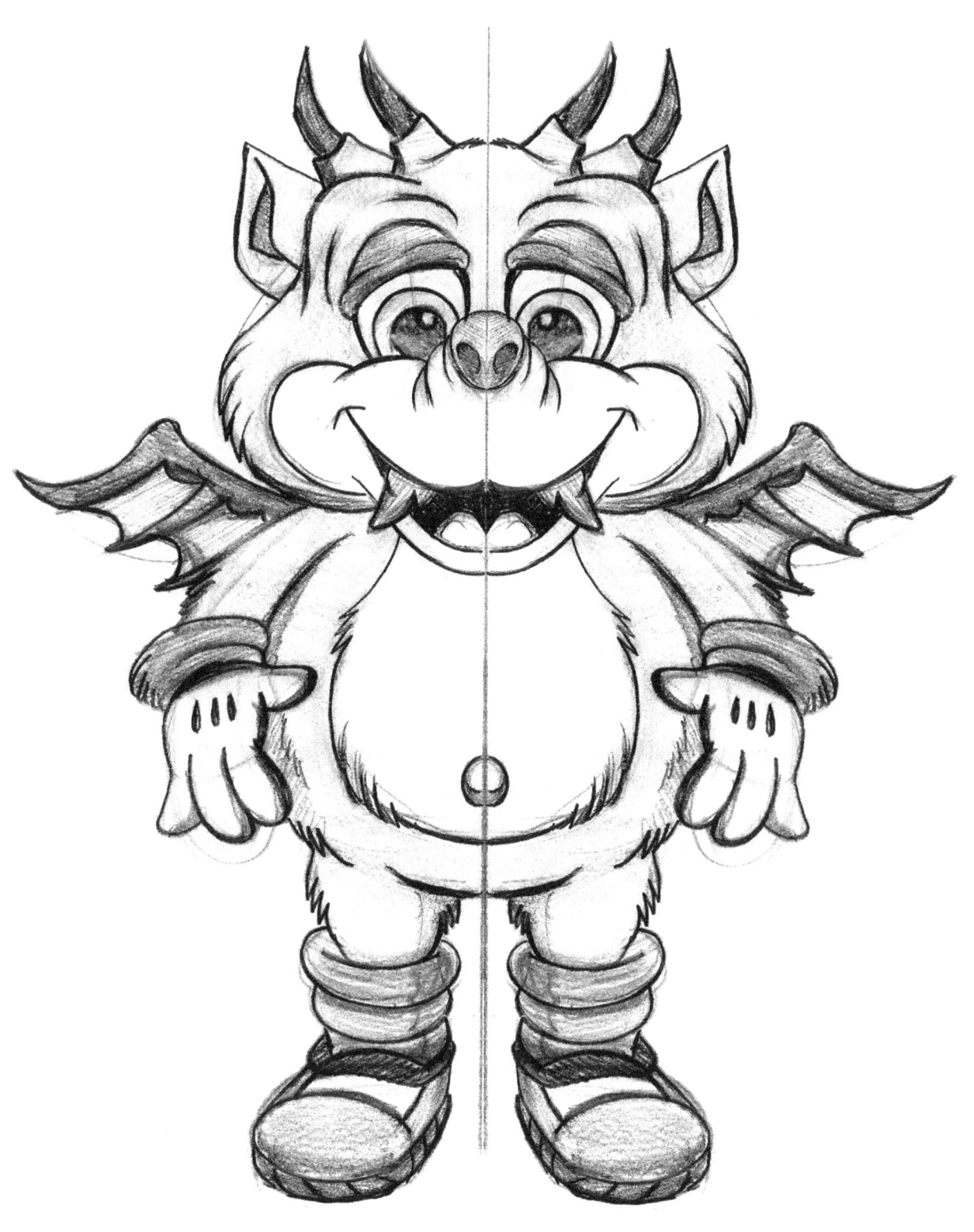

Doogy The Dragon

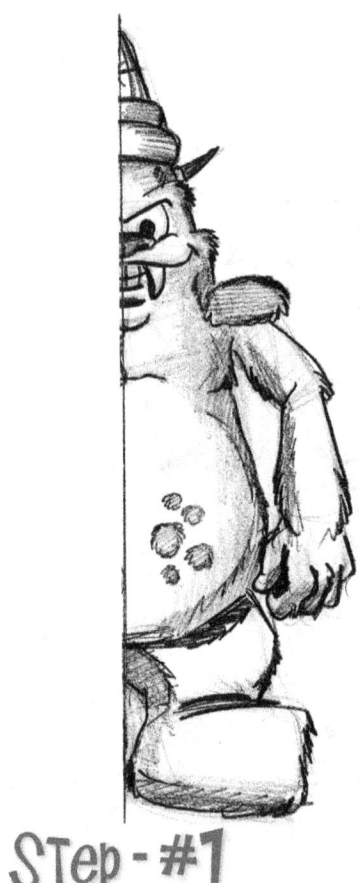

Step - #1

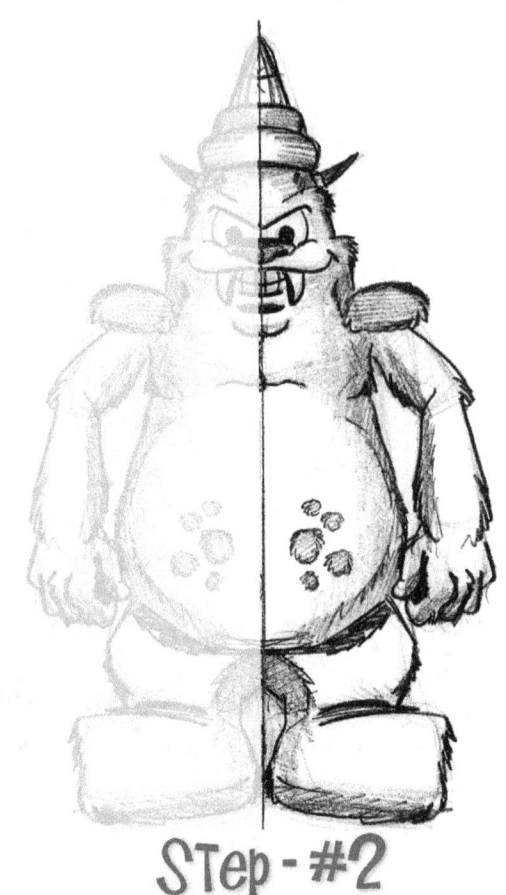

Step - #2

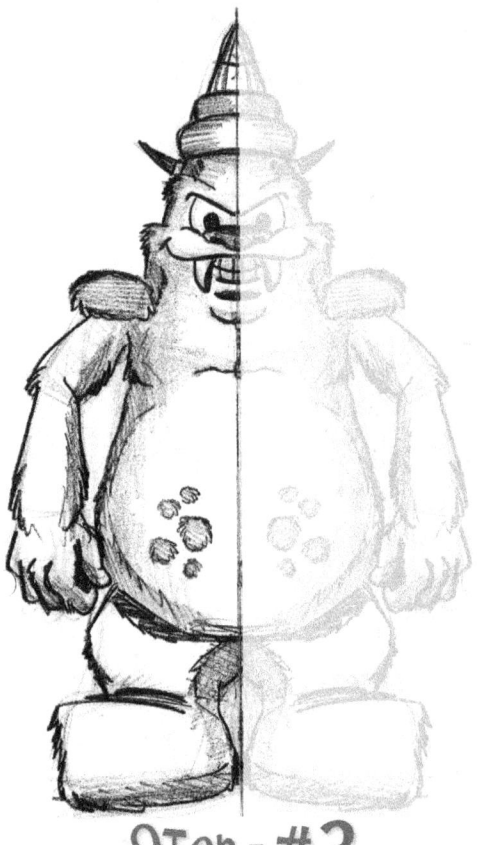

Step - #3

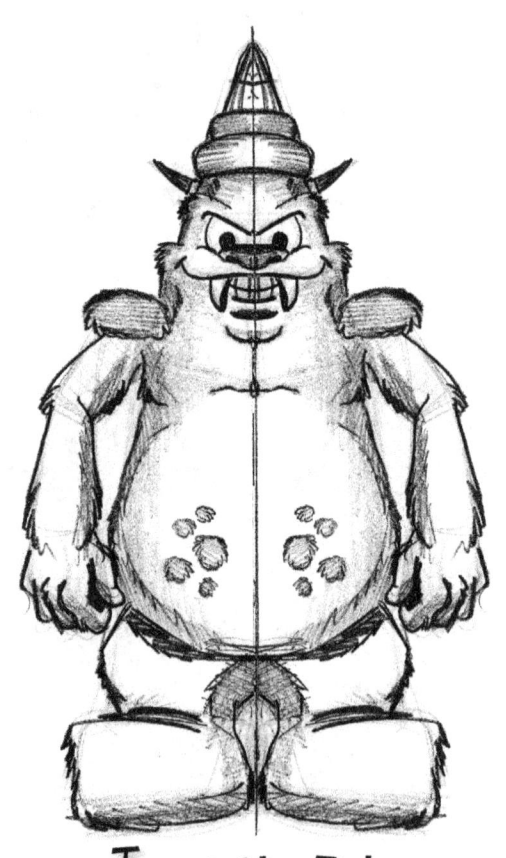

Toon sketch

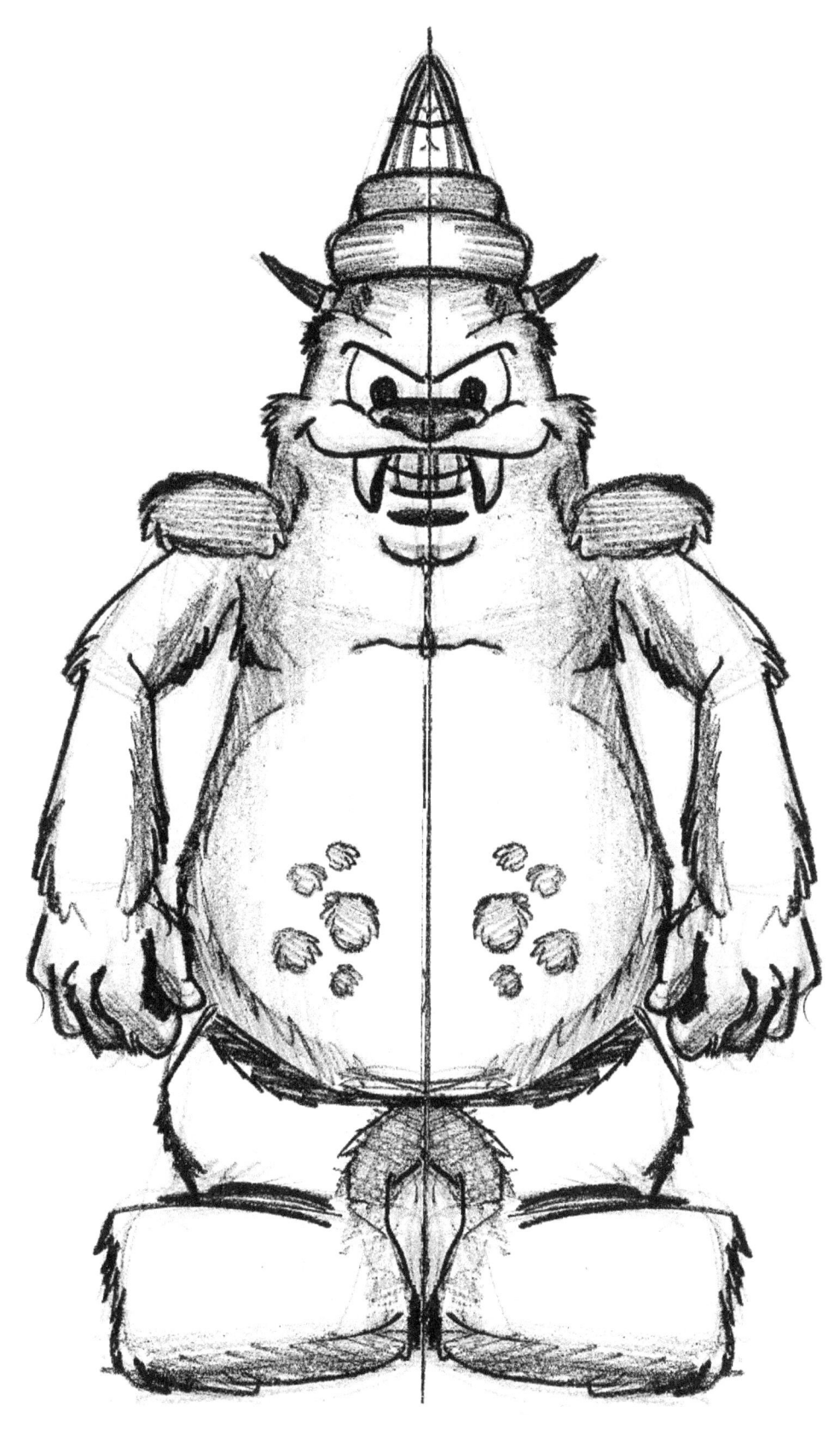

Cooper Stooper

139.

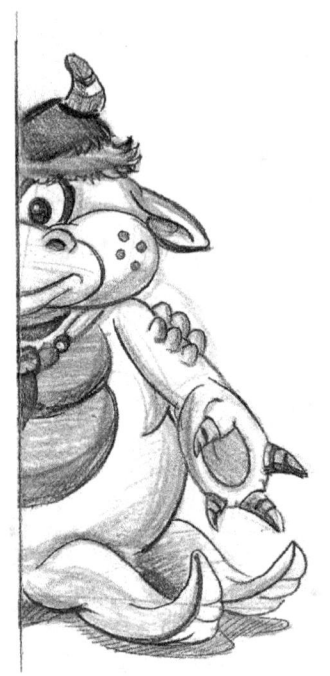

Step - #1

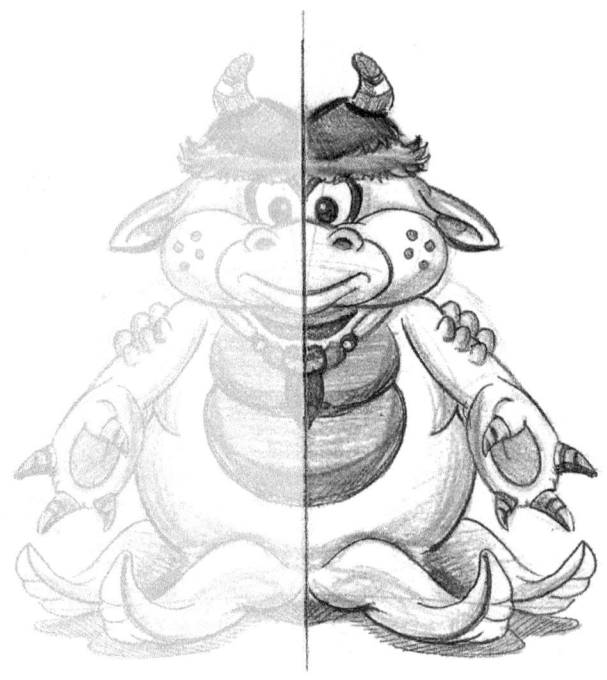

Step - #2

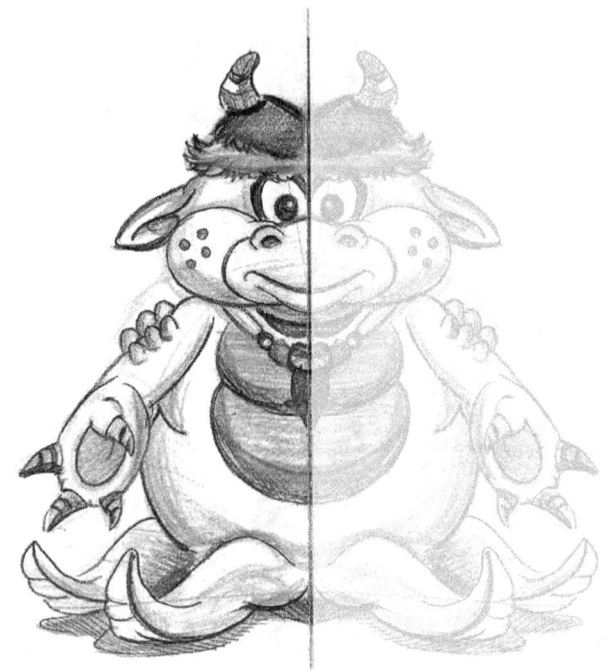

Step - #3

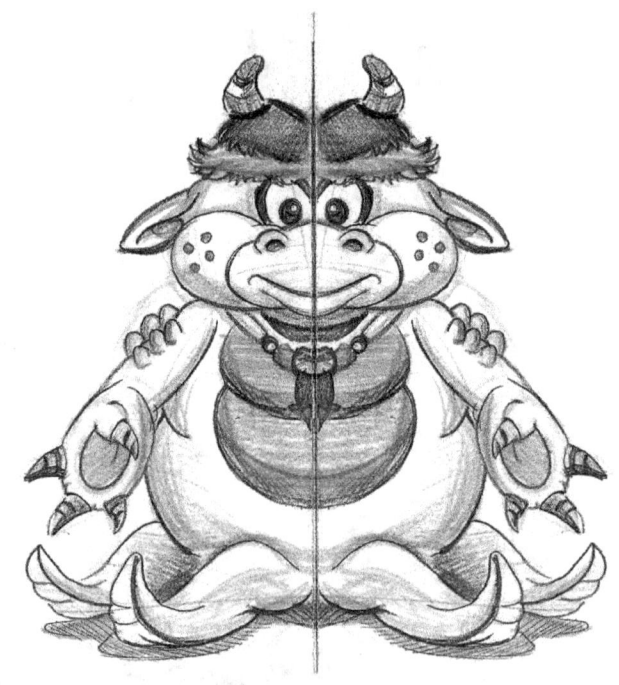

Toon sketch

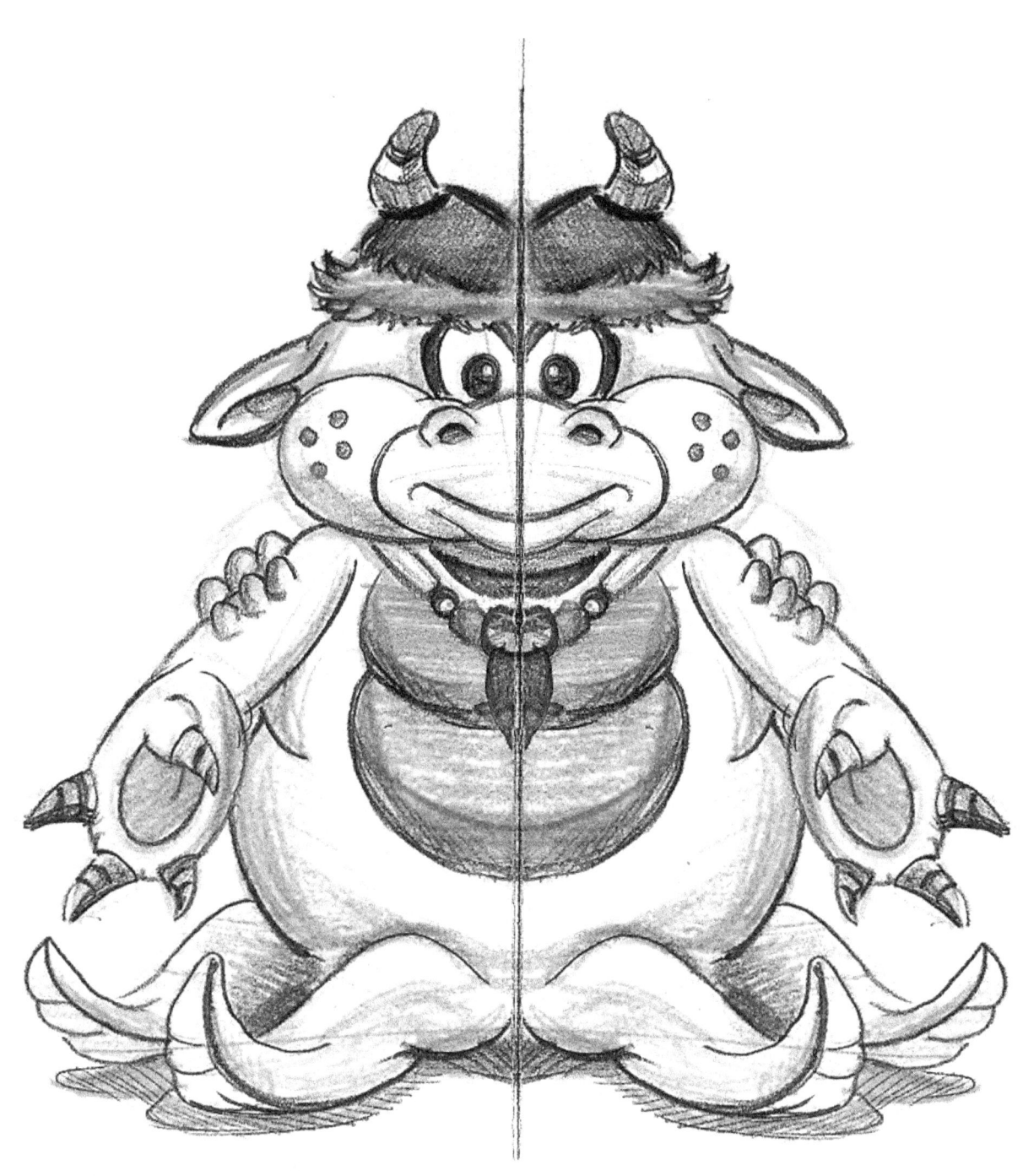

Artie-Ten-Tickles

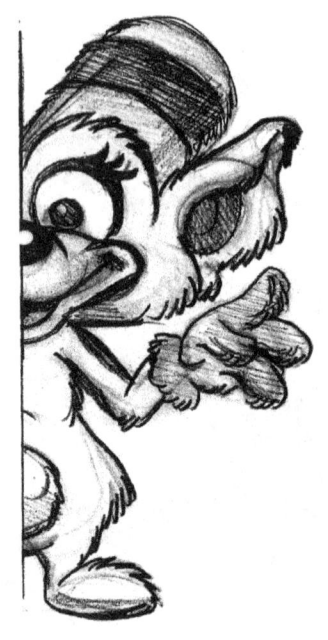

STep - #1

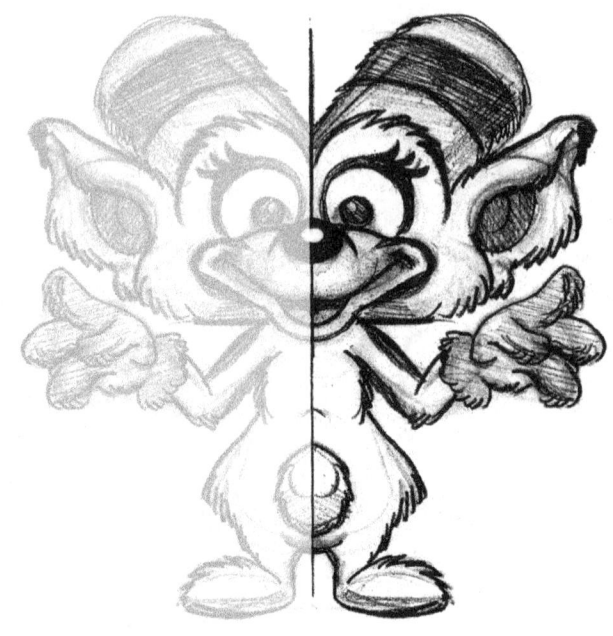

STep - #2

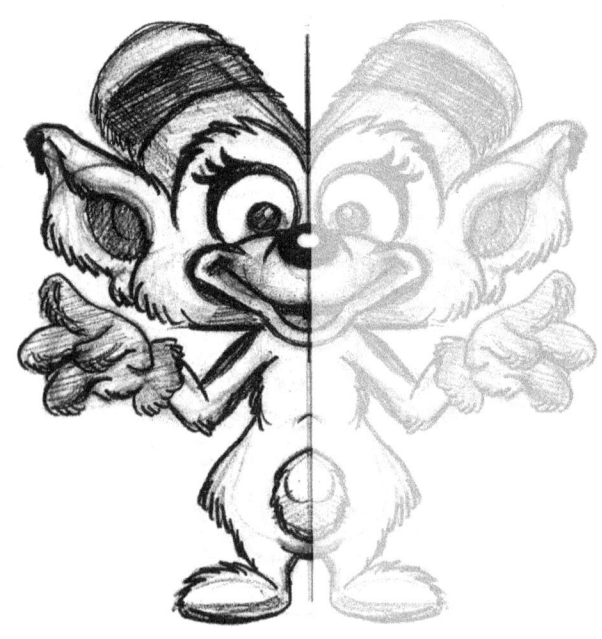

STep - #3

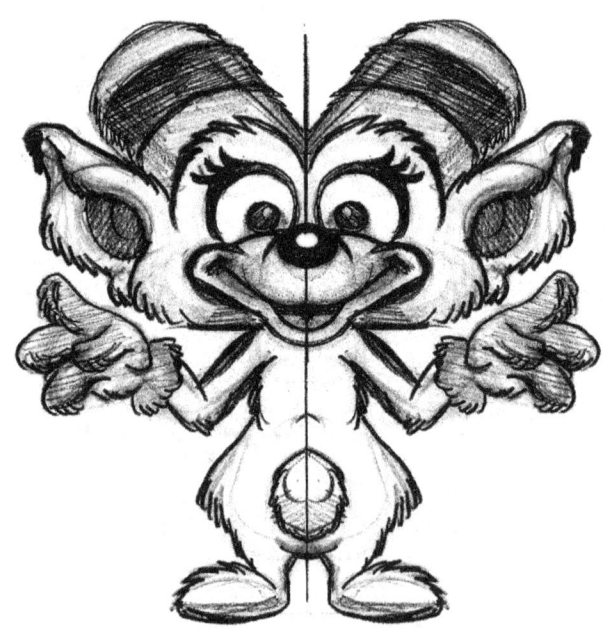

Toon sketch

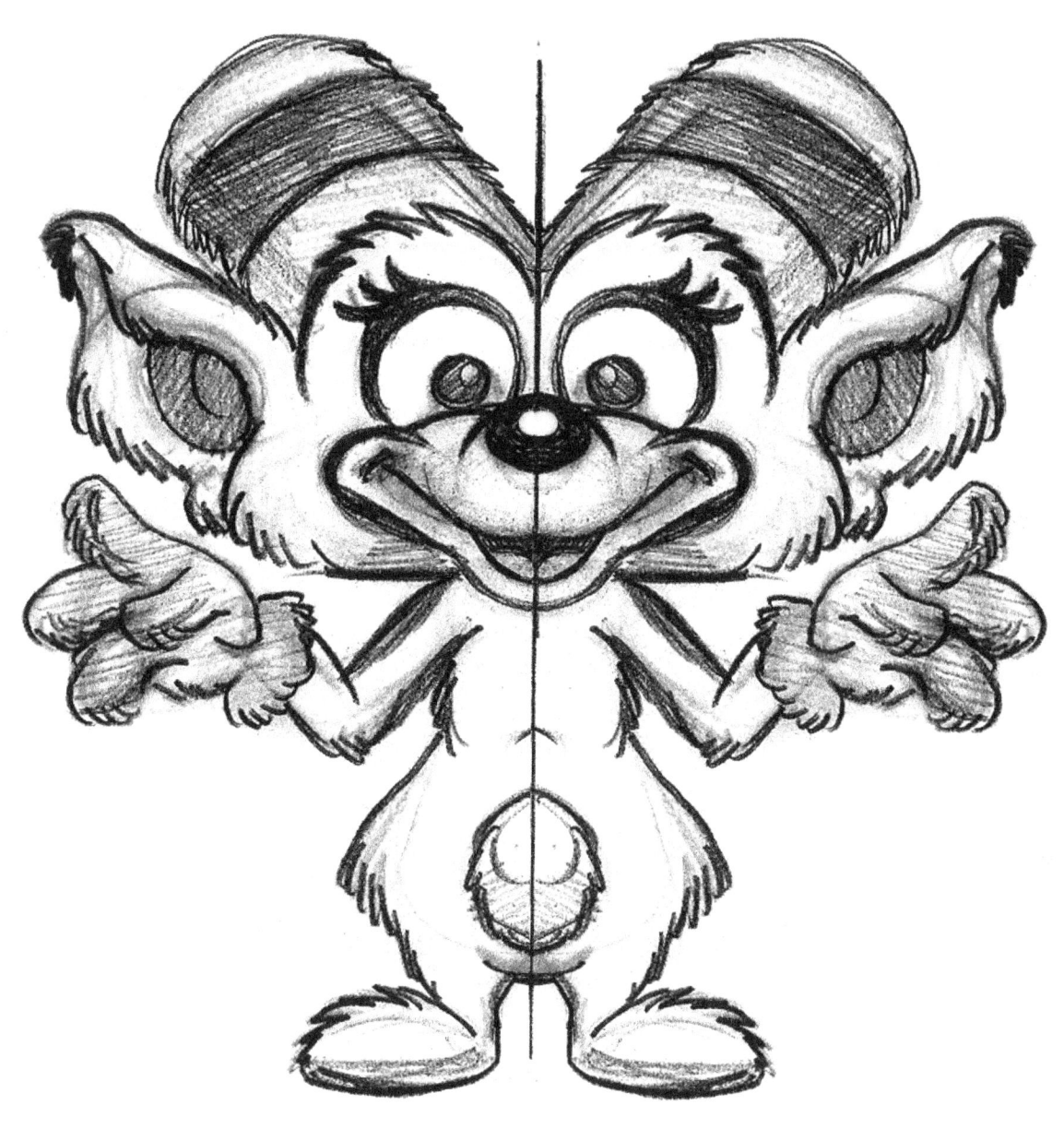

Sweet Sue

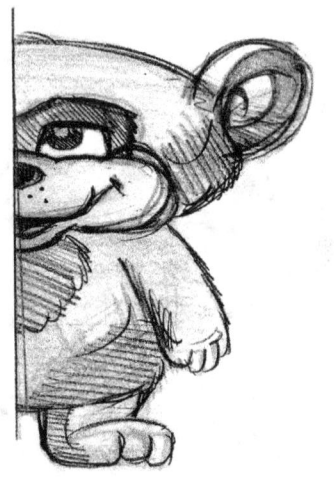

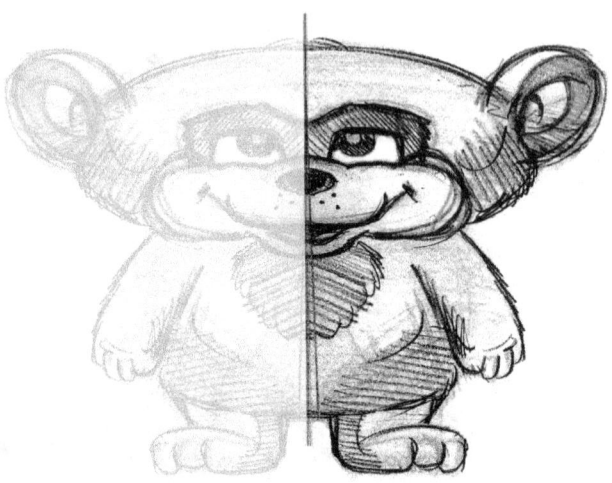

Step - #1

Step - #2

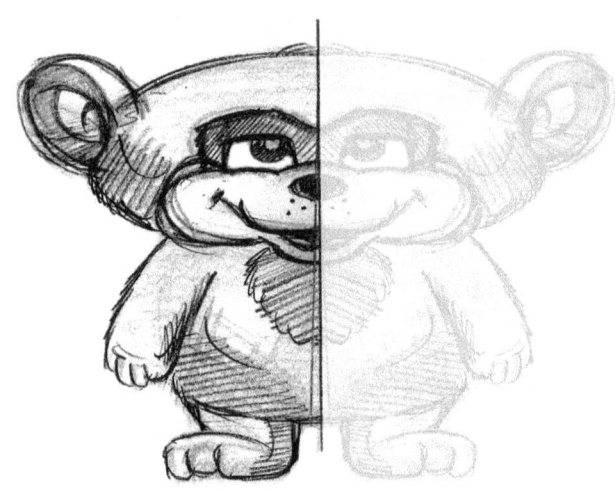

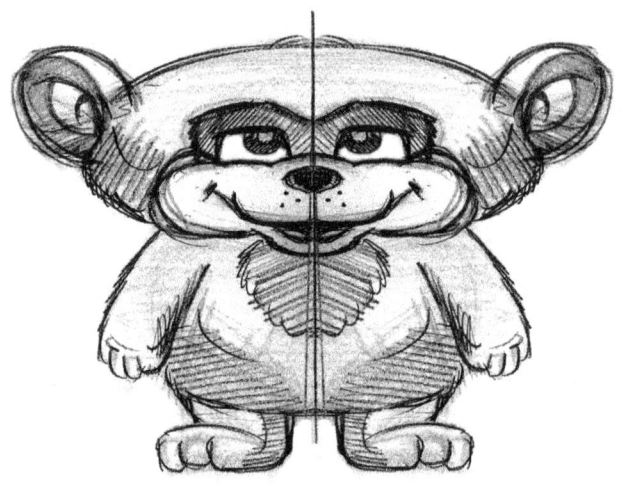

Step - #3

Toon sketch

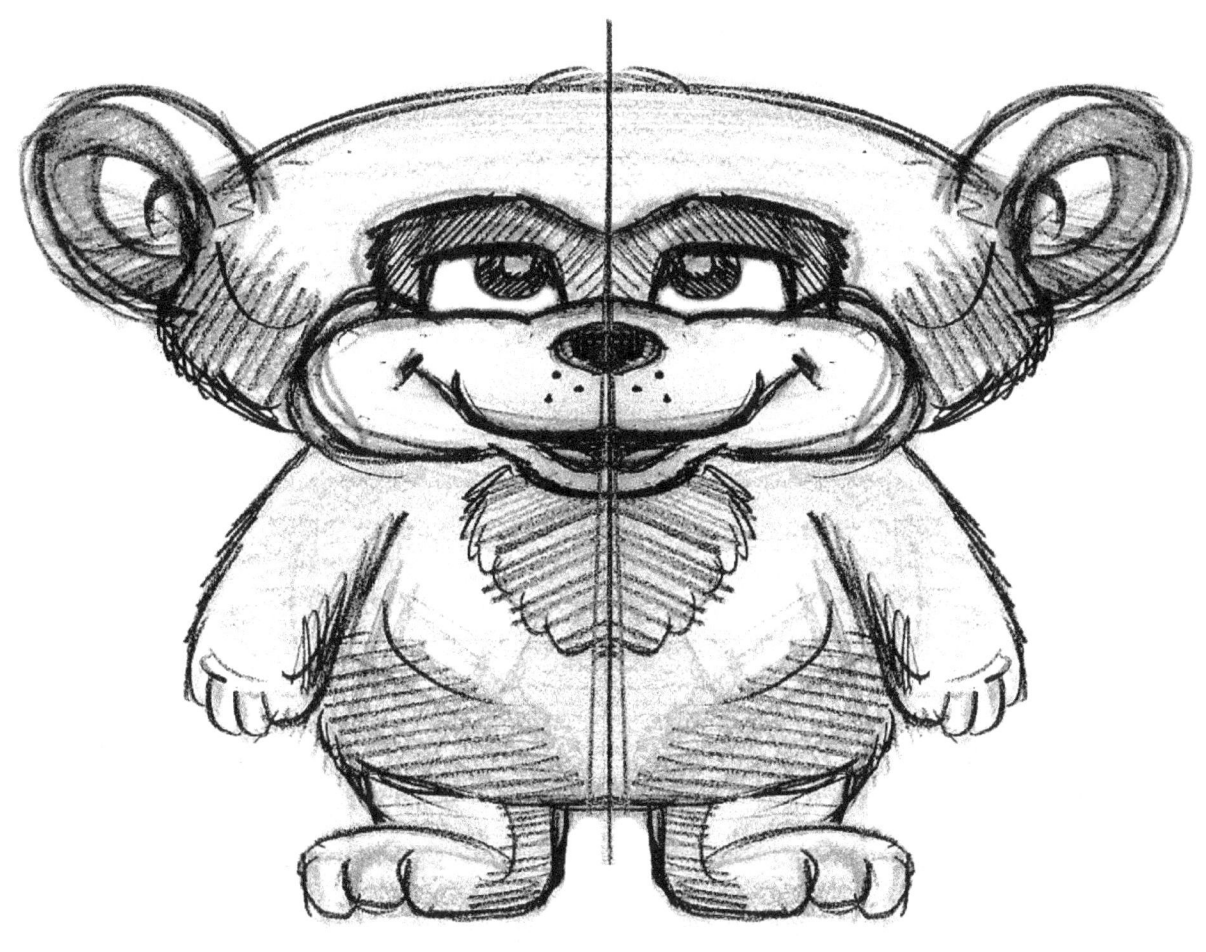

LiL-Boopie

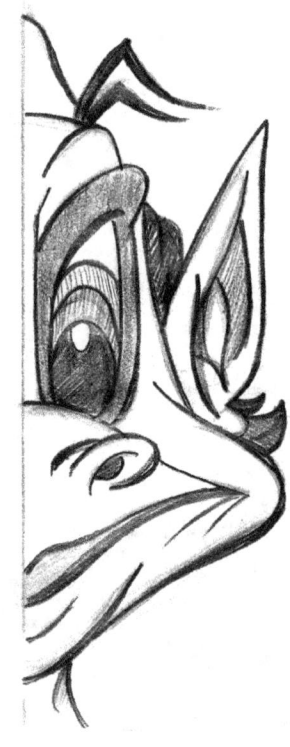

Step - #1

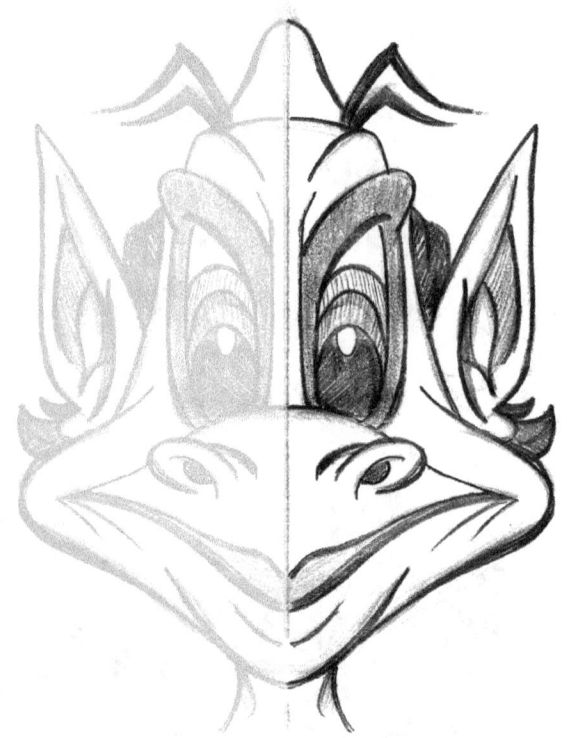

Step - #2

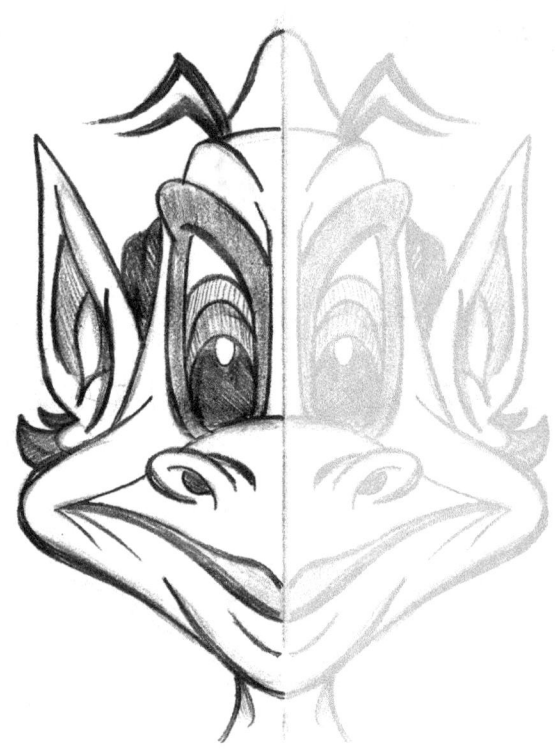

Step - #3

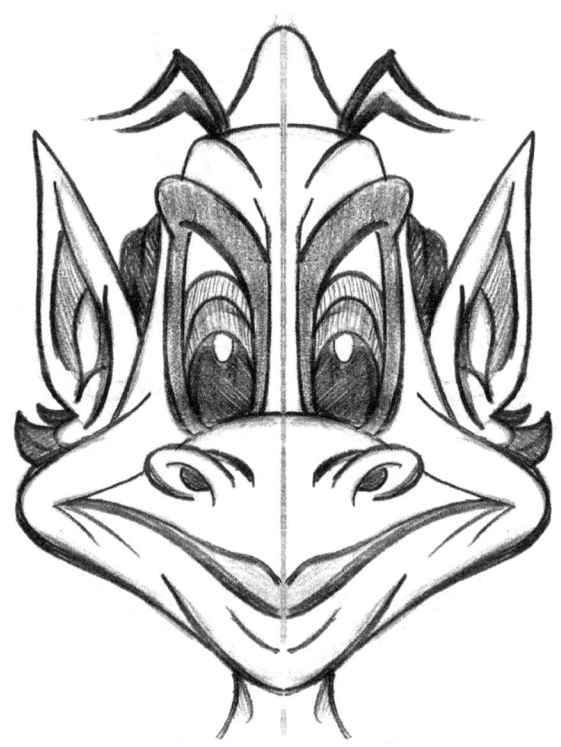

Toon sketch

146.

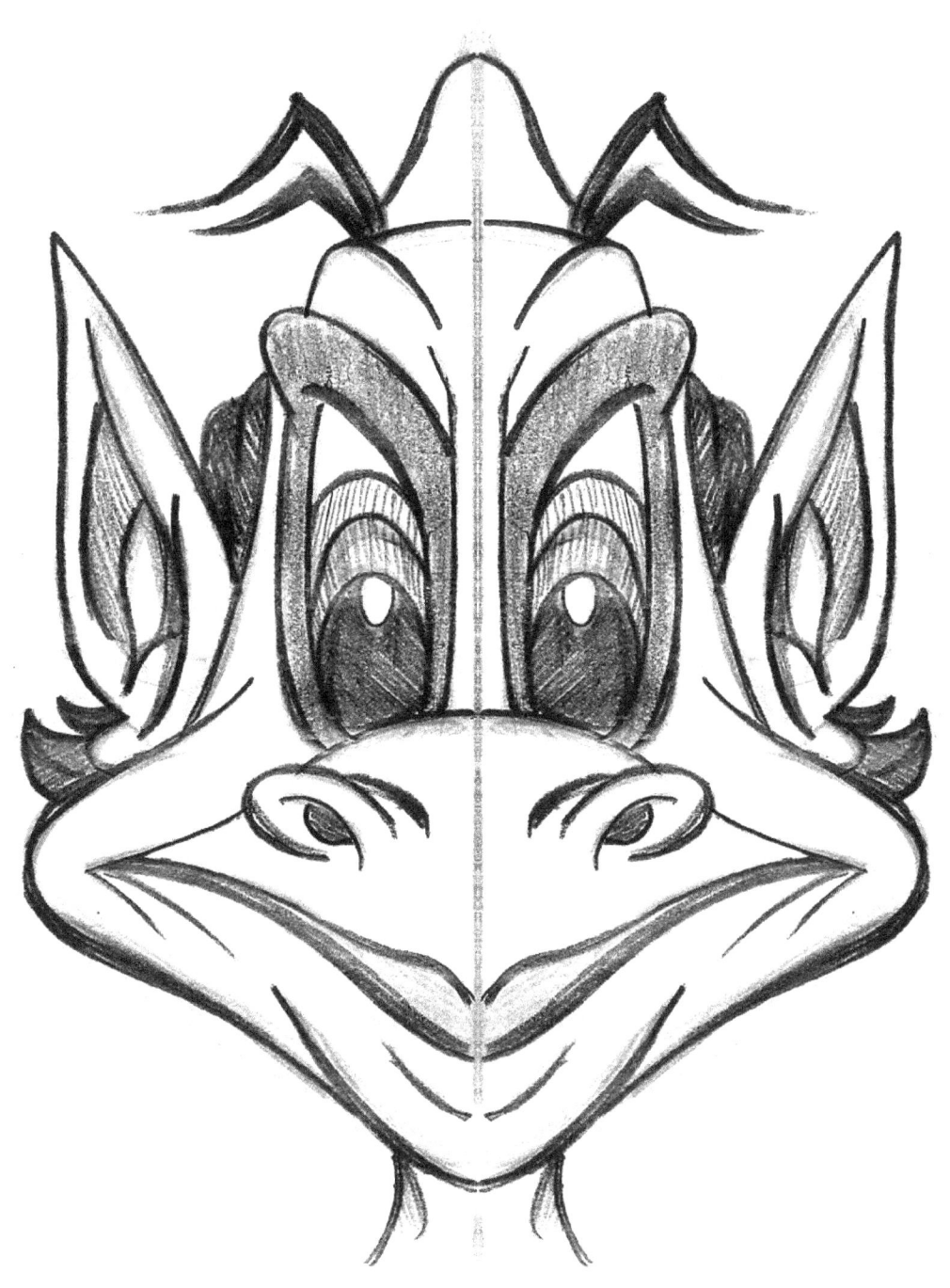

Mc MiLLenium

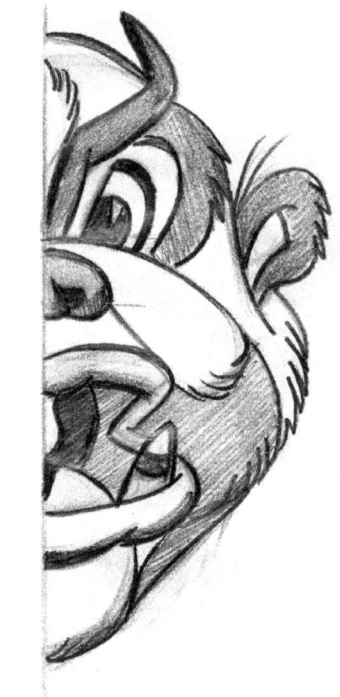

Step - #1

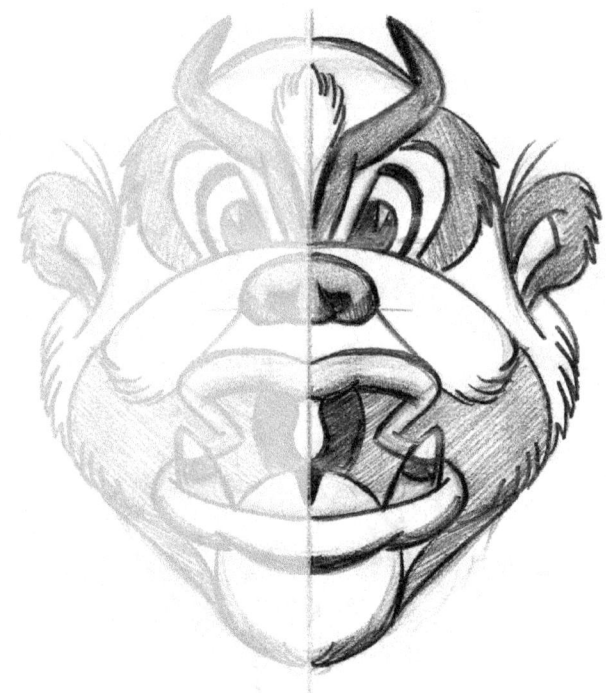

Step - #2

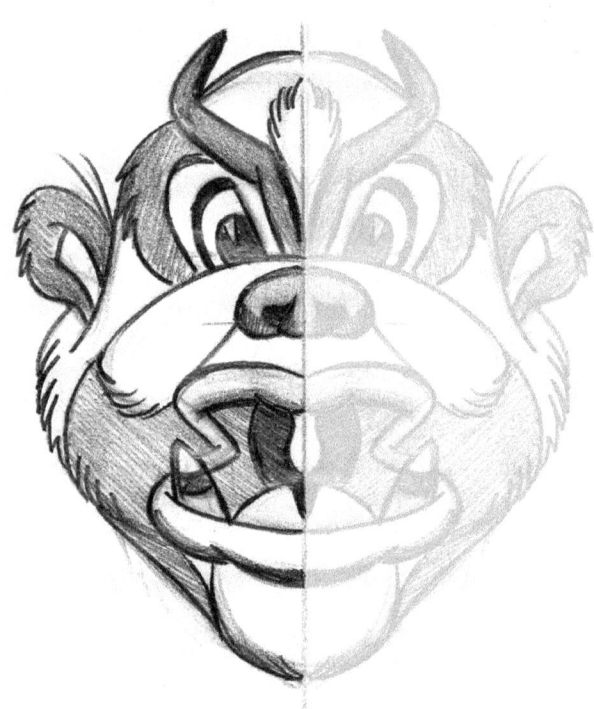

Step - #3

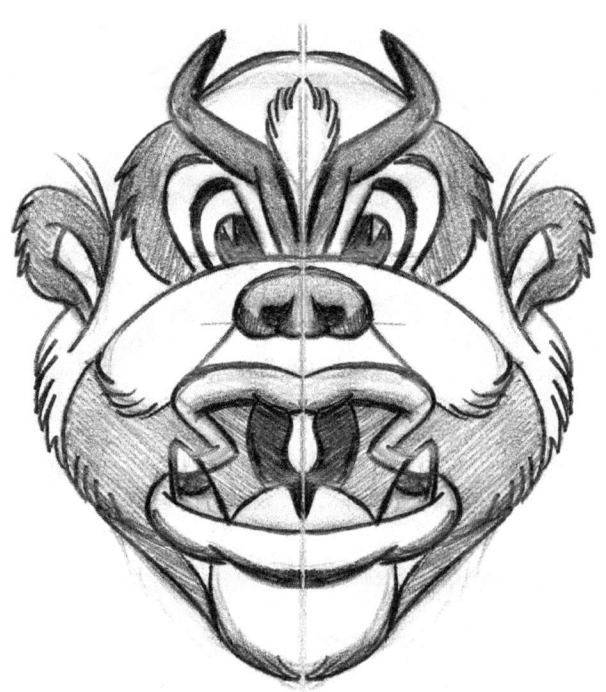

Toon sketch

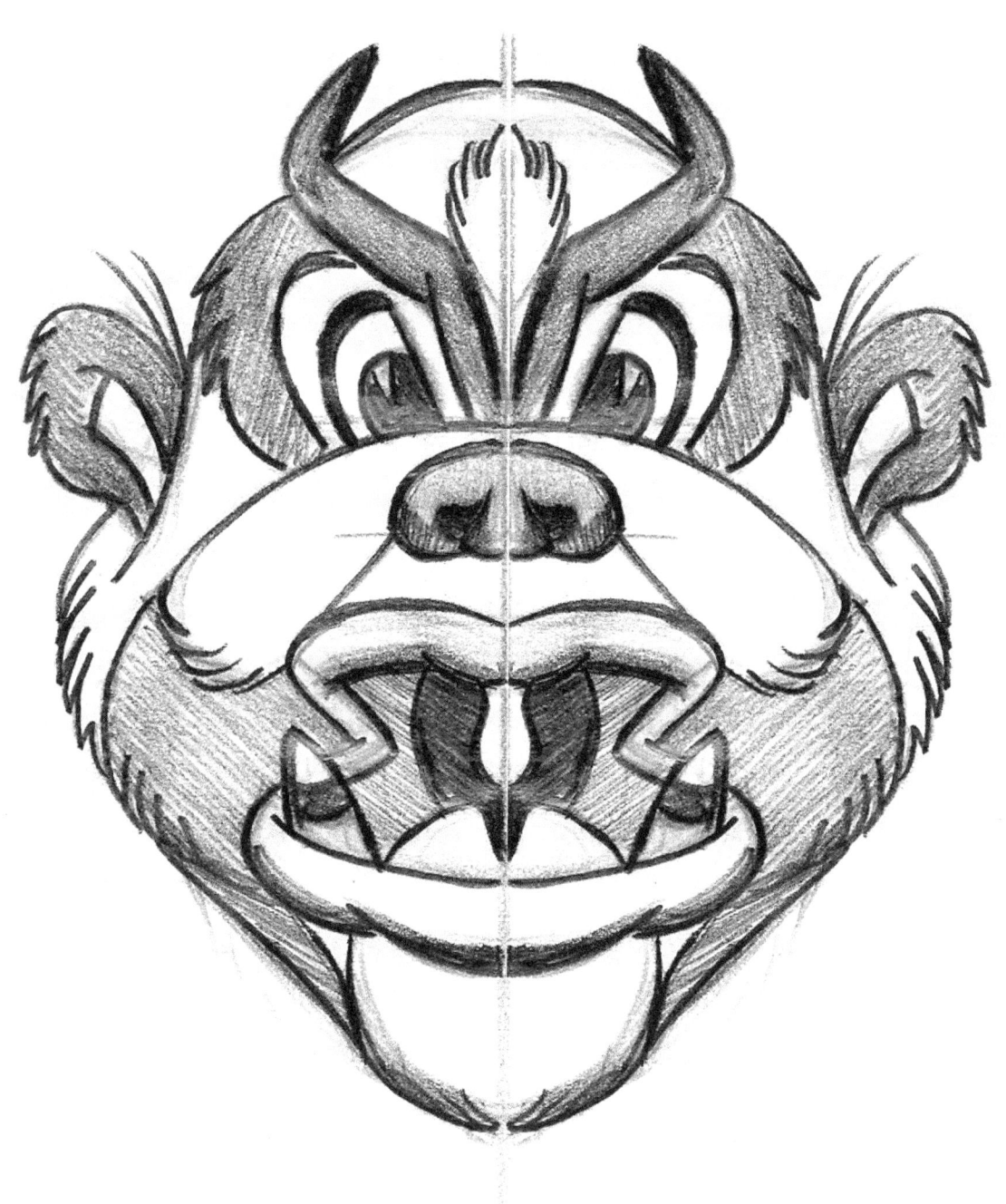

Bear-Nard-Dough

149.

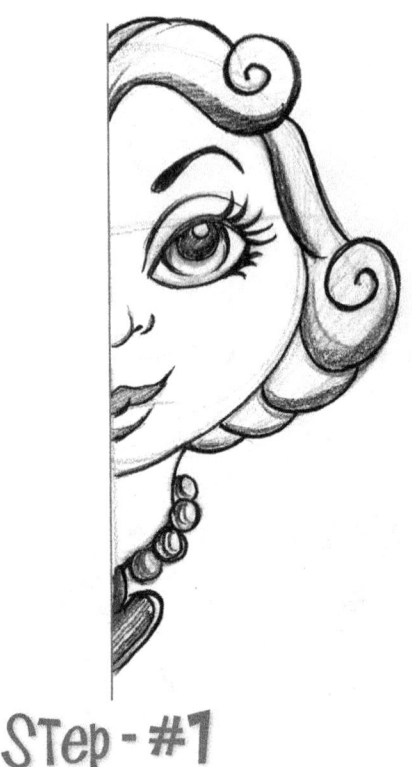

STep - #1

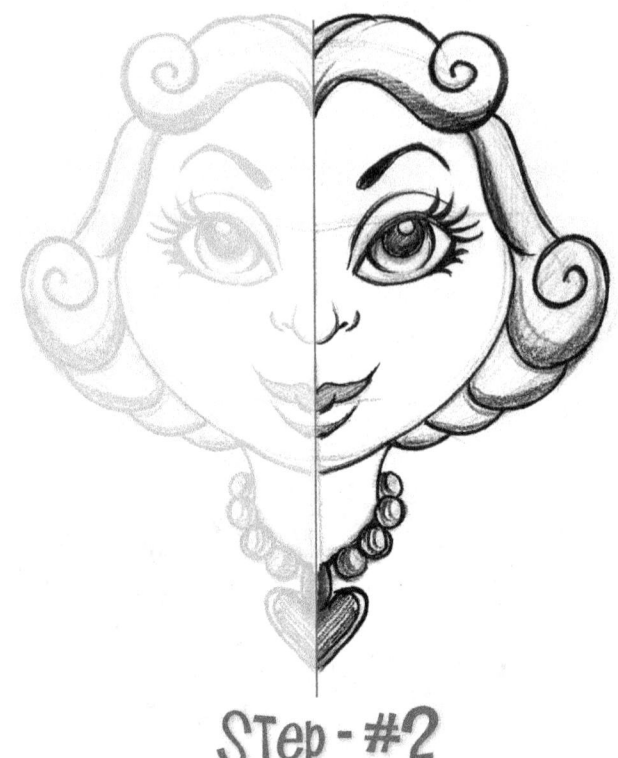

STep - #2

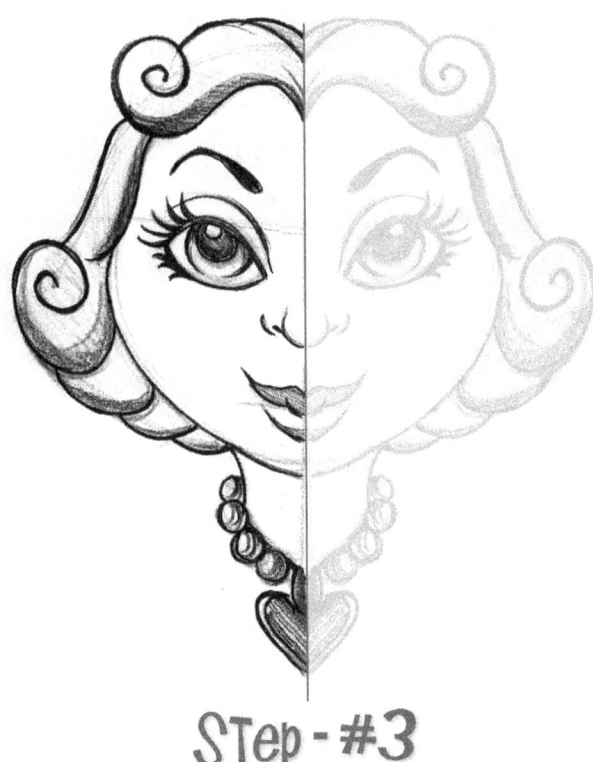

STep - #3

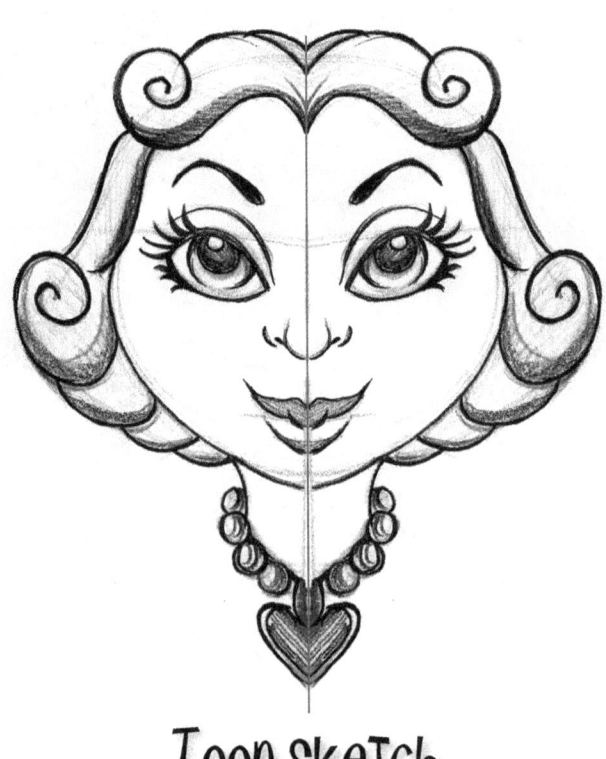

Toon sketch

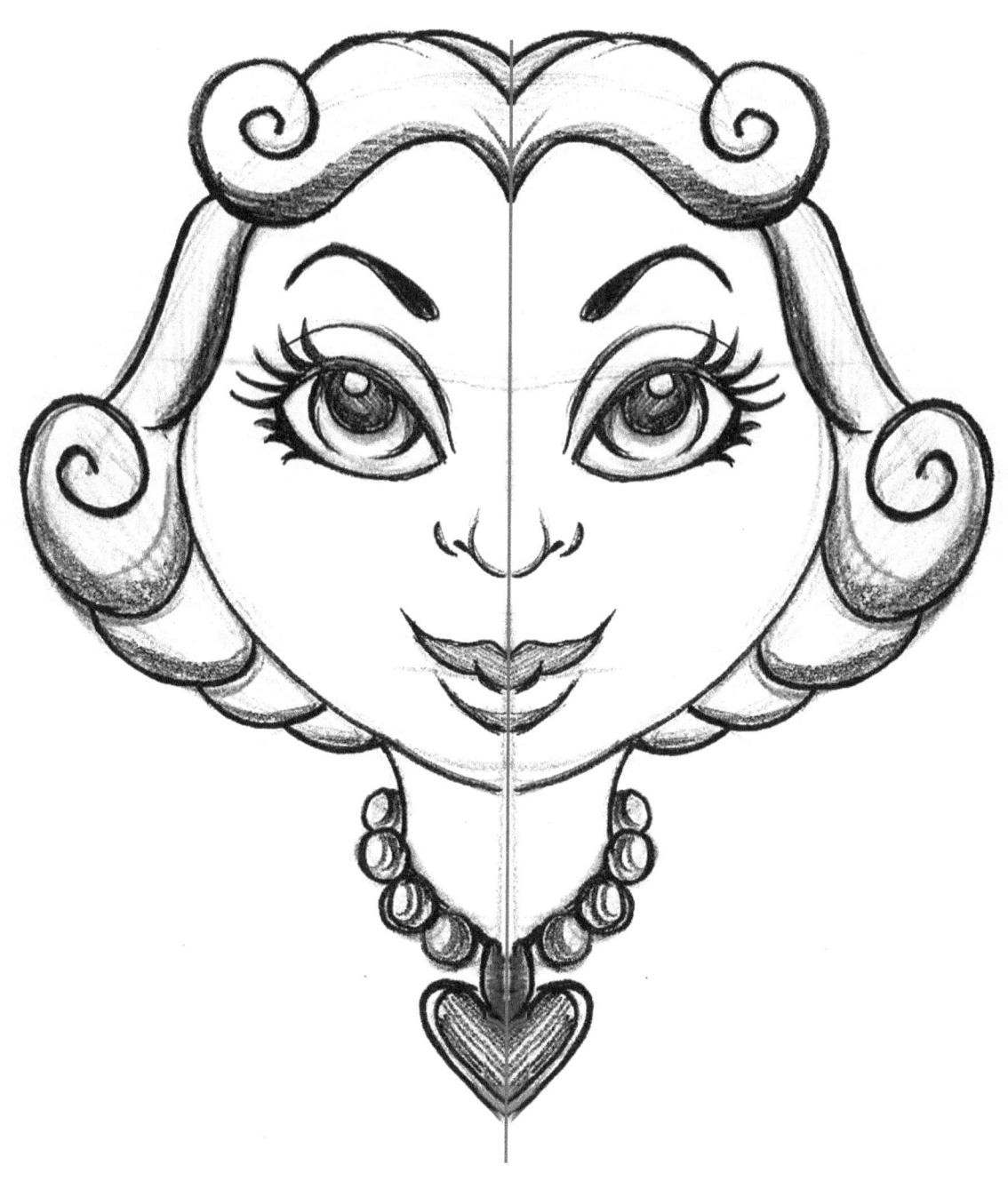

AunT-EviL-Lynn

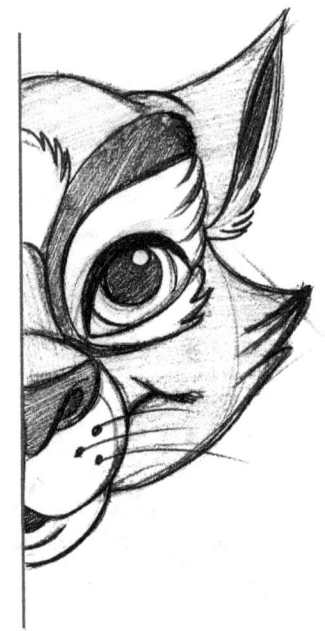

Step - #1

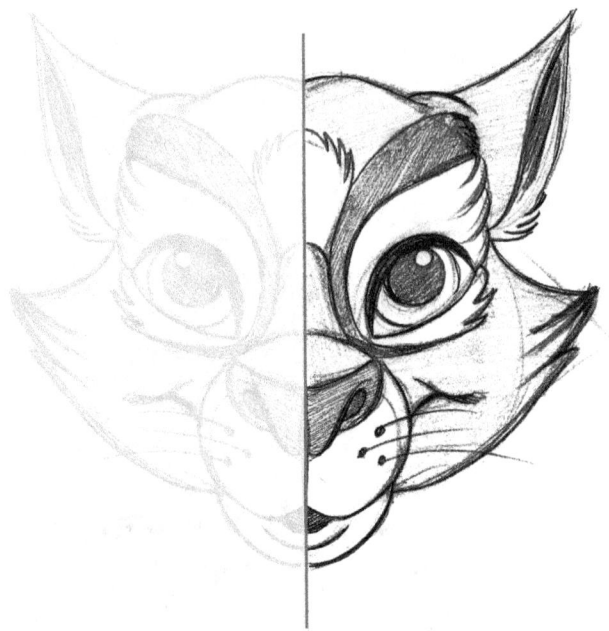

Step - #2

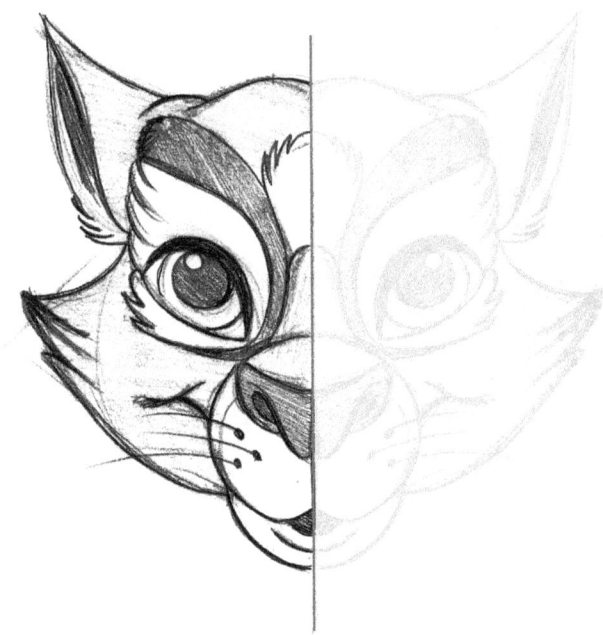

Step - #3

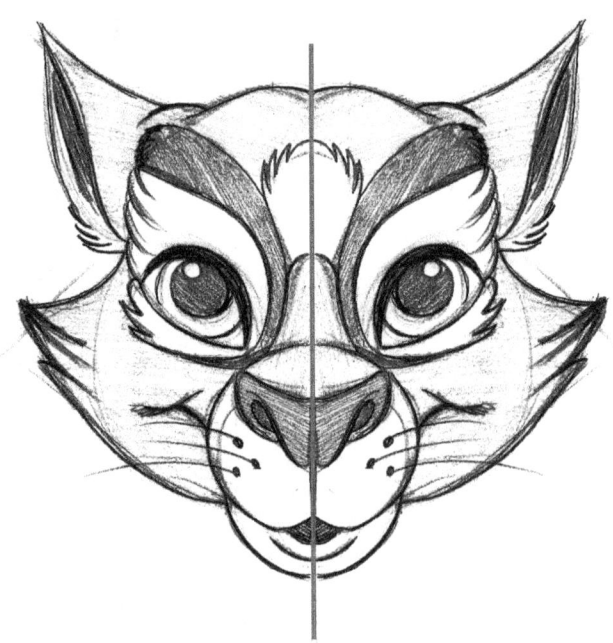

Toon sketch

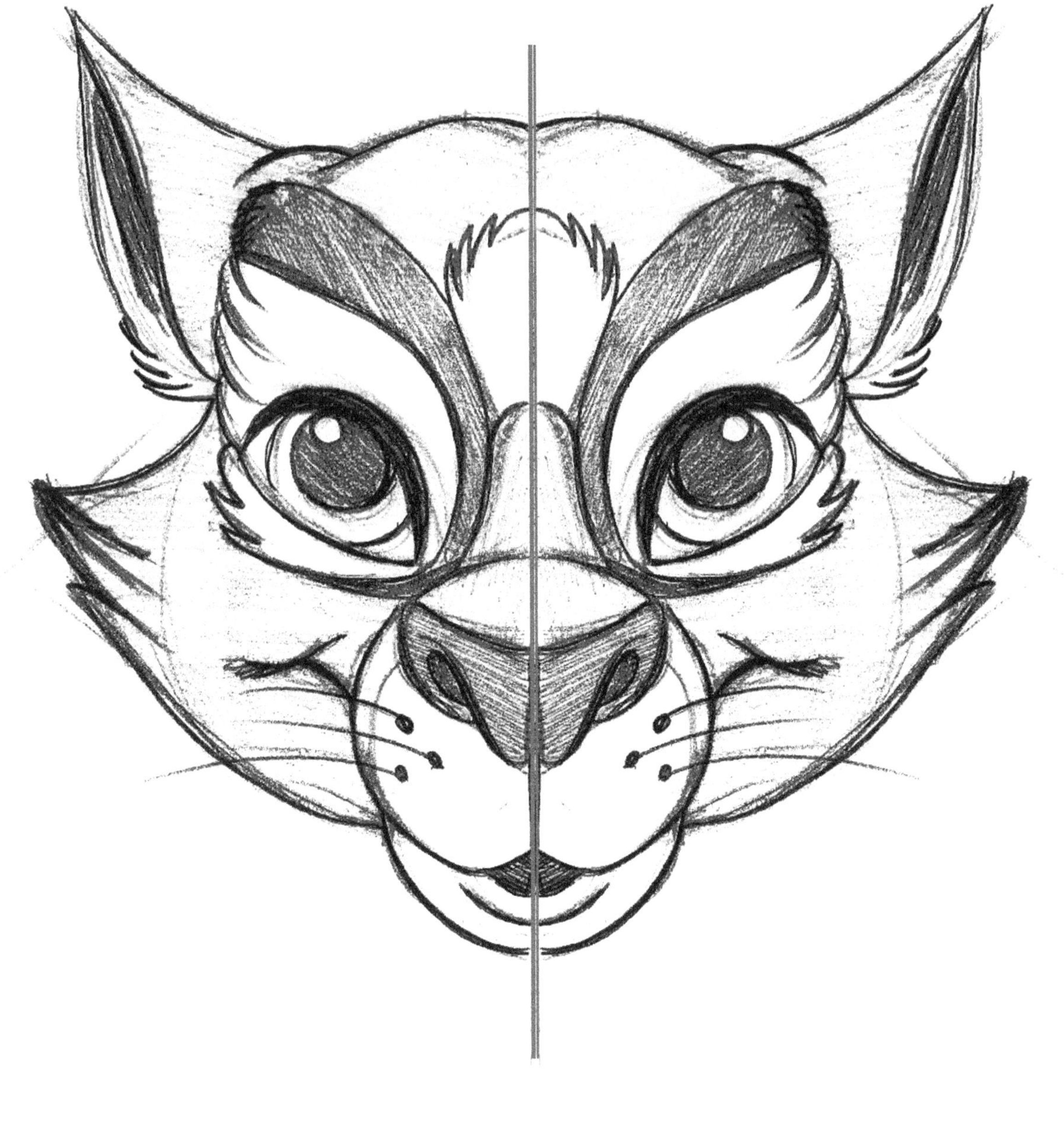

EL GaTiLLo

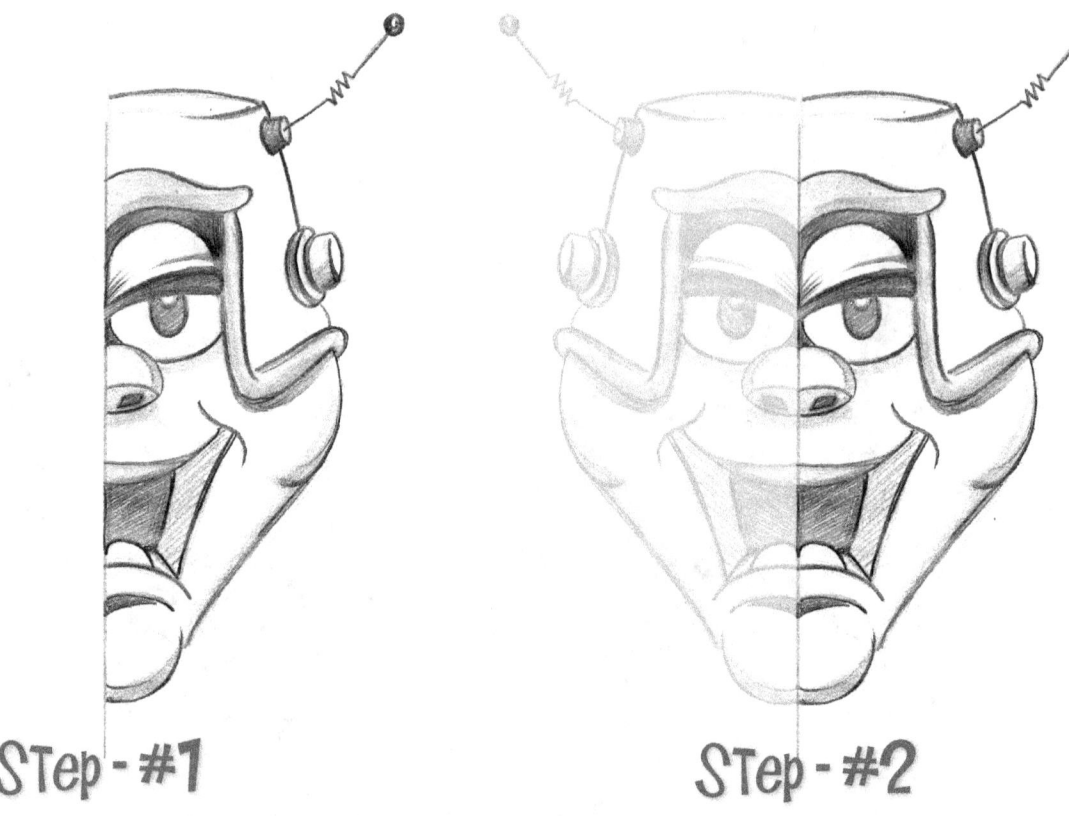

Step - #1

Step - #2

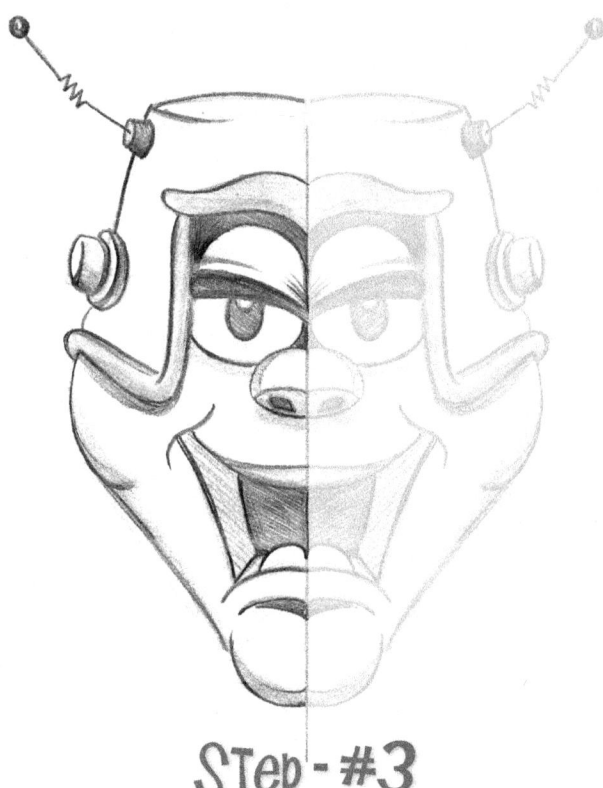

Step - #3

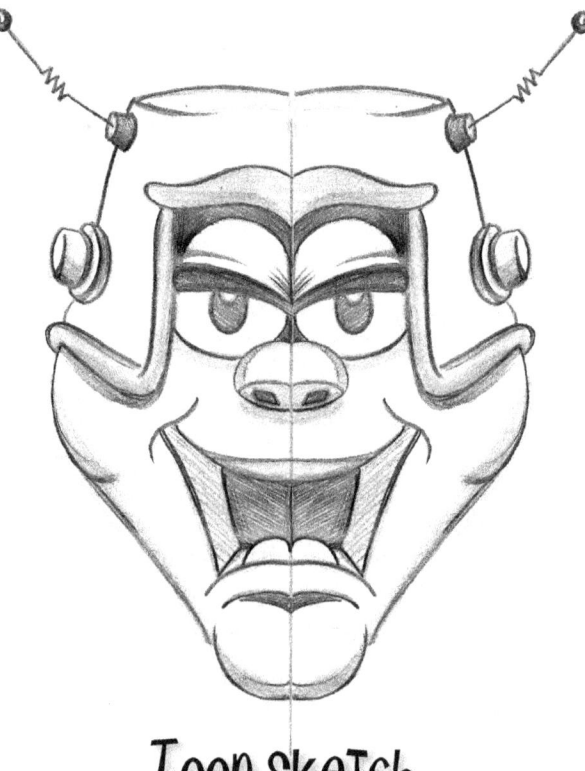

Toon sketch

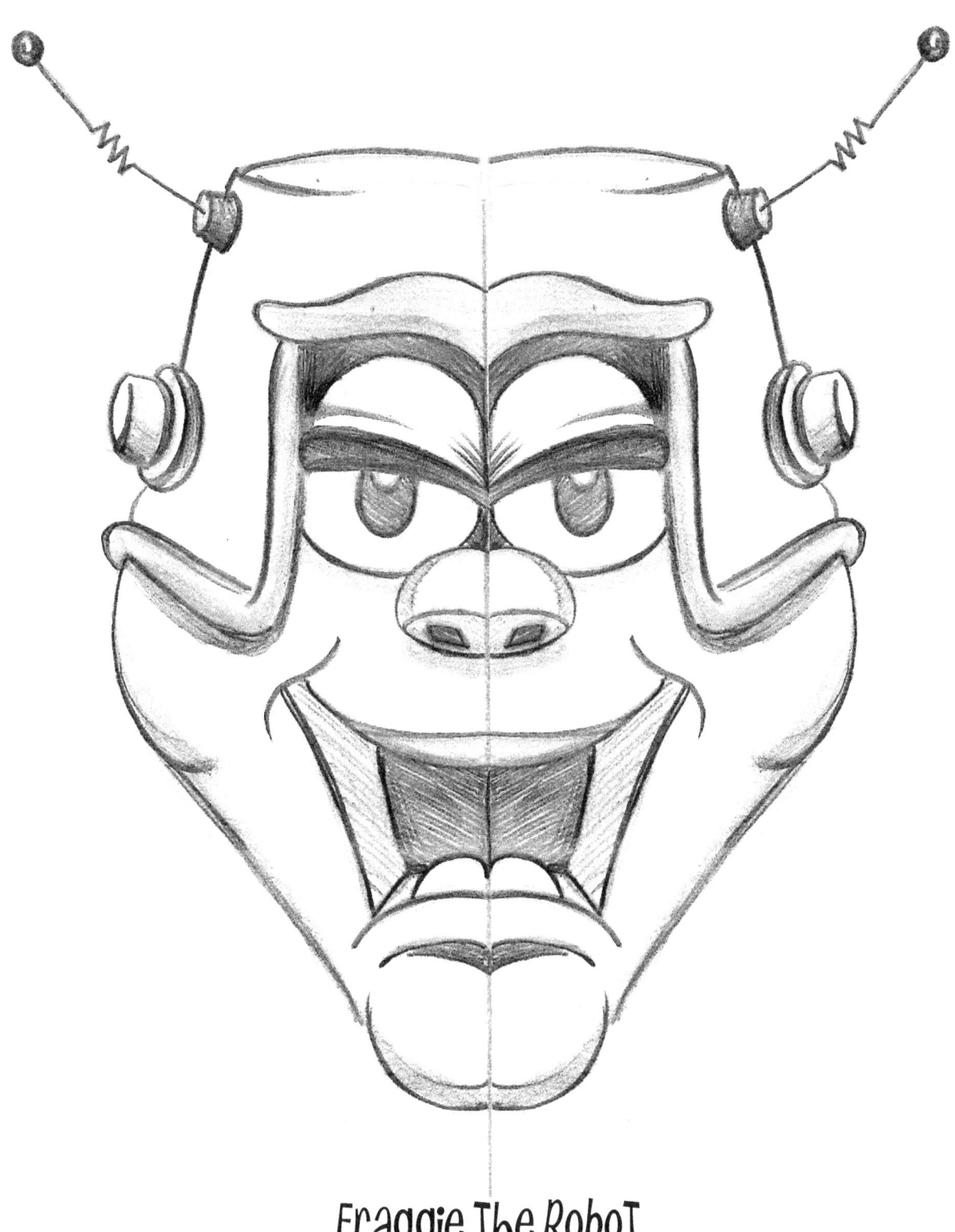

Fraggie The Robot

# Drawing Space

# Chapter 6 Render And Clean-Up

## Two character Turn arounds
## using 360 degrees

Step 1. Start by drawing The 3/4 view of
The character, also called The front perspective view.

Step 2. Using a ruler draw reference Lines across your page.
These will help you Line up important parts such as ; eyes,
head, total size and other important Landmarks
as well as body features.

Step 3. Using your reference Lines complete The
other views of The character. Include front, perspective front,
side, perspective back and back views. These views are also
referred To as The 5 point Turnaround of
a character or The 360 degree Turn.

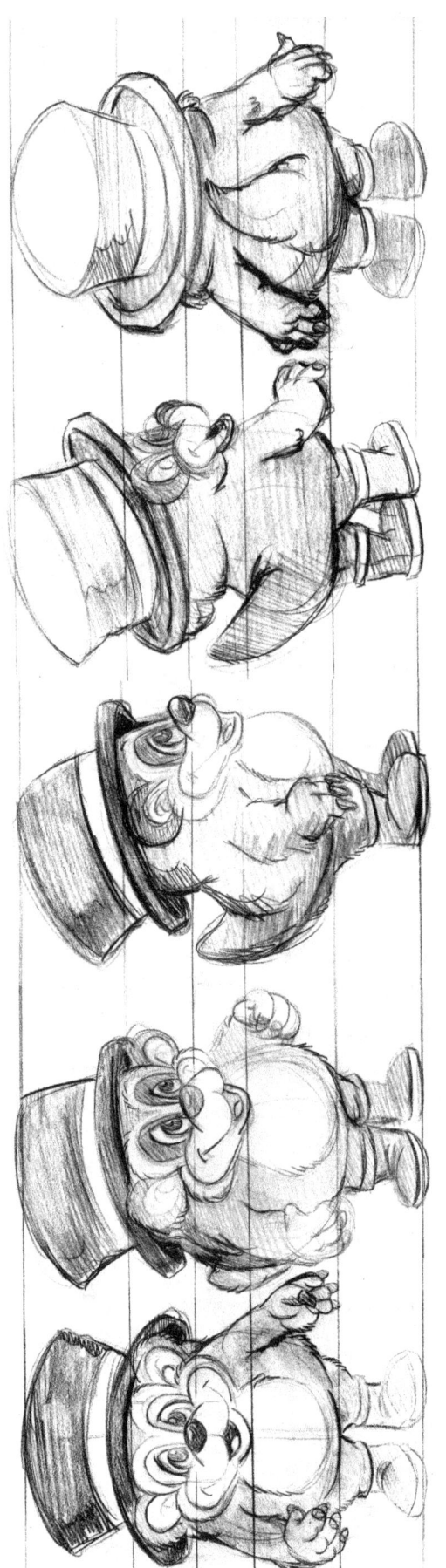

Align & compLeTe ViewS

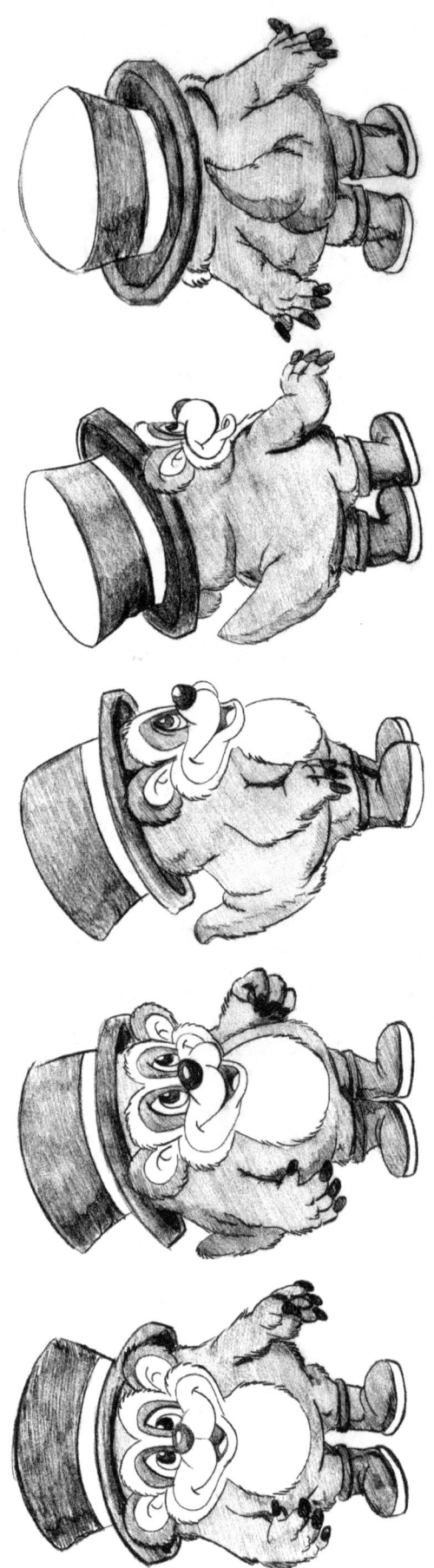

5 poinT Turnaround ViewS compLeTe

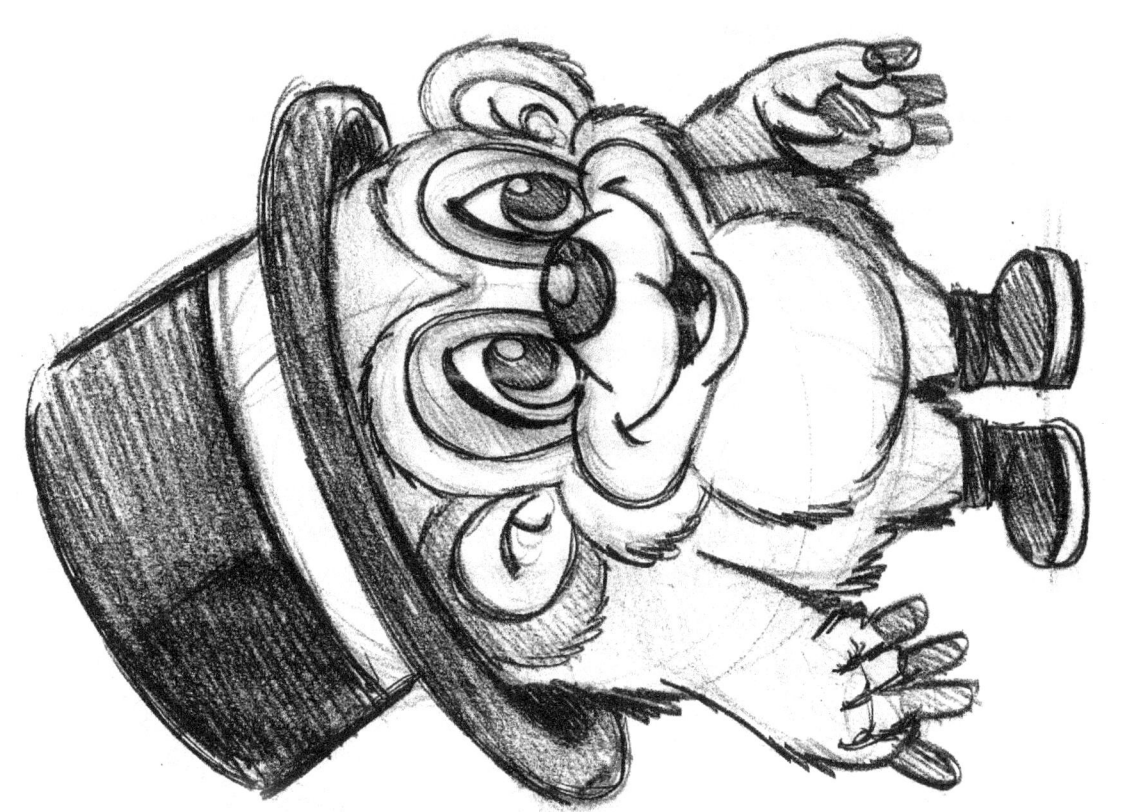

create the characters perspective view

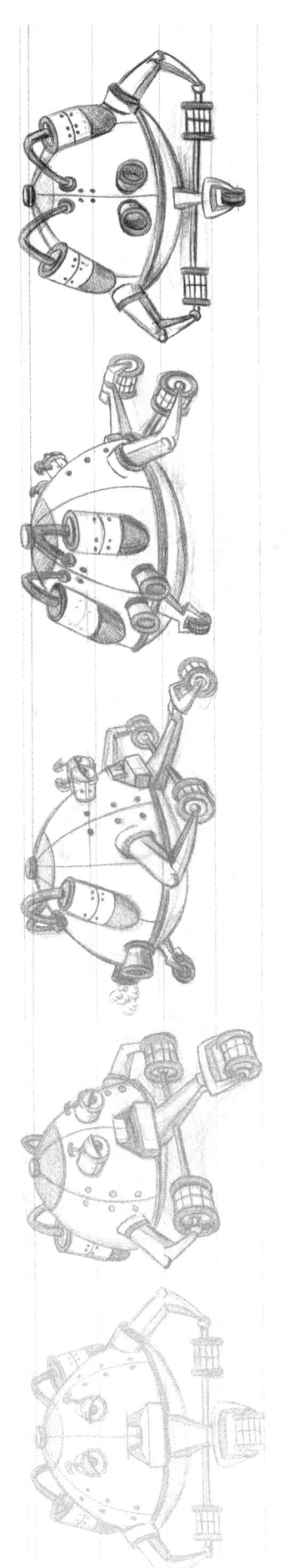

*Align & Complete Views*

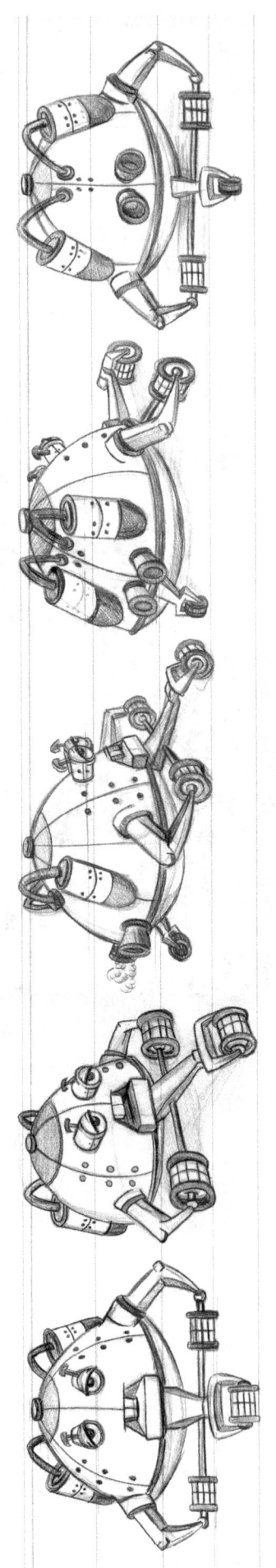

*5 Point Turnaround Views Complete*

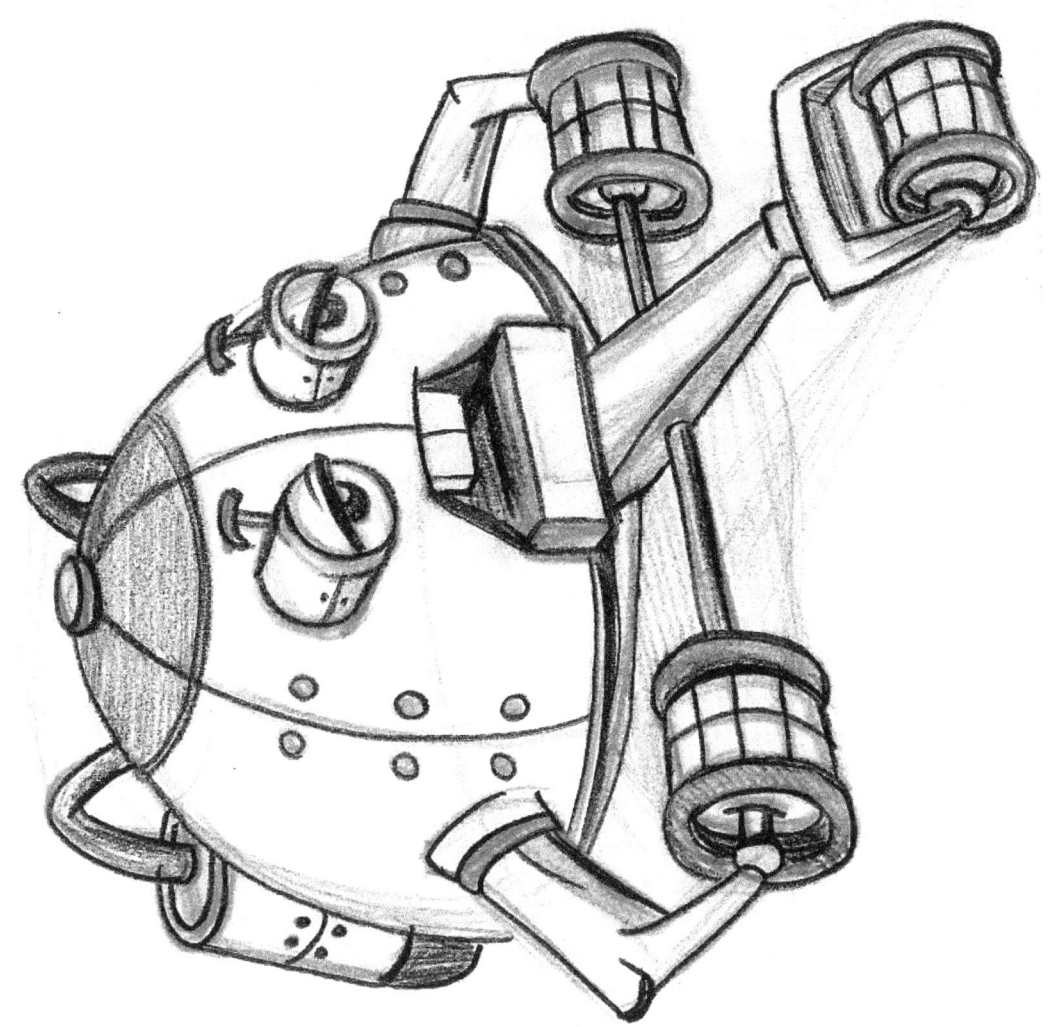

Create the characters perspective view

# Drawing Space

# Four Rendered Characters
# and Toon Clean-Up

STep 1. Choose The Lines ThaT beST define your characters
while Tracing and rendering your arT. ALways use
Tracing paper or an animaTion LighT TabLe.

STep 2. Improvise when possibLe by disTorTing shapes
and adding addiTionaL deTaiL Lines. ALways sharpen aLL
rough Lines and fix The appearance of The characTer.

STep 3. Finish The overaLL design by suggesTing vaLue and shades.
You may aLso use fine crosshaTches buT appLy wiTh precision on The
finaL arT and cLean up. AppLy Thick Lines, Thin Lines and dark shaded
regions on The characTer To improve dimensions and The finaL
deveLopmenT of your now perfecT Toon drawing.

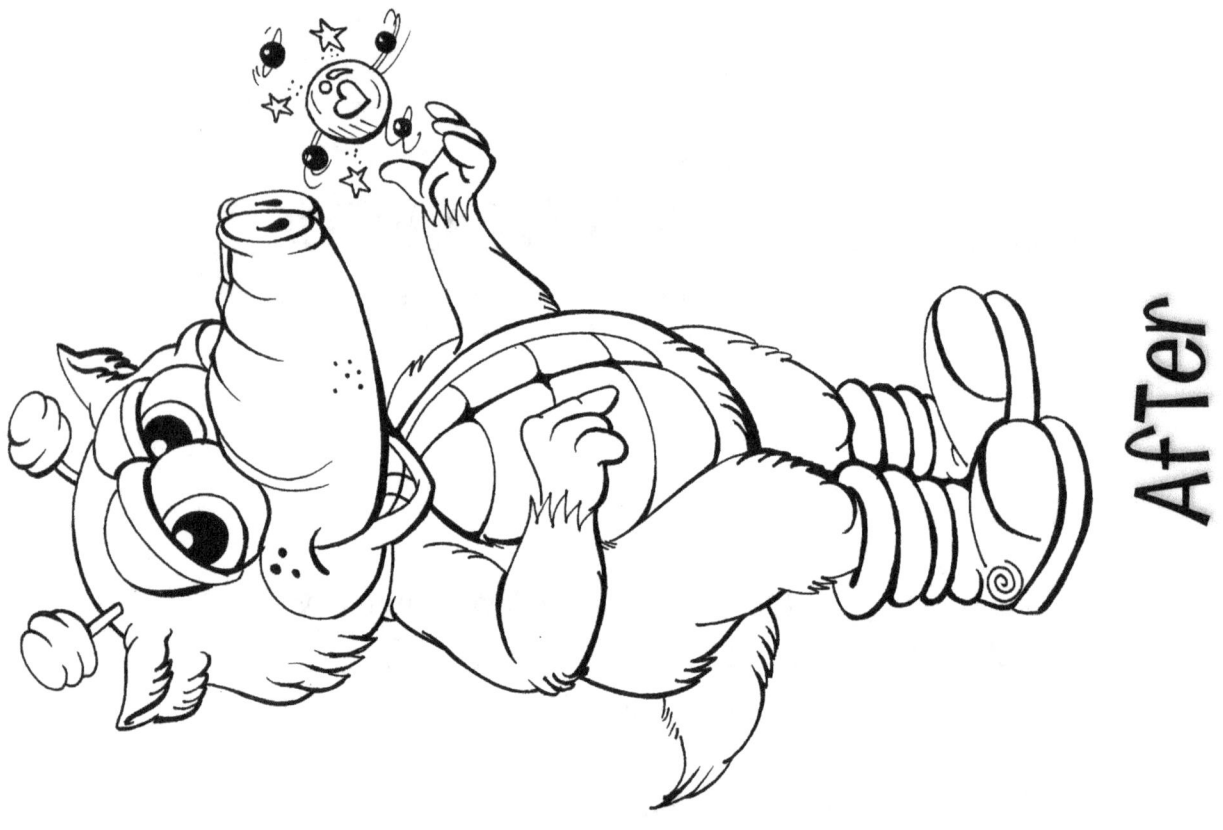

After

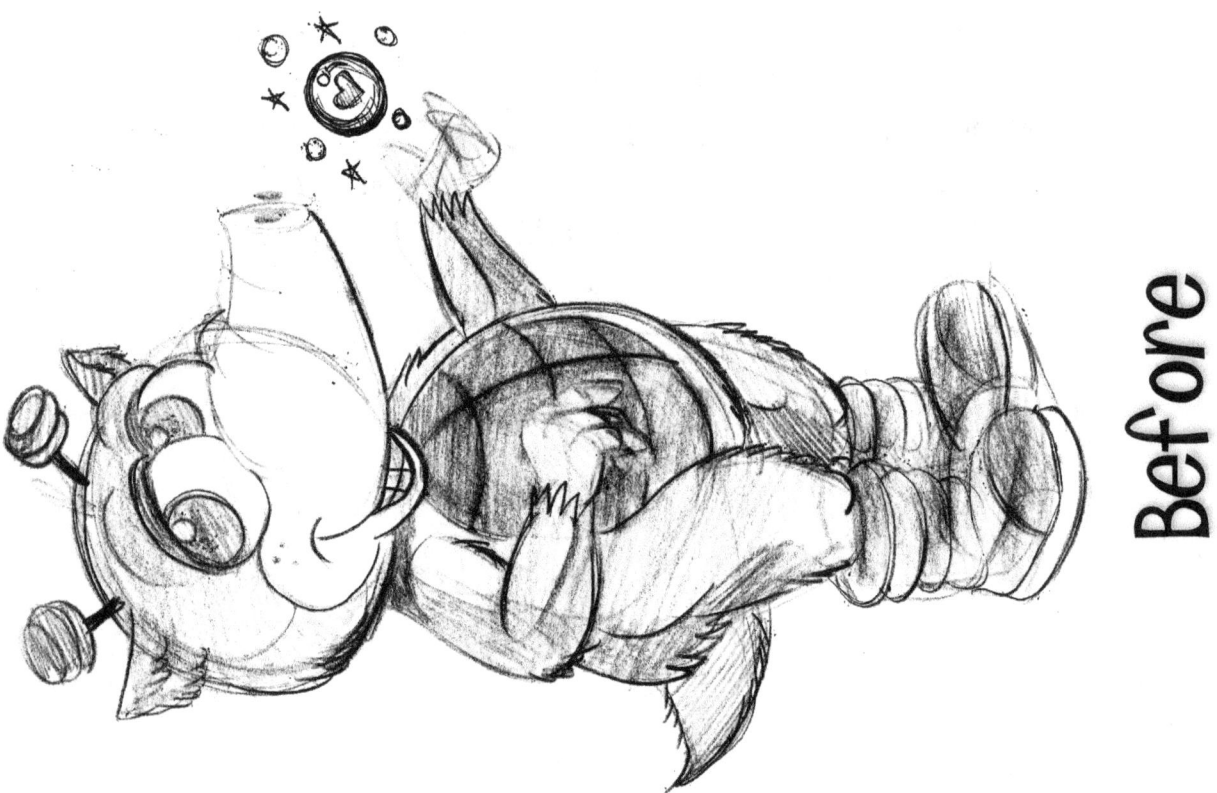

Before

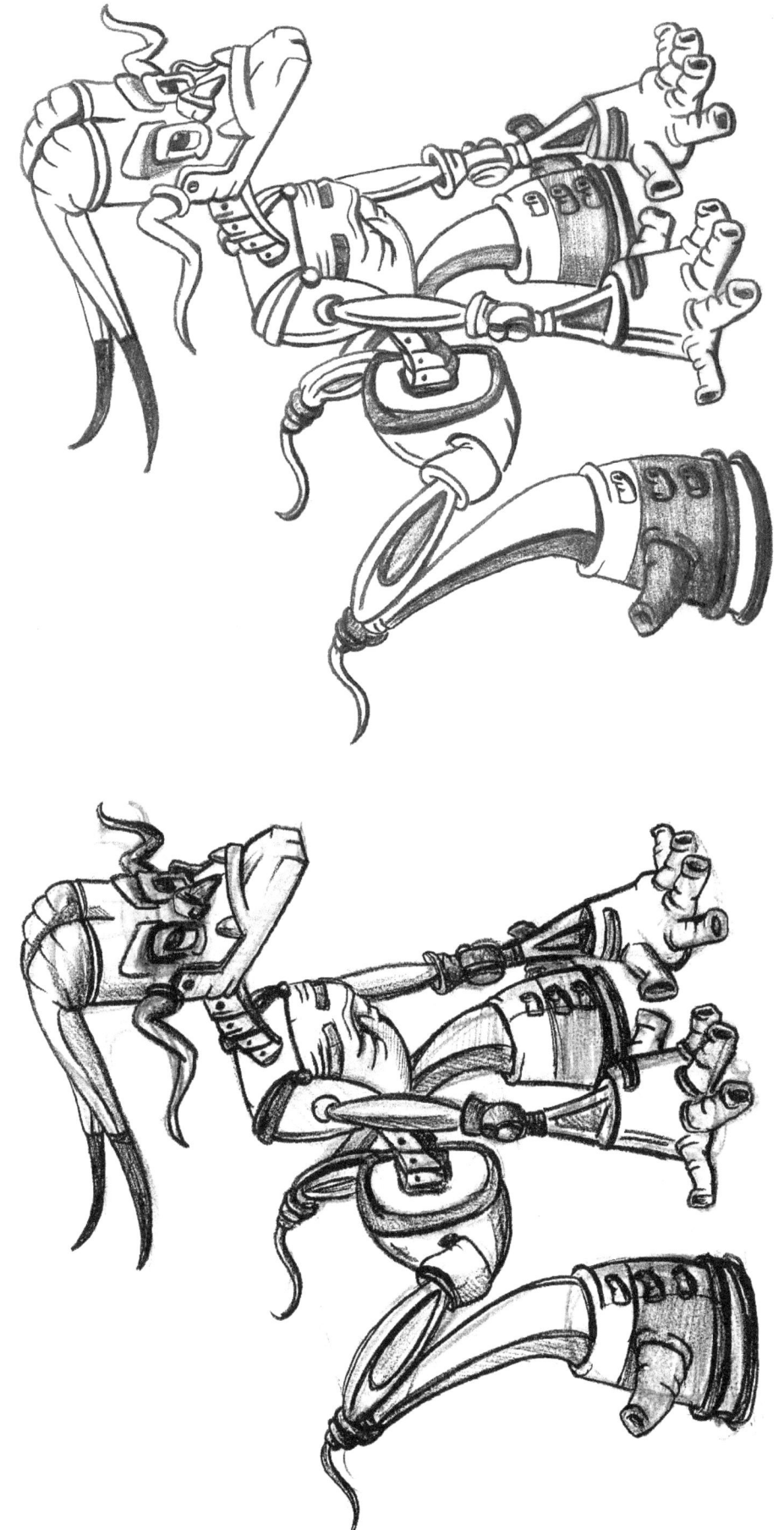

After

Before

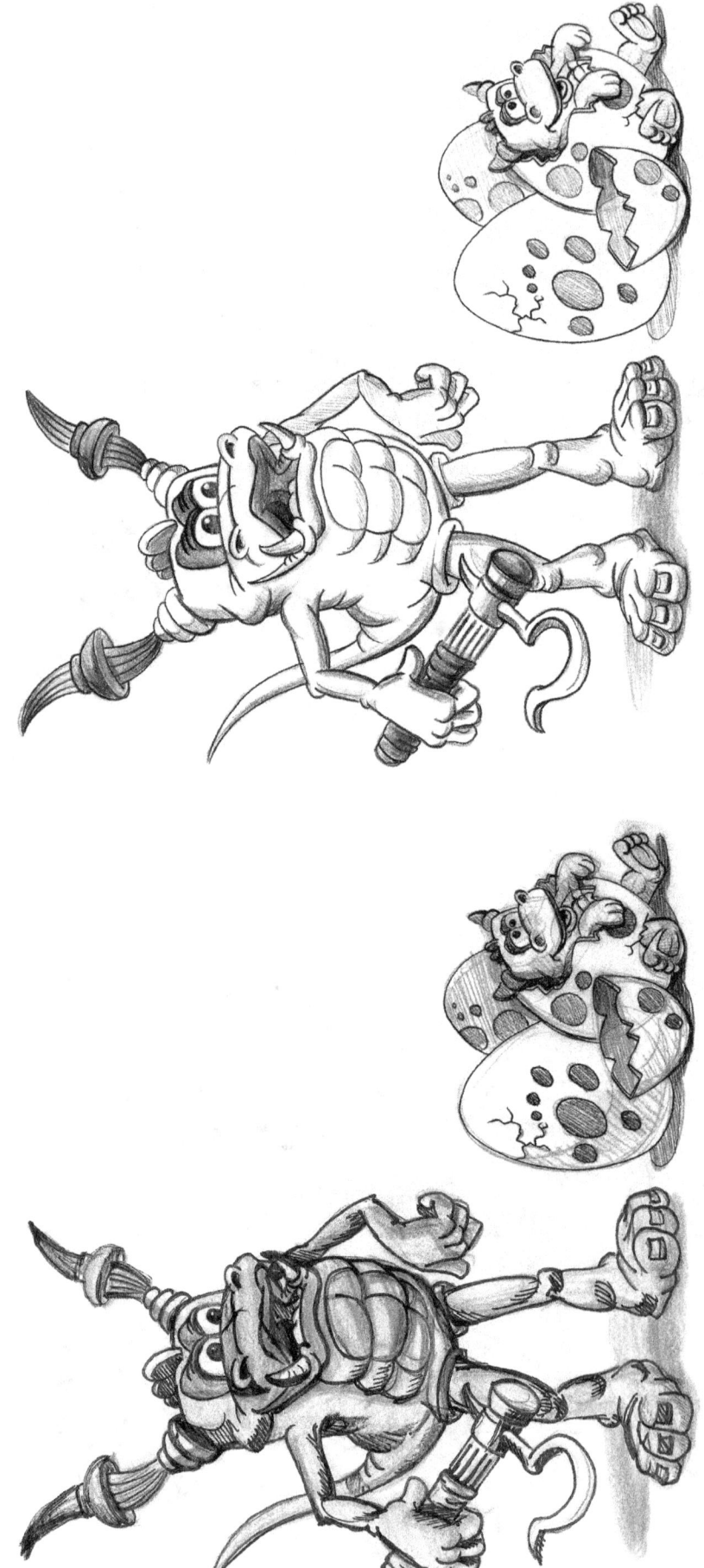

After

Before

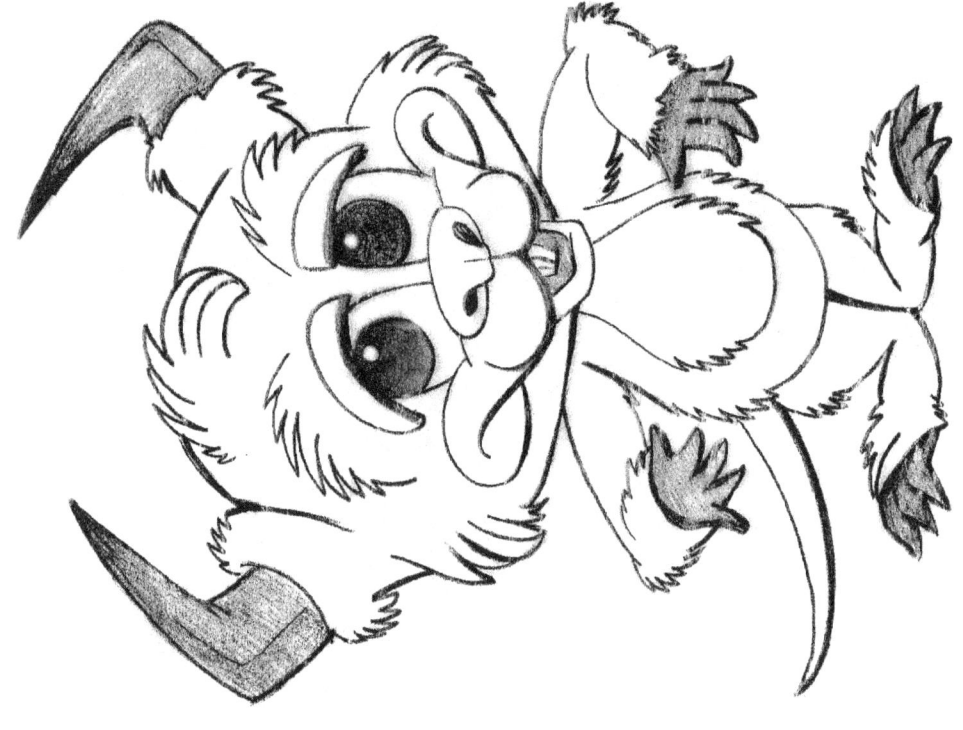

After

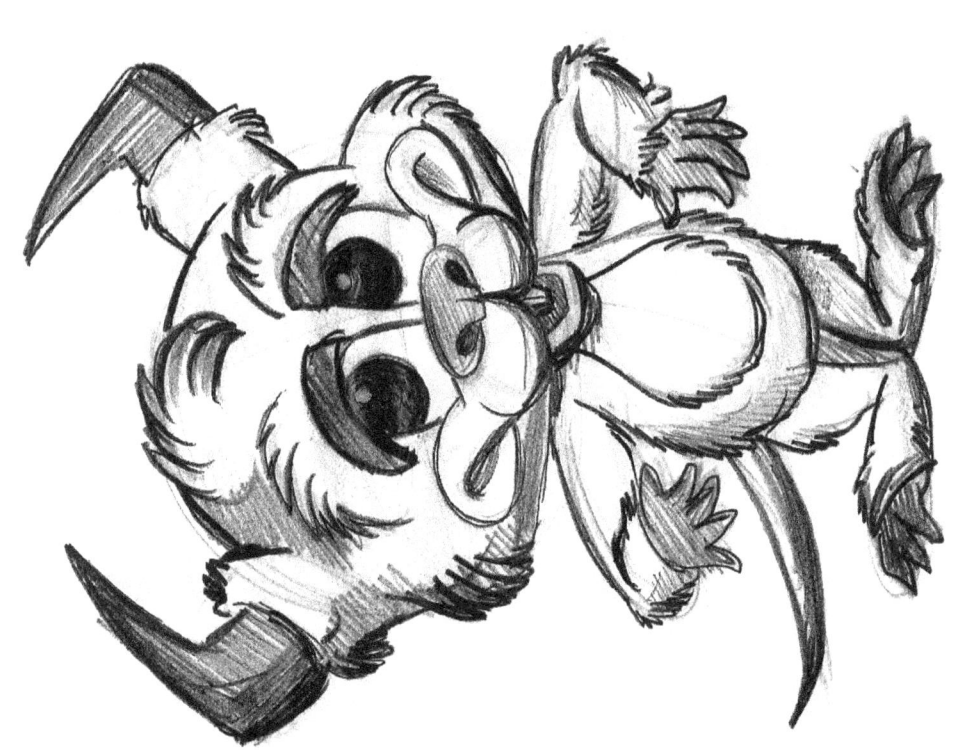

Before

## Creating Fur Lines

## Add Textures & Variations

## Hold Your Pencil at 30° Angle

## Shade with Lines, Crosshatches & Zig-Zags

# Chapter 7 Helpful Hints

## Drawing Fur

Step - 1. Draw all your character construction lines by using regular straight lines. Remember always sketch your lines and shapes and do not begin with hard solid lines.

Step - 2. On the character shapes, use small lines or curves to represent hair strokes. Also try using small x hatches to define fur.

Step - 3. You can then connect lines to make zigzags, or draw small triangular points on all desired areas or on curved masses.

## Shading Masses

Step - 1. Shade towards the bottom of masses to create a shadow effect. Shade much darker to distinguish overlapping parts.

Step - 2. Shade your toons pupils and inner mouth shapes dark. This will express dark inner structures. To create three dimensional toons it is important to shade according to the contour of your characters body parts and shapes.

Step - 3. Always start shading by applying a light shade divider line as your reference. This will guide your shaded areas. Use a rough jagged outline or zigzags when making fur or other textured body parts. You can also experiment with curved lines, hatches or crosshatches

Step - 3 1/2. Always hold your pencil lead against your paper at a 30 degree angle for best results. Press light for light shading and press harder for darker shading, but not hard enough to break the lead. Try shading from dark to light showing transitions of gray values.

# Cartoon Definitions:

**Center Axis:** An Imaginary line equally distant from the sides or outer boundaries of something; the middle in a given formal structure, about which a form, area, or plane is organized.

**Contour:** The outline of a figure or body; the edge or line that defines or bounds a shape or object.

**Oblongs:** Enlongated, usually from the square or circular form.

**Exaggerated:** To represent as greater than is actually the case or To enlarge or increase to an abnormal degree.

**Distorting:** To bend far from natural or normal and to twist out of a proper or natural relation of parts; misshape.

**Limbs:** One of the jointed appendages of an animal, such as an arm, leg, wing, or flipper, used for locomotion or grasping.

**Render:** To fully represent (a perspective view of a projected construction such as a toon) in drawing or painting.

**Value:** In Fine Arts And Animation: a.degree of lightness or darkness in a color or gray scale. b.the relation of light and shade in a painting, drawing, or the like.

**Shading:** The representation of the different values of color or light and dark in a painting or drawing. In cartoon characters adding form by adding shadows and shades of dark and light.

**Crosshatches:** To mark or shade with two or more intersecting series of parallel lines.

**Overlapping:** To lie over and partly cover something.

**Reference point:** An indicator that orients you generally. In art a mark that serves as a guide.

**Facial Features:** Any of the distinct parts of the face, as the eyes, nose, or mouth.

**Proportions:** To form the parts of with balance or symmetry.

**Appearance:** The outward or visible aspect of something.

**Technique:** The manner and ability with which an artist, writer, dancer, athlete, or the like employs the technical skills of a particular art or field of endeavor.

# Useful Materials List
## And
## Combinations of Media

1. Cole erase pencil on sketch book. Use Red, Blue, and Green.
2. Design ebony black pencils or prisma pencils on Tracing paper.
3. Tracing paper with charcoal pencils, pastels or crayons.
4. Rough New sprint pad with a soft 4B charcoal pencil.
5. Pens, pilot pen or fine sharpie on glossy, acetate or photo papers.
6. Mechanical Pencils for final lining 3mm, 5mm, and 7mm leads.
7. Pentel ink brush on watercolor paper or Photo papers.
8. Light Table or small light box for Tracing.
9. Magic eraser, kneaded eraser & pencil sharpener.
10. Standard #2 Pencil and Drafting pencils on drawing paper.

# Follow Your Dreams

When one strives to be a great designer or an artist, it is very important to never give up on your dreams. When I started developing my ability and strengthening my talent, it never failed for an obstacle to arise. Sometimes there are hurdles or hills that must be climbed in order to reach the glory on the other side. I often thought that there would be no way out. People also tried to convince me that art would not make me a day-to-day living, and that an artist is most likely to end up being the first to starve in today's rough world. This just was not enough for me to give up on my goals. I love to draw and I believe that there is nothing I like better than seeing the world in a creative perspective. In a world where trash becomes art materials for crafts. Pencil lines become 3-D shapes that are infinite in depth and in combinations. My mind and my heart always made me sure that I was born to be an artist. I almost did not complete college because the process of becoming an artist was also a challenge. There was math, as well as the other areas of education of which I never wanted to be a part. All I wanted to practice was art until it all started making sense. Education slowly gave me an understanding as to why math, art, and all the other aspects of formal education were required to follow my dreams as a designer. We gain intelligence so that we can continue following the path with all its strenuous bumps, uphill and downhill trails. Now that I have a skilled foundation, I can create anything I want to create. Imagination turns into reality in the end, but only if you have the heart to follow your dreams. Dream big and you can overcome all the difficult experiences throughout your entire art career. Then when you reach your glory, nothing can stop you from sharing it with the world.

Love Always,
Rene D'Erazo

# Inspirational Phrases.

Cartoons are fun!

Never stop sketching!

Creating means innovating.

Reach your goals with a pencil!!

Build many ideas and illustrate them.

Drawing can make you happy.

The possibilities in art are endless!

Characters are cool like people.

Always love your artwork!!

# Imagination. Is. Key.

Drawing is giving, while sketching
is fun,
It's how we created all that is
Under the sun.

Art is relaxing
Painting is too,
It's what makes us happy when
We feel blue.

Sketching is magic as you're
Making a toon,
It's why we draw circles as big
As the moon.

Creating is power as the pencils are
Ever ready and sharp,
It's how we express the lines in our heart.

Imagination is key
Vision is exciting,
And when we can't draw, well, we just
Put it in writing.

Designing is talent manifested when you invent
a cartoon,
It's why we need paper to doodle on soon.

Do not keep the ideas contained in your head, allow them to be free
And prance upon the ledge.
Let them take flight, share them with all. Don't hide them away
or make them too small.

Hold on to the wonder of creation.
Cease to be at ease with only what you see.
Remember these three words always:

Imagination. Is. Key.

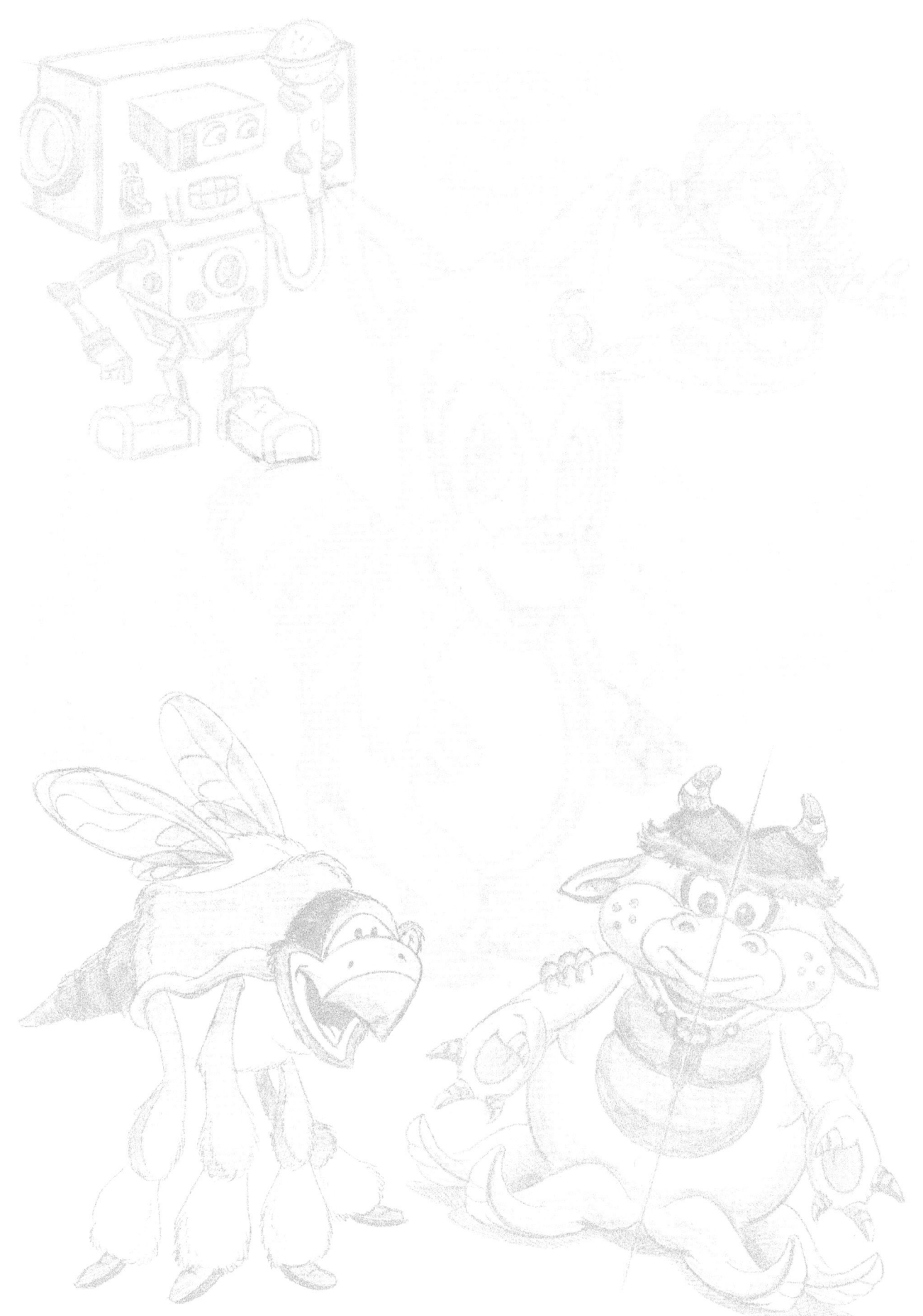

# Draw Around My Picture

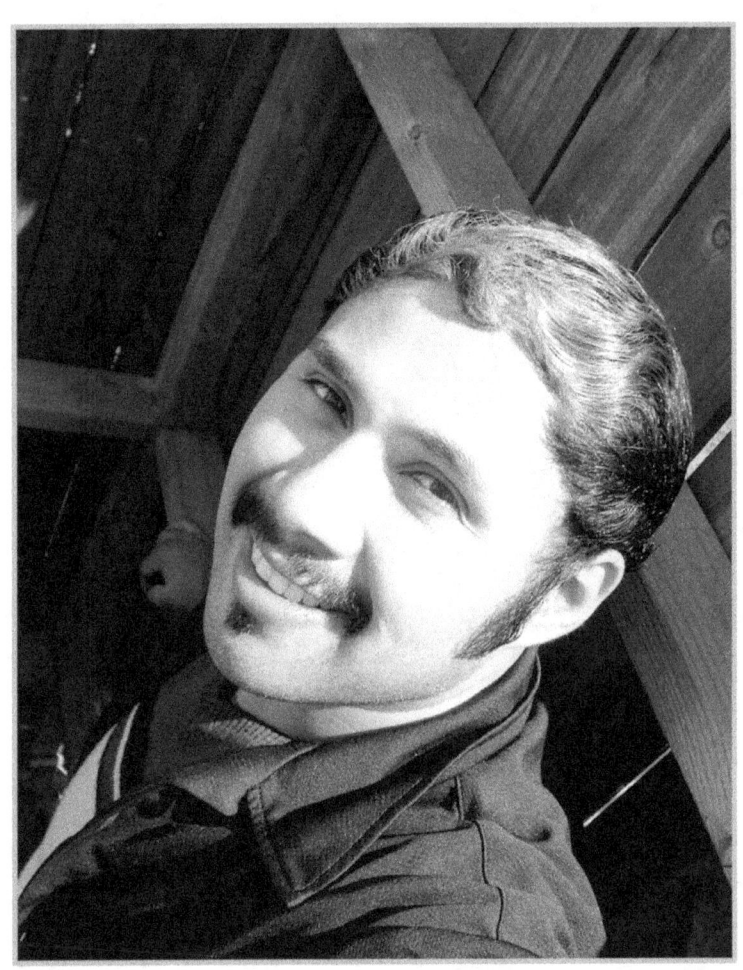

# Rene Daniel Erazo *1979

# About The Toon Artist.

Rene Erazo was born in Los Angeles, Ca. on the day of June 13, 1979. After college completion, he continued on an exciting roller coaster ride of learning new things and innovating ideas by utilizing his skills as well as his animation expertise. Although his education prepared him to become a cartoon animator, he has broadened his capabilities by sharing his talent with a wide range of design industries.

"Design can be expressed in many different ways. An artist can make a design that fits in any form of artwork as long as it's embellished to fit into a theme, style or category which will help portray the main idea or provide a clear visualization to the viewer." - Rene Erazo

This drawing book is his first written and illustrated book published in the year 2011. This book has been made possible with all the guidance and support given by his family, friends and people that have been inspired by Rene's self determination. As a special thanks, he shares the following words of hope with his readers.

"My mission is to embrace the inner love that I have for cartoon characters by creating over 45 new innovative characters that I can share with today's generation of aspiring artists. One of my strongest beliefs is that growth is possible only if knowledge is passed from one individual to another, therefore; my goal is to produce a book showing all the steps that I know which are important in the development of new characters. My book has been designed to guide new talent through all the vital steps of character art. I hope my book helps reach into the minds of talented and striving artists in ways that will expand their cartooning and visualization skills, as well as their observation and practical skills. This book will also allow me as a toon animator, to share my professional art experience with those that desire be a great artist, too." - Rene Erazo

Although drawing cartoon characters is his favorite past time, this talented artist creates many other visual types of concepts. Some of his other professional skills include: toy design, graphic illustration, floral, product development, hobby crafting and new inventions through layout of 3-Dimensional presentations. When not behind the drawing table, he spends his spare time collecting Disney collectibles and developing new displays of hand crafted art work or dioramas.

"I love Disney and my world literally revolves around Walt Disney and his inspiring art and characters, it's all so intriguing. He is my ultimate inspiration and has been the most impressive artist of my lifetime. I am so thankful to be a part of a world that never stops growing or innovating new and amazing things, Thank you,
Walt." - Rene Erazo

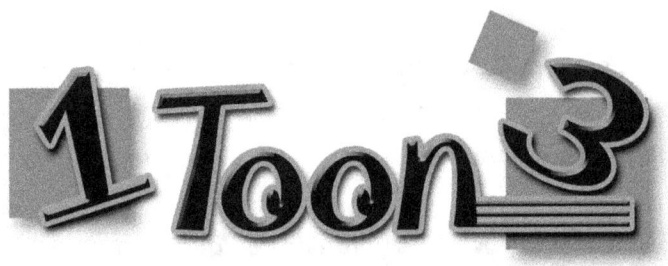

You Are Now A Toon Artist.

www.ingramcontent.com/pod-product-compliance
Lightning Source LLC
Chambersburg PA
CBHW081258170526
45165CB00011B/3342